From the Isles of Dream

Visionary Stories and Poems of the Celtic Renaissance

Selected by
John Matthews

Foreword by Robin Williamson

Floris Books

First published in 1993 by Floris Books.
© John Matthews 1993
The copyrights listed under the acknowledgments
form a part of the copyright of this volume.
All rights reserved. No part of this publication may
be reproduced without the prior permission of
Floris Books, 15 Harrison Gardens, Edinburgh.

British Library CIP Data available

ISBN 0-86315-523-5

Printed in Great Britain
by The Cromwell Press, Melksham, Wiltshire SN12 8PH

Contents

Acknowledgments

Thanks to Robin Williamson for taking time out of his busy schedule to write the foreword; to Caitlín Matthews for allowing me to quote from her unpublished essay; to Faber and Faber Ltd for permission to reprint *Princes of the Twilight* by Henry Treece; to the estate of John Cowper Powys and Laurence Pollinger Ltd for permission to reprint "Taliessin Pen Beirdd" from *Porius*; to the estate of Ella Young for permission to reprint "The Weird of Fionavar"; to Devin-Adair Publishers Inc. for permission to include "The White Hound of the Mountain" by Thomas J. Kiernan. Whilst every effort has been made to locate the copyright holders of certain texts, this has not always proved possible. Any omissions will be corrected in future editions wherever possible.

John Matthews
Oxford 1993

Foreword

The writers represented in this anthology have often been lumped together under the heading of "Celtic Twilight" — a term I've always disliked as premature or downright inaccurate. For — despite wholesale clearances of the population of Gaelic Scotland, famine, pestilence, feud and oppression in Ireland, and determined suppression of all levity in the folk-muse as works of the Devil by the chapels of Wales — Celtic art has been enjoying both a continuation and a new dawn throughout the twentieth century.

These writers manifest a prime quality of "Celtic-ness"; the sense of the invisible which then permeates the outer world. They have the power and wizardry to make great treasures literally out of the air. They carry into English the spirit of Gaelic and Welsh bards who imbued every hill with an inner kingdom, every lake with a King-Under-Wave, and who trusted that fairy-land might be found round every corner of every road of the world.

The works of Fiona Macleod, Lord Dunsany, George Macdonald, "AE" and especially W.B. Yeats have been an inspiration to me in my own work since I was a boy. I'm delighted to see some of them gathered and presented here under the sure hands of John Matthews.

Robin Williamson

So they came riding
In red and in gold,
With laughter and harping,
Over the world.

No sword was among them,
They fought with a song,
Safe in their kingdom,
The children of Spring.

From "The Warrior Bards" by Henry Treece

Introduction
Companions of the Sidhe

Till the soil — bid cities rise —
Be strong, O Celt — be rich, be wise —
But still, with those divine grave eyes,
Respect the realm of Mysteries.

Fiona Macleod: *The Book of Orm*

All of the writers represented in this collection have one thing in common: they draw for their inspiration on Celtic roots. They collectively form the spearhead of what has been called the Celtic Revival, or Renaissance. That this was no such thing, but rather a continuing presence which had maintained its validity throughout centuries of oppression and neglect, is part of the wonder of Celtic art and vision.

As Caitlín Matthews has stated in her essay "Guardians of Deep Memory" :

> All societies need their gifted ones, their artists and mystics: without them the land becomes weary and disenchanted. Traditional Celtic society enshrined and maintained an Otherworldly enchantment by supporting its gifted people — sometimes in secret, always with honour. The tradition of the primal note by which creation comes into being is well attested in many spiritualities. The first utterance of the gods gives forth vibrations and harmonies whose interweaving causes variety within creation. These vibratory rates are distinguished by colour, number and qualitative functions which influence the whole of our life. Music is the first ordering of chaos, and it is present in the "singing" of many of the voices which make up this

collection. When the music of enchantment ceases, chaos returns.

There is a strong tradition that both druids and Christians maintained "perpetual choirs of song," which helped preserve the sacred order. In Celtic tradition these were maintained by the poets and bards whose voices were trained to utter the enchantments of the Otherworld, and to maintain the song lines of the land with sacred story. In Celtic Christian tradition this custom continued. Within monastic foundations choirs of monks and nuns sang the Divine Office, combining the Psalms of David with prayers, canticles and sacred readings. In secular society, the telling of stories appropriate to circumstances continued despite attempts of the various incoming conquerors to prevent it. Even among the ordinary people, the regulation of the daily round of work by incantatory prayer and song was maintained.

The use of "enchantment" here is specific. Like other terms, such as "imagination," it has lost its currency. To enchant means also to "re-enchant," to bind the reader into a new and mystical awareness of the magic and wonder inherent in the mythology and spirituality of the Celtic world. In this context it also means "to infuse with song." The importance of song as a channel for tradition is as important as speech.

Thus no part of the enchantment was allowed to fail, and the light of the Celtic vision was kept alight despite everything — though after the ending of the Middle Ages it no longer shone in the halls of kings and princes but was rather maintained by itinerant story-tellers who wandered the roadways of the Celtic lands.

The vision that they bodied forth, which in their words sprang into vital being, was of a culture continually aware of its interrelationship with the Otherworld. Gods and Goddesses, heroes and champions, the spirits of tree and stone and water, were everywhere daily present. The unified vision of creation thus evinced is embodied in poems dating from the earliest written texts of the Celtic peoples. Fionn's seventh century "Poem of

May-Day" given below may be a far cry from the elaborate language of Macpherson — but both share the dream of a world where everything is alive:

> May: fair-aspected,
> perfect season;
> blackbirds sing
> where the sun glows.
>
> The hardy cuckoo calls
> a welcome to noble Summer;
> ends the bitter storms
> that strip the trees of the wood.
>
> Summer cuts the streams;
> swift horses seek water;
> the heather grows tall;
> fair foliage flourishes.
>
> The hawthorn sprouts;
> smooth flows the ocean —
> Summer causing it to sleep;
> blossom covers the world …
>
> The true man sings
> gladly in the bright day,
> sings loudly of May —
> fair aspected season!

(my translation)

That the vision survived at all is itself a wonder. When the Romans invaded these lands in the first century AD, they outlawed the bards and singers, killed off the Druid priesthood and overlaid the spirituality of the Celts with their own. Still the vision survived. When the Saxons finally overran the last pockets of resistance after the departure of Arthur in the sixth century, they brought a new and powerful culture which did its best to dilute the brief resurgence of Celtic tradition. Still the vision survived. The incoming Saxons were not proof against the beauty of the Celtic vision. They learned from the Celtic saints and incorporated their vision into the Christianizing of Britain. This process of integration might have sustained the Celtic presence, but the Synod of Whitby in AD 664 favoured Roman rather than local Celtic Christianity.

The pursuit of the Celtic vision did not lie in possessing the land, but in celebrating the rich gifts of the spirit, in being part of creation. Yet this vision was to encounter the very real dispossession from land, language and culture. When the Normans invaded England in the eleventh century, they imposed a feudal law over their subject peoples. Ireland was conquered soon afterwards, losing its autonomy. Wales was unified with England in 1543. Scotland, after centuries of acrimonious combat, was finally incorporated into England in 1707 by the Act of Union. The language, ideas and vision of the conquered Celtic peoples were devalued as less important than the predominant English vision of conquest and empire. But still the vision survived.

As long as there are a few voices left to communicate the vision, spiritual survival and recovery are possible. In Wales and Scotland, the stories were preserved in valley and mountain, wherever there were people to listen. The few surviving native bards and singers of Ireland were outlawed and forbidden to tell the old stories, often teaching children in proscribed hedge schools. Yet still, the vision survived. The poets of Ireland still sought the inspiration of their land and vision, invoking the Goddess of the Land as the Aisling or Vision Woman of the hills, a spirit who wandered outcast. The eighteenth century onwards saw the iniquitous "clearances" in Scotland and the nineteenth century famines throughout Ireland, further eroding the indigenous traditions of these lands, enriching the shores of Canada and America, of Australia and New Zealand. Those who remained, suffered the customary privations of indigenous peoples the world over — loss of land, loss of language, loss of soul. Some defiantly withstood oppression by political action or by the more subversive song and story, but the majority stood in

12

much the same case as native Americans of the nineteenth and twentieth centuries — poised on the verge of cultural extinction. Yet the vision, in however fragmented a form, survived. It did so because it was based on a spiritual reality.

Then, in the eighteenth century, came the first stirrings of renewal. The fires, for so long banked down, began to burn with a new fierceness, aided and abetted by a team of rescuers. Before a culture totters into dereliction, there are always a few enlightened souls who realize the wealth of what is about to be lost. Time and again, we see this extraordinary and timely rescue throughout history: the documentary evidence of classical Greek worship and sites by Pausanius just before the wholesale conversion of the Roman Empire to Christianity; the antiquarian witness of Camden and Stukely to ancient British sacred sites before the industrialization and destruction of the countryside. Now began an extraordinary renascence, sometimes fuelled, it must be admitted, by the re-invention of the Celtic tradition.

Rendered politically harmless by the fruitless attempts of the Old and Young Stuart Pretenders to re-establish their dynasty, Scotland lay in shock. The clan leaders were either dead or had become more English than the English. But Gaelic was still spoken in the Highlands and Islands, and the old stories and songs were still told. The work of one man helped fan the flames into a conflagration which illuminated the Celtic tradition for a new generation.

The man in question was James Macpherson (1736–96), author of the controversial "Ossian" poems. It is appropriate that we begin this collection of writings by the leading lights of the Celtic renascence with an extract from his work.

Macpherson was an arch popularizer. He rewrote the Celtic vision in such a way that the non-Celtic reading public from Napoleon to Goethe were delighted and enthused. The Gaels of Macpherson's writing had become noble and heroic in the manner of the romantic "Red Indian" of the eighteenth century: savage yet loving, passionate yet tender, vanquished yet noble in defeat. His books sold in a way that is difficult for us to believe today, when poetry has been relegated to the realm of a polite hobby. More than 80 000 copies of *Fingal* were sold in the first year of publication. It, and the volumes which followed, were romantic, colourful, and visionary. They had titles like: *Cath-Loda, The Death of Cuthullin, The Battle of Lora*, and they dealt with episodes from the lives of the great heroes of the Celtic world. In their time they were the favourite reading of no less a person than Napoleon Buonaparte, who declared that they were one of the reasons why he wanted to conquer England!

The works which, collectively, make up Macpherson's *Poems of Ossian* (1760–63) were the first sign of a cultural renascence among the Celts. They were, and have been, much vilified by purists who found them to be clumsily expressed, wanting in inspiration and, worst of all, probable forgeries. All of these criticisms are, to some extent, justified. Macpherson was not a great poet — though he could occasionally rise to considerable heights, as the extract from *Fingal* included here demonstrates (pp. 21ff).

The accusation of forgery, levelled at "Ossian" is also, to some extent, true. Macpherson claimed to have discovered certain manuscripts during his extensive travels through Western Scotland, which he then translated and edited into a series of epics. Undoubtedly, most present day authorities would agree that these manuscripts were largely the invention of Macpherson's vivid imagination, though based on the oral tales of Fionn Mac Cumhail and his fianna, which were still widely recited in the Gaelic West Highlands. Like his equally famous and equally notorious Welsh counterpart, Iolo Morgannwg, Macpherson began as a translator and collector of these genuine Gaelic poems, and ended as a forger. Where there were "gaps" he filled them in from his own imagination and from a liberal knowledge of Celtic myth and legend.

So, if we regard the works as, in a certain sense, "fictions" we are correct. But — and this is a very big but — we should also be aware of the contribution they made to Celtic art and literature. Not only did they (as did Iolo's work) help to focus the attention of the world upon Celtic literature — writers as famous and distant as Goethe defended them — with the result that we have far more Celtic literature today than we might have had — but Macpherson also added a dimension to the old stories which they had always possessed, but which had been hitherto neglected — that of the visionary, the magical, and the wondrous.

Like those who followed in his footsteps, writers such as William Sharp (Fiona Macleod) and George Russell (AE), Macpherson saw that beyond the Celtic myths and legends lay spiritual and magical qualities which had something to say to all people. His writings carry a charge of Celtic magical energy which is present in all the works included in this collection.

If we view Macpherson as beginning the Celtic Renaissance, then Matthew Arnold's influential essay on "The Study of Celtic Literature" (1868) contributed a further and powerful incentive. Arnold, an English poet who spoke none of the native Celtic tongues, wrote passionately of the beauties and subtleties of the ancient literatures of Ireland, Scotland, and Wales. His work prompted a wave of revivalist concern for the "lost" literature of the Celts — which had, of course, never really been lost at all — but which now, under the banner of "rediscovery" flourished again. Coincidentally, archaeologists and antiquarians began to study the artefacts of the Bronze Age, coins and inscriptions were studied and the findings published in newly founded journals like *Revue Celtique, Scottish Gaelic Studies* and *Y Cymmrodor.* New translations of the ancient bardic works began to appear. Many, like those of Iolo Morgannwg, were either inaccurate or downright forgeries. Some, like the works of Celticists such as Kuno Meyer, Whitley Stokes, and Douglas Hyde, were carefully researched and scholarly. Others, like the writings of Fiona Macleod, AE, James Stephens, Ella Young and Kenneth Morris, drew upon the wisdom of the traditional Celtic bards and myth-makers to create new visions.

The Celtic Renaissance had no formal organization, no elected leaders — though it did have its high priests, the foremost of these being the poet and statesman W.B. Yeats and the visionary genius George Russell, who wrote under the persona

15

of "AE." These two, more than any, spearheaded the resurgence of national pride in the heritage of Celtic Ireland.

"A nation," wrote Russell in 1937, "is a collective imagination held with intensity, an identity of culture or consciousness among millions, which makes them act as a single entity in relation to other human groups ... It is a spirit created by the poets, historians, musicians, by the utterances of great men, the artists in life. The mysterious element of beauty, of a peculiar beauty, exists in every nation and is the root cause of the love felt for it by its citizens, just as the existence of spirit, the most mysterious and impalpable thing, is the fountain of the manifold activities of the body."

For these men, and for the poets, writers, painters and visionaries who together brought into being the renascence of the Celtic spirit, the land and the ancient mythologies which grew out of it were of central importance. It was to the myths of the gods and goddesses that they turned to rediscover for themselves the powerful spirit of the old world, which they renewed for their generation and those which followed.

It is the writings of these, and others like them, dating from the middle of the eighteenth century to the 1940s, which make up the contents of this collection. Though they constituted no formal group, several knew each other and derived inspiration from each other's work. Sharp met with Russell, Standish O'Grady, Douglas Hyde and Lady Gregory in 1897 — though in 1901 he and Russell were to enter into an astringent public debate over the question of whether it was possible to call oneself a Celt without espousing Nationalism. Russell, though he well knew that Fiona Macleod was a pseudonym for Sharp, attacked "Miss Macleod" for "her" timidity and "moral platitudes," stating that: "A number of our rapidly dwindling race have their backs to a wall; they are making a last stand for freedom."[*] This freedom he saw, as did many of his fellows, represented in a return to the themes and heroes of the glorious Celtic past. Sharp, on the other hand, espoused a

---

[*] "Irish Ideals and Fiona Macleod," *All Ireland Review*, August, 1900.

gentler, more spiritual approach which, while it is very much present within all his work, none the less presents as much pride in the deeper qualities of the land as anything that Russell produced.

That Sharp was able to do this has much to do with a particular approach to these vital inner qualities. This is summed up in the use of the term "visionary," which may be applied to all of the writers included here. It is an aspect of their work which grew out of an association with various mystical or esoteric organizations. Thus Ella Young, Kenneth Morris and Russell were all, at one time or another, associated with the Theosophical Society; while Yeats and Russell were prime movers in the founding of the esoteric Order of the Golden Dawn, and Morris and Young adhered to the school of the Theosophist Katherine Tingley. This concentrated their intuitive understanding of the inner myths of the land in a mystical fashion. It was as though a battle was fought at some level between a nationalistic and a mystical approach to art, in which the latter won by embracing the former and thus changing it in various subtle ways.

In many instances the writers whose work is represented here were led deeper into the realm of Celtic myth and spirituality through their association with such groups as those named above. This not only gave new strength to their work, but also linked them in a way that is given to writers who espouse the *deeper* nationalism of their county's inner traditions.

I have deliberately sought out the most visionary of their works — though each contributed material in other areas of literature as well — which reflect a unique vision of the Celtic peoples. Some of these writers are well known still, like the painter Edward Burne-Jones represented here by an early short story "The Druid and the Maiden." Others, such as Fiona Macleod, George Macdonald, and AE, once had large followings but have since fallen into neglect. There are scholars, diplomats and statesmen here, as well as mystics, visionaries and poets. The earliest is Macpherson himself; the latest Henry Treece, who died in 1961 but was a true inheritor of the traditions of his spiritual brethren.

That their view of the past was not always historically accurate does not matter, any more than it matters that they sometimes reflect the curious romantic miasma which extended over all the arts, from poetry to painting, at this time. It was known, perhaps unkindly, as "the Celtic twilight," although this is a somewhat facile critical epithet which applies just as much to Victorian classical art or the work of the Pre-Raphaelites — where it is found perfectly acceptable — as to the writings of the Celtic revival. It seems that while it was considered appropriate to deal with heroic subjects (usually from Classical or Biblical sources) in a romanticized or even sentimental way within the other arts, to write of Celtic heroes or gods in the same way was considered either excessive or silly.

There is certainly a kind of sorrowful, misty quality to much of the work of the Celtic revivalists. It grows out of a sense of regret for a past which, in truth, never existed — at least, not in the way they chose to perceive it. Not that they were consciously re-inventing the past. They simply selected from the broken littoral of Celtic myth, spirituality and literature those things which they wanted — and from them re-created a world which was only partly like that of their ancestors. A poem by the nineteenth century Breton poet, Hervé Noel le Breton, perfectly describes the qualities of this vision.

> This is our doom. To walk for ever and ever
>   The wilderness unblest,
> To weary soul and sense in vain endeavour
>   And find no coign of rest ...
>
> To weave fantastic webs that shrink and crumble
>   Before they leave the loom,
> To build with travail aery towers that tumble
>   And temples like the tomb ...
>
> (The Burden of Lost Souls)

In works such as this, as in the stories and poems assembled here,

18

the Celtic revivalists succeeded in transcending the insularity of nationalism and of a romanticized view of the past, bringing into being something which spoke to people of other cultures also.

That they were able to do this is largely due to the way in which they perceived the past — not as a set of historical verities, but as a mystical whole which was as much the product of their own spiritual heritage — a heritage which they felt through the soles of their feet, from the land itself.

Thus when Yeats wrote that "in our land, there is no river or mountain that is not associated in the memory with some event or legend," he was speaking the truth: the *Dindshencas*, a vast body of literature dealing with local legends, had already begun to be edited by E.J. Gwynne — but more than this there was a deeper and abiding sense of the land as a living being. In early Celtic mythology Ireland was represented as "Eriu," a sovereignty-bearing woman with whom would-be kings must sleep to substantiate their claim. The writers of the Celtic Renaissance may not have been required to "marry the land" in this way, but they sought out the sovereign mysteries of their native culture with every bit as much devotion and single-mindedness.

It is this which informs all they wrote, and it is a voice that can be heard — if listened for with care — in most of the writing which follows. Each of the writers chosen to represent the Celtic revival was at home in the Hollow Hills, the faery palaces where the ancient gods and goddesses, the *Sidhe*, the Lordly Ones, had their home. They are thus all, in one way or another, "companions" of the Sidhe, who have visited the Otherworld and returned with stories of the wonders they have seen. To spend a little time in their company is to take a step outside the world in which we daily find ourselves — to a place where there is no time, no death, no war or famine or murder. Yet it is no dreamy paradise. Rather, it offers us a reflection of our own world as we have perhaps never seen it before. In this the works included here are truly visionary — they give back to us a sense of the numinous which we have mostly lost. We too become, for a time, companions of the Sidhe, and wander in the realms of the infinite from which it is not possible to return unchanged.

In conclusion I would echo the words of William Sharp in the introduction to his wife's 1896 anthology *Lyra Celtica.* It was, he maintained, compiled "not for the specialist but for the lover of poetry." From it one might gain a glimpse "into a strange and beautiful land wherein, as in a certain design by William Blake, the sun, the moon, and the morning star all shine together, and where the horizons are spanned by fugitive rainbows ever marvellously dissolving and more marvellously re-forming."

John Matthews
Oxford, 1993

The Night-Song of the Bards

James Macpherson

James Macpherson (1736–96) was as much a composer as he was a collector of Celtic tradition. Though he never admitted to having forged most of the material attributed to the third century bard "Ossian," there can be little doubt that he built upon no more than a skeletal core of genuine poetry and myth to create a wholly new work of art. Much of the voluminous poetry is scarcely readable with enjoyment today, but Macpherson often succeeded in capturing the essence of the ancient tradition which obsessed him. For this reason, and because of his importance as a forerunner of the Celtic revival, I have included the following extract from the epic poem "Fingal," originally published in 1762 and reprinted as part of The Poems of Ossian *in 1846. Here five bards, passing the night in the house of a chieftain who is himself a poet, go out to make observations of the night and on returning make their extempore description of what they have seen.*

From *The Poems of Ossian,* by James Macpherson. Patrick Geddes & Co. Edinburgh 1896.

Mildred R. Lamb

The Night-Song of the Bards

[Five bards passing the night in the house of a chief, who was a poet himself, went severally to make their observations on, and returned with an extempore description of, night.]

FIRST BARD.

Night is dull and dark. The clouds rest on the hills. No star with green trembling beam; no moon looks from the sky. I hear the blast in the wood, but I hear it distant far. The stream of the valley murmurs; but its murmur is sullen and sad. From the tree at the grave of the dead the long-howling owl is heard. I see a dim form on the plain! It is a ghost! it fades, it flies. Some funeral shall pass this way: the meteor marks the path.

The distant dog is howling from the hut of the hill. The stag lies on the mountain moss: the hind is at his side. She hears the wind in his branchy horns. She starts, but lies again.

The roe is in the cleft of the rock; the heath-cock's head is beneath his wing. No beast, no bird is abroad, but the owl and the howling fox: she on a leafless tree; he in a cloud on the hill.

Dark, panting, trembling, sad, the traveller has lost his way. Through shrubs, through thorns, he goes, along the gurgling rill. He fears the rock and the fen. He fears the ghost of night. The old tree groans to the blast; the falling branch resounds. The wind drives the withered burrs, clung together, along the grass. It is the light tread of a ghost! He trembles amidst the night.

Dark, dusky, howling, is night, cloudy, windy, and full of ghosts! The dead are abroad! my friends, receive me from the night.

SECOND BARD.

The wind is up, the shower descends. The spirit of the mountain shrieks. Woods fall from high. Windows flap.* The growing river

---

* i.e. the sheepskin or deerskin coverings for apertures, still used in some remote shielings.

23

roars. The traveller attempts the ford. Hark! that shriek! he dies! The storm drives the horse from the hill, the goat, the lowing cow. They tremble as drives the shower, beside the shouldering bank.

The hunter starts from sleep, in his lonely hut; he wakes the fire decayed. His wet dogs smoke around him. He fills the chinks with heath. Loud roar two mountain streams which meet beside his booth.[*]

Sad on the side of a hill the wandering shepherd sits. The tree resounds above him. The stream roars down the rock. He waits for the rising moon to guide him to his home.

Ghosts ride on the storm tonight. Sweet is their voice between the squalls of wind. Their songs are of other worlds.

The rain is past. The dry wind blows. Streams roar, and windows flap. Cold drops fall from the roof. I see the starry sky. But the shower gathers again. The west is gloomy and dark. Night is stormy and dismal; receive me, my friends, from night.

THIRD BARD.
The wind still sounds between the hills, and whistles through the grass of the rock. The firs fall from their place. The turfy hut is torn. The clouds, divided, fly over the sky, and show the burning stars. The meteor, token of death! flies sparkling through the gloom. It rests on the hill. I see the withered fern, the dark-browned rock, the fallen oak. Who is that in his shroud beneath the tree, by the stream?

The waves dark-tumble on the lake, and lash its rocky sides. The boat is brimful in the cove; the oars on the rocking tide. A maid sits sad beside the rock, and eyes the rolling stream. Her lover promised to come. She saw his boat, when yet it was light, on the lake. Is this his broken boat on the shore? Are these his groans on the wind?

Hark! the hail rattles around. The flaky snow descends. The tops of the hills are white. The stormy winds abate. Various is the night and cold; receive me, my friends, from night.

[*] Shed.

FOURTH BARD.

Night is calm and fair; blue, starry, settled is night. The winds, with the clouds, are gone. They sink behind the hill. The moon is up on the mountain. Trees glister, streams shine on the rock. Bright rolls the settled lake; bright the stream of the vale.

I see the trees overturned; the shocks of corn on the plain. The wakeful hind rebuilds the shocks, and whistles on the distant field.

Calm, settled, fair is night! Who comes from the place of the dead? That form with the robe of snow, white arms, and dark-brown hair! It is the daughter of the chief of the people: she that lately fell! Come, let us view thee, O maid! Thou that hast been the delight of heroes! The blast drives the phantom away; white, without form, it ascends the hill.

The breezes drive the blue mist, slowly, over the narrow vale. It rises on the hill, and joins its head to heaven. Night is settled, calm, blue, starry, bright with the moon. Receive me not, my friends, for lovely is the night.

FIFTH BARD.

Night is calm, but dreary. The moon is in a cloud in the west. Slow moves that pale beam along the shaded hill. The distant wave is heard. The torrent murmurs on the rock. The cock is heard from the booth.* More than half the night is past. The house-wife, groping in the gloom, re-kindles the settled fire. The hunter thinks that day approaches, and calls his bounding dogs. He ascends the hill, and whistles on his way. A blast removes the cloud. He sees the starry plough of the north. Much of the night is to pass. He nods by the mossy rock.

Hark! the whirlwind is in the wood! A low murmur in the vale! It is the mighty army of the dead returning from the air.

The moon rests behind the hill. The beam is still on that lofty rock. Long are the shadows of the trees. Now it is dark over all. Night is dreary, silent, and dark; receive me, my friends, from night.

*Here probably the byre.

25

THE CHIEF.

Let clouds rest on the hills: spirits fly, and travellers fear. Let the winds of the woods arise, the sounding storms descend. Roar streams and windows flap, and green-winged meteors fly! Rise the pale moon from behind her hills, or inclose her head in clouds! Night is alike to me, blue, stormy, or gloomy the sky. Night flies before the beam, when it is poured on the hill. The young day returns from his clouds, but we return no more.

Where are our chiefs of old? Where are our kings of mighty name? The fields of their battles are silent. Scarce their mossy tombs remain. We shall also be forgot. This lofty house shall fall. Our sons shall not behold the ruins in grass. They shall ask of the aged, "Where stood the walls of our fathers?"

Raise the song, and strike the harp; send round the shells of joy. Suspend a hundred tapers on high. Youths and maids begin the dance. Let some grey bard be near me, to tell the deeds of other times; of kings renowned in our land, of chiefs we behold no more. Thus let the night pass until morning shall appear in our halls. Then let the bow be at hand, the dogs, the youths of the chase. We shall ascend the hill with day, and awake the deer.

The Heart of the Spring

W B Yeats

William Butler Yeats (1865–1939) was a poet and playwright, a scholar and mystic of the highest order. As well as contributing some of the finest poetry of this or any age, he was an active politician who campaigned energetically for the Nationalist cause in Ireland. He also collected faery lore and was a leading light in the Hermetic Order of the Golden Dawn. This group of like-minded individuals, who included A.E. Waite, MacGregor Mathers and W. Wynn Westcott, was founded in 1886 with the avowed intention of exploring the inner realms and in seeking there the mystery which informed the whole of creation. Yeats' own researches and findings, some of them obtained through his wife's mediumistic skills, appeared in A Vision *(1937), an extraordinary and powerful re-statement of the archetypal order of the universe. Yeats' stories reflect both his love of mythology and his perceptions of the eternal mystery just beneath the surface of life. The story printed here comes from an early collection,* The Secret Rose *(1897) and combines both Yeats' hermetic or esoteric interests and his love of traditional lore. Another collection,* The Celtic Twilight, *very probably gave rise to the description attached to much of the mystical and romantic writings of this period.*

From *The Secret Rose* by W. B. Yeats. Macmillan, London 1897.

The Heart of the Spring

A very old man, whose face was almost as fleshless as the foot of a bird, sat meditating upon the rocky shore of the flat and hazel-covered isle which fills the widest part of Lough Gill. A russet-faced boy of seventeen years sat by his side, watching the swallows dipping for flies in the still water. The old man was dressed in threadbare blue velvet and the boy wore a frieze coat and had a rosary about his neck. Behind the two, and half hidden by trees, was a little monastery. It had been burned down a long while before by sacrilegious men of the Queen's party, but had been roofed anew with rushes by the boy, that the old man might find shelter in his last days. He had not set his spade, however, into the garden about it, and the lilies and the roses of the monks had spread out until their confused luxuriance met and mingled with the narrowing circle of the fern. Beyond the lilies and the roses the ferns were so deep that a child walking among them would be hidden from sight, even though he stood upon his toes; and beyond the fern rose many hazels and small oak-trees.

"Master," said the boy, "this long fasting, and the labour of beckoning after nightfall to the beings who dwell in the waters and among the hazels and oak-trees, is too much for your strength. Rest from all this labour for a little, for your hand this day seemed more heavy upon my shoulder and your feet less steady than I have known them. Men say that you are older than the eagles, and yet you will not seek the rest that belongs to age."

He spoke eagerly, as though his heart were in the words; and the old man answered slowly and deliberately, as though his heart were in distant days and events.

"I will tell you why I have not been able to rest," he said. "It is right that you should know, for you have served me faithfully these five years, and even with affection, taking away thereby a little of the doom of loneliness which always falls upon the wise. Now, too, that the end of my labour and the triumph of my hopes is at hand, it is more needful for you to have this knowledge."

"Master, do not think that I would question you. It is my life to keep the fire alight, and the thatch close that the rain may not come in, and strong, that the wind may not blow it among the trees; and to take down the heavy books from the shelves, and to possess an incurious and reverent heart. God has made out of His abundance a separate wisdom for everything which lives, and to do these things is my wisdom."

"You are afraid," said the old man, and his eyes shone with a momentary anger.

"Sometimes at night," said the boy, "when you are reading, with a stick of mountain ash in your hand, I look out of the door and see, now a great grey man driving swine among the hazels, and now many little people in red caps who come out of the lake driving little white cows before them. I do not fear these little people so much as the grey man; for, when they come near the house, they milk the cows, and they drink the frothing milk, and begin to dance; and I know there is good in the heart that loves dancing; but I fear them for all that. And I fear the tall white-armed ladies who come out of the air, and move slowly hither and thither, crowning themselves with the roses or with the lilies, and shaking about them their living hair, which moves, for so I have heard them tell the little people, with the motion of their thoughts, now spreading out and now gathering close to their heads. They have mild, beautiful faces, but I am afraid of the Sidhe, and afraid of the art which draws them about us."

"Why," said the old man, "do you fear the ancient gods who made the spears of your father's fathers to be stout in battle, and the little people who came at night from the depth of the lakes and sang among the crickets upon their hearths? And in our evil day they still watch over the loveliness of the earth. But I must tell you why I have fasted and laboured when others would sink into the sleep of age, for without your help once more I shall have fasted and laboured to no good end. When you have done for me this last thing, you may go and build your cottage and till your fields, and take some girl to wife, and forget the ancient gods, for I shall leave behind me in this little house money to make strong the roof-tree of your cottage and to keep cellar and larder full. I have sought through all my life to find the secret of life. I was not happy in my youth, for I knew that it would pass; and I was not happy in my manhood, for I knew that age was coming; and so I gave myself, in youth and manhood and age, to the search for the Great Secret. I longed for a life whose abundance would fill centuries, I scorned the life of fourscore winters. I would be—no, I *will* be!—like the ancient gods of the land. I read in my youth, in a Hebrew manuscript I found in a Spanish monastery, that there is a moment after the Sun has entered the Ram and before he has passed the Lion, which trembles with the Song of the Immortal Powers, and that whosoever finds this moment and listens to the Song shall become like the Immortal Powers themselves; I came back to Ireland and asked the faery men, and the cow-doctors, if they knew when this moment was; but though all had heard of it, there was none could find the moment upon the hour-glass. So I gave myself to magic, and spent my life in fasting and in labour that I might bring the gods and the Men of Faery to my side; and now at last one of the Men of Faery has told me that the moment is at hand. One, who wore a red cap and whose lips were white with the froth of the new milk, whispered it into my ear. Tomorrow, a little before the close of the first hour after dawn, I shall find the moment, and then I will go away to a southern land and build myself a palace of white marble amid orange-trees, and gather the brave and the beautiful about me, and enter into the eternal kingdom of my youth. But, that I may hear the whole Song, I was told by the little fellow with the froth of the new milk on his lips that you must bring great masses of green boughs and pile them about the door and the window of my room; and you must put fresh green rushes upon the floor, and cover the table and the rushes with the roses and the lilies of the monks. You must do this tonight, and in the morning at the end of the first hour after dawn, you must come and find me."

"Will you be quite young then?" said the boy.

"I will be as young then as you are, but now I am still old and tired, and you must help me to my chair and to my books."

When the boy had left the wizard in his room, and had lighted the lamp which, by some contrivance, gave forth a sweet odour as of strange flowers, he went into the wood and began cutting green boughs from the hazels, and great bundles of rushes from the western border of the isle, where the small rocks gave place to gently sloping sand and clay. It was nightfall before he had cut enough for his purpose, and well nigh midnight before he had carried the last bundle to its place, and gone back for the roses and the lilies. It was one of those warm, beautiful nights when everything seems carved of precious stones. Sleuth Wood away to the south looked as though cut out of green beryl, and the waters that mirrored it shone like pale opal. The roses he was gathering were like glowing rubies, and the lilies had the dull lustre of pearl. Everything had taken upon itself the look of something imperishable, except a glow-worm, whose faint flame burnt on steadily among the shadows, moving slowly hither and thither, the only thing that seemed alive, the only thing that seemed perishable as mortal hope. The boy gathered a great armful of roses and lilies, and thrusting the glow-worm among their pearl and ruby, carried them into the room, where the old man sat in a half-slumber. He laid armful after armful upon the floor and above the table, and then, gently closing the door, threw himself upon his bed of rushes, to dream of a peaceful manhood with a desirable wife and laughing children.

At dawn he got up, and went down to the edge of the lake, taking the hour-glass with him. He put some bread and wine into the boat, that his master might not lack food at the outset of his journey, and then sat down to wait the close of the first hour after dawn. Gradually the birds began to sing, and when the last grains of sand were falling, everything suddenly seemed to overflow with their music. It was the most beautiful and living moment of the year; one could listen to the spring's heart beating in it. He got up and went to find his master. The green boughs filled the door, and he had to make a way through them. When he entered the room the sunlight was falling in flickering circles on floor and walls and table, and everything was full of soft green shadows. But the old man sat clasping a mass of roses and lilies in his arms, and with his head sunk upon his breast.

On the table, at his left hand, was a leather wallet full of gold and silver pieces, as for a journey, and at his right hand was a long staff. The boy touched him and he did not move. He lifted the hands, but they were quite cold, and they fell heavily.

"It were better for him," said the lad, "to have said his prayers and kissed his beads!" He looked at the thread-bare blue velvet, and he saw it was covered with the pollen of the flowers, and while he was looking at it a thrush, who had alighted among the boughs that were piled against the window, began to sing.

The Dàn-nan-Ròn

Fiona Macleod

*Fiona Macleod was the pseudonym of William Sharp (1855–1905)
— a much protected secret during his lifetime. During his
comparatively brief life he travelled widely and produced a large
collection of works — all of them tinged with a mystical and eloquent
perception of the Celtic tradition. His curious double life — as, on the
one hand, the successful and popular female writer of fantasies and
poetry and, on the other, as a respected critic and defender of the Celtic
spirit, gave rise to an underlying tension in all his work which saves
it from sentimentality and bathos. Macleod/Sharp was at the centre of
the Edinburgh movement: artists and writers who constellated around
the scholar and publisher Patrick Geddes — producing many of the
best works of the Celtic revival. His most popular work was
undoubtedly "The Immortal Hour", a play about the Sidhe, the
god-like faery race of Ireland. This was turned into a hugely successful
opera with music by Rutland Boughton (1920) which has recently
been re-recorded to popular acclaim. Of all the writers represented by
this collection, Macleod deserves a special place in the hearts of all
who love the mystery and beauty of the Celtic world. The title of the
story included here refers to a fateful tune, perhaps borrowed from the
faery people, which when played always brought bad luck in its wake.*

From *The Hills of Ruel. Duffield & Co. New York 1921.*

Margery H. Lawrence

The Dàn-nan-Ròn

I

When Anne Gillespie, that was my friend in Eilanmore, left the island after the death of her uncle, the old man Robert Achanna, it was to go far west.

Among the men of the Outer Isles who for three summers past had been at the fishing off Eilanmore there was one named Mànus MacCodrum. He was a fine lad to see, but though most of the fisherfolk of the Lews and North Uist are fair, either with reddish hair and grey eyes, or blue-eyed and yellow-haired, he was of a brown skin with dark hair and dusky brown eyes. He was, however, as unlike to the dark Celts of Arran and the Inner Hebrides as to the Northmen. He came of his people, sure enough. All the MacCodrums of North Uist had been brown-skinned and brown-haired and brown-eyed: and herein may have lain the reason why, in bygone days, this small clan of Uist was known throughout the Western Isles as the *Sliochd-nan-Ròn*, the offspring of the seals.

Not so tall as most of the men of North Uist and the Lews, Mànus MacCodrum was of a fair height, and supple and strong. No man was a better fisherman than he, and he was well liked of his fellows, for all the morose gloom that was upon him at times. He had a voice as sweet as a woman's when he sang, and he sang often, and knew all the old runes of the islands, from the Obb of Harris to the Head of Mingulay. Often, too, he chanted the beautiful *orain spioradail* of the Catholic priests and Christian Brothers of South Uist and Barra, though where he lived in North Uist he was the sole man who adhered to the ancient faith.

It may have been because Anne was a Catholic too, though, sure, the Achannas were so also, notwithstanding that their forebears and kindred in Galloway were Protestant (and this because of old Robert Achanna's love for his wife, who was of the old faith, so it is said)—it may have been for this reason, though I think her lover's admiring eyes and soft speech and sweet singing had more to do with it, that she pledged her troth to Mànus. It was a south wind for him as the saying is; for with her rippling brown hair and soft, grey eyes and cream-white skin, there was no comelier lass in the isles.

So when Achanna was laid to his long rest, and there was none left upon Eilanmore save only his three youngest sons, Mànus MacCodrum sailed north-eastward across the Minch to take home his bride. Of the four eldest sons, Alasdair had left Eilanmore some months before his father died, and sailed westward, though no one knew whither or for what end or for how long, and no word had been brought from him, nor was he ever seen again in the island which had come to be called Eilan-nan-Allmharachain, the Isle of the Strangers; Allan and William had been drowned in a wild gale in the Minch; and Robert had died of the white fever, that deadly wasting disease which is the scourge of the Isles. Marcus was now "Eilanmore," and lived there with Gloom and Seumas, all three unmarried, though it was rumoured among the neighbouring islanders that each loved Marsail nic Ailpean,[1] in Eilean-Rona of the Summer Isles hard by the coast of Sutherland.

When Mànus asked Anne to go with him she agreed. The three brothers were ill-pleased at this, for apart from their not wishing their cousin to go so far away, they did not want to lose her, as she not only cooked for them and did all that a woman does, including spinning and weaving, but was most sweet and fair to see, and in the long winter nights sang by the hour together, while Gloom played strange wild airs upon his *feadan*, a kind of oaten pipe or flute.

She loved Mànus, I know; but there was this reason also for her going, that she was afraid of Gloom. Often upon the moor or on the hill she turned and hastened home, because she heard

[1] Marsail nic Ailpean is the Gaelic of which an English translation would be Marjory MacAlpine. *Nic* is a contraction for *nighean mhic*, "daughter of the line of."

the lilt and fall of that feadan. It was an eerie thing to her, to be going through the twilight when she thought the three men were in the house, smoking after their supper, and suddenly to hear beyond and coming towards her the shrill song of that oaten flute, playing "The Dance of the Dead," or "The Flow and Ebb," or "The Shadow-Reel."

That, sometimes at least, he knew she was there was clear to her, because, as she stole rapidly through the tangled fern and gale, she would hear a mocking laugh follow her like a leaping thing.

Mànus was not there on the night when she told Marcus and his brothers that she was going. He was in the haven on board the *Luath*, with his two mates, he singing in the moonshine as all three sat mending their fishing gear.

After the supper was done, the three brothers sat smoking and talking over an offer that had been made about some Shetland sheep. For a time Anne watched them in silence. They were not like brothers, she thought. Marcus, tall, broad-shouldered, with yellow hair and strangely dark blue-black eyes and black eyebrows; stern, with a weary look on his sun-brown face. The light from the peats glinted upon the tawny curve of thick hair that trailed from his upper lip, for he had the *caisean-feusag* of the Northmen. Gloom, slighter of build, dark of hue and hair, but with hairless face; with thin, white, long-fingered hands that had ever a nervous motion, as though they were tide-wrack. There was always a frown on the centre of his forehead, even when he smiled with his thin lips and dusky, unbetraying eyes. He looked what he was, the brain of the Achannas. Not only did he have the English as though native to that tongue, but could and did read strange unnecessary books. Moreover, he was the only son of Robert Achanna to whom the old man had imparted his store of learning, for Achanna had been a schoolmaster in his youth, in Galloway, and he had intended Gloom for the priesthood. His voice, too, was low and clear, but cold as pale-green water running under ice. As for Seumas, he was more like Marcus than Gloom, though not so fair. He had the same brown hair and shadowy hazel eyes, the same pale and smooth face, with something of the same intent look which characterized the long-time missing, and probably dead, eldest brother, Alasdair. He, too, was tall and gaunt. On Seumas's face there was that indescribable, as to some of course imperceptible, look which is indicated by the phrase, "the dusk of the shadow," though few there are who know what they mean by that, or, knowing, are fain to say.

Suddenly, and without any word or reason for it, Gloom turned and spoke to her.

"Well, Anne, and what is it?"

"I did not speak, Gloom."

"True for you *mo cailinn.* But it's about to speak you were."

"Well, and that is true, Marcus, and you, Gloom, and you, Seumas, I have that to tell which you will not be altogether glad for the hearing. 'Tis about—about—me and—and Mànus."

There was no reply at first. The three brothers sat looking at her like the kye at a stranger on the moor-land. There was a deepening of the frown on Gloom's brow, but when Anne looked at him his eyes fell and dwelt in the shadow at his feet. Then Marcus spoke in a low voice:

"Is it Mànus MacCodrum you will be meaning?"

"Ay, sure."

Again silence. Gloom did not lift his eyes, and Seumas was now staring at the peats. Marcus shifted uneasily.

"And what will Mànus MacCodrum be wanting?"

"Sure, Marcus, you know well what I mean. Why do you make this thing hard for me? There is but one thing he would come here wanting. And he has asked me if I will go with him; and I have said yes; and if you are not willing that he come again with the minister, or that we go across to the kirk in Berneray of Uist in the Sound of Harris, then I will not stay under this roof another night, but will go away from Eilanmore at sunrise in the *Luath,* that is now in the haven. And that is for the hearing and knowing, Marcus and Gloom and Seumas!"

Once more silence followed her speaking. It was broken in a strange way. Gloom slipped his feadan into his hands, and so to his mouth. The clear, cold notes of the flute filled the flame-lit room. It was as though white polar birds were drifting before the coming of snow.

The notes slid into a wild, remote air: cold moonlight on the dark o' the sea, it was. It was the *Dàn-nan-Ròn.*

Anne flushed, trembled, and then abruptly rose. As she leaned on her clenched right hand upon the table, the light of the peats showed that her eyes were aflame.

"Why do you play *that,* Gloom Achanna?"

The man finished the bar, then blew into the oaten pipe, before, just glancing at the girl, he replied:

"And what harm will there be in *that,* Anna-ban?"

"You know it is harm. That is the 'Dàn-nan-Ròn'!"

"Ay, and what then, Anna-ban?"

"What then? Are you thinking I don't know what you mean by playing the 'Song o' the Seals'?"

With an abrupt gesture Gloom put the feadan aside. As he did so, he rose.

"See here, Anne," he began roughly, when Marcus intervened.

"That will do just now, Gloom. Anne-à-ghraidh, do you mean that you are going to do this thing?"

"Ay, sure."

"Do you know why Gloom played the 'Dàn-nan-Ròn'?"

"It was a cruel thing."

"You know what is said in the isles about—about—this or that man, who is under *gheasan,* who is spell-bound, and—and—about the seals—"

"Yes, Marcus, it is knowing it that I am: '*Tha iad a' cantuinn gur h-e daoine fo gheasan a th' anns no roin.*' "

" '*They say that seals*', " he repeated slowly, " '*They say that seals are men under magic spells.*' And have you ever pondered that thing, Anne, my cousin?"

"I am knowing well what you mean."

"Then you will know that the MacCodrums of North Uist are called the *Sliochd-nan-Ròn?*"

"I have heard."

"And would you be for marrying a man that is of the race of

39

the beasts, and himself knowing what that *geas* means, and who may any day go back to his people?"

"Ah, now, Marcus, sure it is making a mock of me you are. Neither you nor any here believe that foolish thing. How can a man born of a woman be a seal, even though his *sinnsear* were the offspring of the sea-people? which is not a saying I am believing either, though it may be; and not that it matters much, whatever, about the far-back forebears."

Marcus frowned darkly, and at first made no response. At last he answered, speaking sullenly:

"You may be believing this or you may be believing that, Anna-nic-Gilleasbuig, but two things are as well known as that the east wind brings the blight and the west wind the rain. And one is this: that long ago a seal-man wedded a woman of North Uist, and that he or his son was called Neil MacCodrum; and that the sea-fever of the seal was in the blood of his line ever after. And this is the other: that twice within the memory of living folk, a MacCodrum has taken upon himself the form of a seal, and has so met his death, once Neil MacCodrum of the Ru' Tormaid, and once Anndra MacCodrum of Berneray in the Sound. There's talk of others, but these are known of us all. And you will not be forgetting now that Neildonn was the grandfather, and that Anndra was the brother of the father of Mànus MacCodrum?"

"I am not caring what you say, Marcus. It is all foam of the sea."

"There's no foam without wind or tide, Anne, an' it's a dark tide that will be bearing you away to Uist, and a black wind that will be blowing far away behind the east, the wind that will be carrying his death-cry to your ears."

The girl shuddered. The brave spirit in her, however, did not quail.

"Well, so be it. To each his fate. But, seal or no seal, I am going to wed Mànus MacCodrum, who is a man as good as any here, and a true man at that, and the man I love, and that will be my man, God willing, the praise be His!"

Again Gloom took up the feadan, and sent a few cold, white

notes floating through the hot room, breaking, suddenly, into the wild, fantastic, opening air of the "Dàn-nan-Ròn."

With a low cry and passionate gesture Anne sprang forward, snatched the oat-flute from his grasp, and would have thrown it in the fire. Marcus held her in an iron grip, however.

"Don't you be minding Gloom, Anne," he said quietly, as he took the feadan from her hand and handed it to his brother; "sure, he's only telling you in *his* way what I am telling you in mine."

She shook herself free, and moved to the other side of the table. On the opposite wall hung the dirk which had belonged to the old Achanna. This she unfastened. Holding it in her right hand, she faced the three men.

"On the cross of the dirk I swear I will be the woman of Mànus MacCodrum."

The brothers made no response. They looked at her fixedly.

"And by the cross of the dirk I swear that if any man comes between me and Mànus, this dirk will be for his remembering in a certain hour of the day of the days."

As she spoke, she looked meaningly at Gloom, whom she feared more than Marcus or Seumas.

"And by the cross of the dirk I swear that if evil comes to Mànus, this dirk will have another sheath, and that will be my milkless breast; and by that token I now throw the old sheath in the fire."

As she finished, she threw the sheath on to the burning peats. Gloom quietly lifted it, brushed off the sparks of flame as though they were dust, and put it in his pocket.

"And by the same token, Anne," he said, "your oaths will come to nought."

Rising, he made a sign to his brothers to follow. When they were outside he told Seumas to return, and to keep Anne within, by peace if possible, by force if not. Briefly they discussed their plans, and then separated. While Seumas went back, Marcus and Gloom made their way to the haven.

Their black figures were visible in the moonlight, but at first they were not noticed by the men on board the *Luath*, for Mànus was singing.

When the islesman stopped abruptly, one of his companions asked him jokingly if his song had brought a seal alongside, and bid him beware lest it was a woman of the sea-people.

His face darkened, but he made no reply. When the others listened they heard the wild strain of the "Dàn-nan-Ròn" stealing through the moonshine. Staring against the shore, they could discern the two brothers.

"What will be the meaning of that?" asked one of the men uneasily.

"When a man comes instead of a woman," answered Mànus slowly, "the young corbies are astir in the nest."

So, it meant blood. Aulay MacNeil and Donull MacDonull put down their gear, rose, and stood waiting for what Mànus would do.

"Ho, there!" he cried.

"Ho-ro!"

"What will you be wanting, Eilanmore?"

"We are wanting a word of you, Mànus MacCodrum. Will you come ashore?"

"If you want a word of me, you can come to me."

"There is no boat here."

"I'll send the *bàta-beag.*"

When he had spoken, Mànus asked Donull, the younger of his mates, a lad of seventeen, to row to the shore.

"And bring back no more than one man," he added, "whether it be Eilanmore himself or Gloom-mhic-Achanna."

The rope of the small boat was unfastened, and Donull rowed it swiftly through the moonshine. The passing of a cloud dusked the shore, but they saw him throw a rope for the guiding of the boat alongside the ledge of the landing-place; then the sudden darkening obscured the vision. Donull must be talking, they thought, for two or three minutes elapsed without sign, but at last the boat put off again, and with two figures only. Doubtless the lad had had to argue against the coming of both Marcus and Gloom.

This, in truth, was what Donull had done. But while he was speaking Marcus was staring fixedly beyond him.

"Who is it that is there?" he asked, "there, in the stern?"

"There is no one there."

"I thought I saw the shadow of a man."

"Then it was my shadow, Eilanmore."

Achanna turned to his brother.

"I see a man's death there in the boat."

Gloom quailed for a moment, then laughed low.

"I see no death of a man sitting in the boat, Marcus, but if I did I am thinking it would dance to the air of the 'Dàn-nan-Ròn,' which is more than the wraith of you or me would do."

"It is not a wraith I was seeing, but the death of a man."

Gloom whispered, and his brother nodded sullenly. The next moment a heavy muffler was round Donull's mouth; and before he could resist, or even guess what had happened, he was on his face on the shore, bound and gagged. A minute later the oars were taken by Gloom, and the boat moved swiftly out of the inner haven.

As it drew near Mànus stared at it intently.

"That is not Donull that is rowing, Aulay!"

"No: it will be Gloom Achanna, I'm thinking."

MacCodrum started. If so, that other figure at the stern was too big for Donull. The cloud passed just as the boat came alongside. The rope was made secure, and then Marcus and Gloom sprang on board.

"Where is Donull MacDonull?" demanded Mànus sharply.

Marcus made no reply, so Gloom answered for him.

"He has gone up to the house with a message to Anne-nic-Gilleasbuig."

"And what will that message be?"

"That Mànus MacCodrum has sailed away from Eilanmore, and will not see her again."

MacCodrum laughed. It was a low, ugly laugh.

"Sure, Gloom Achanna, you should be taking that feadan of yours and playing the *Codhail-nan-Pairtean*, for I'm thinkin' the crabs are gathering about the rocks down below us, an' laughing wi' their claws."

"Well, and that is a true thing," Gloom replied slowly and

43

quietly. "Yes, for sure I might, as you say, be playing the 'Meeting of the Crabs.' Perhaps," he added, as by a sudden afterthought, "perhaps, though it is a calm night, you will be hearing the *comh-thonn.* The 'slapping of the waves' is a better thing to be hearing than the 'Meeting of the Crabs.' "

"If I hear the *comh-thonn* it is not in the way you will be meaning, Gloom-mhic-Achanna. 'Tis not the 'up sail and good-bye' they will be saying, but 'Home wi' the Bride.' "

Here Marcus intervened.

"Let us be having no more words, Mànus MacCodrum. The girl Anne is not for you. Gloom is to be her man. So get you hence. If you will be going quiet, it is quiet we will be. If you have your feet on this thing, then you will be having that too which I saw in the boat."

"And what was it you saw in the boat, Achanna?"

"The death of a man."

"So——. And now" (this after a prolonged silence, wherein the four men stood facing each other) "is it a blood-matter if not of peace?"

"Ay. Go, if you are wise. If not, 'tis your own death you will be making."

There was a flash as of summer lightning. A bluish flame seemed to leap through the moonshine. Marcus reeled, with a gasping cry; then, leaning back, till his face blanched in the moonlight, his knees gave way. As he fell, he turned half round. The long knife which Mànus had hurled at him had not penetrated his breast more than an inch at most, but as he fell on the deck it was driven into him up to the hilt.

In the blank silence that followed, the three men could hear a sound like the ebb-tide in seaweed. It was the gurgling of the bloody froth in the lungs of the dead man.

The first to speak was his brother, and then only when thin reddish-white foam-bubbles began to burst from the blue lips of Marcus.

"It is murder."

He spoke low, but it was like the surf of breakers in the ears of those who heard.

"You have said one part of a true word, Gloom Achanna. It is murder—that you and he came here for!"

"The death of Marcus Achanna is on you, Mànus MacCodrum."

"So be it, as between yourself and me, or between all of your blood and me; though Aulay MacNeil as well as you can witness that though in self-defence I threw the knife at Achanna, it was his own doing that drove it into him."

"You can whisper that to the rope when it is round your neck."

"And what will *you* be doing now, Gloom-mhic-Achanna?"

For the first time Gloom shifted uneasily. A swift glance revealed to him the awkward fact that the boat trailed behind the *Luath*, so that he could not leap into it, while if he turned to haul it close by the rope he was at the mercy of the two men.

"I will go in peace," he said quietly.

"Ay," was the answer, in an equally quiet tone, "in the white peace."

Upon this menace of death the two men stood facing each other.

Achanna broke the silence at last.

"You'll hear the 'Dàn-nan-Ròn' the night before you die, Mànus MacCodrum, and lest you doubt it you'll hear it again in your death-hour."

"*Ma tha sin an Dàn*—if that be ordained." Mànus spoke gravely. His very quietude, however, boded ill. There was no hope of clemency; Gloom knew that.

Suddenly he laughed scornfully. Then, pointing with his right hand as if to some one behind his two adversaries, he cried out: "Put the death-hand on them, Marcus! Give them the Grave!" Both men sprang aside, the heart of each nigh upon bursting. The death-touch of the newly slain is an awful thing to incur, for it means that the wraith can transfer all its evil to the person touched.

The next moment there was a heavy splash. Mànus realized that it was no more than a ruse, and that Gloom had escaped. With feverish haste he hauled in the small boat, leaped into it, and began at once to row so as to intercept his enemy.

Achanna rose once, between him and the *Luath*. MacCodrum crossed the oars in the thole-pins and seized the boat-hook.

The swimmer kept straight for him. Suddenly he dived. In a flash Mànus knew that Gloom was going to rise under the boat, seize the keel, and upset him, and thus probably be able to grip him from above. There was time, and no more, to leap; and, indeed, scarce had he plunged into the sea ere the boat swung right over, Achanna clambering over it the next moment.

At first Gloom could not see where his foe was. He crouched on the upturned craft, and peered eagerly into the moonlit water. All at once a black mass shot out of the shadow between him and the smack. This black mass laughed—the same low, ugly laugh that had preceded the death of Marcus.

He who was in turn the swimmer was now close. When a fathom away he leaned back and began to tread water steadily. In his right hand he grasped the boat-hook. The man in the boat knew that to stay where he was meant certain death. He gathered himself together like a crouching cat. Mànus kept treading the water slowly, but with the hook ready so that the sharp iron spike at the end of it should transfix his foe if he came at him with a leap. Now and again he laughed. Then in his low sweet voice, but brokenly at times between his deep breathings, he began to sing:

The tide was dark, an' heavy with the burden that it bore;
I heard it talkin', whisperin', upon the weedy shore;
Each wave that stirred the seaweed was like a closing door;
'Tis closing doors they hear at last who hear no more, no more,
   My Grief,
   No more!

The tide was in the salt seaweed, and like a knife it tore;
The wild sea-wind went moaning, sooing,
moaning o'er and o'er;
The deep sea-heart was brooding deep upon its ancient lore—
I heard the sob, the sooing sob, the dying sob at its core,
   My Grief,
   Its core!

The white sea-waves were wan and grey its ashy lips before,
The yeast within its ravening mouth was red with streaming gore;
O red seaweed, O red sea-waves, O hollow baffled roar,
Since one thou hast, O dark dim Sea, why callest thou for more,
        My Grief,
        For more?

In the quiet moonlight the chant, with its long, slow cadences, sung as no other man in the isles could sing it, sounded sweet and remote beyond words to tell. The glittering shine was upon the water of the haven, and moved in waving lines of fire along the stone ledges. Sometimes a fish rose, and spilt a ripple of pale gold; or a sea-nettle swam to the surface, and turned its blue or greenish globe of living jelly to the moon dazzle.

The man in the water made a sudden stop in his treading and listened intently. Then once more the phosphorescent light gleamed about his slow-moving shoulders. In a louder chanting voice came once again:

Each wave that stirs the seaweed is like a closing door;
'Tis closing doors they hear at last who hear no more, no more,
        My Grief,
        No more!

Yes, his quick ears had caught the inland strain of a voice he knew. Soft and white as the moonshine came Anne's singing as she passed along the corrie leading to the haven. In vain his travelling gaze sought her: she was still in the shadow, and, besides, a slow-drifting cloud obscured the moonlight. When he looked back again a stifled exclamation came from his lips. There was not a sign of Gloom Achanna. He had slipped noiselessly from the boat, and was now either behind it, or had dived beneath it, or was swimming under water this way or that. If only the cloud would sail by, muttered Mànus, as he held himself in readiness for an attack from beneath or behind. As the dusk lightened, he swam slowly towards the boat, and then swiftly round it. There was no one there. He climbed on to the keel,

47

and stood, leaning forward, as a salmon-leisterer by torchlight, with his spear-pointed boat hook raised. Neither below nor beyond could he discern any shape. A whispered call to Aulay MacNeil showed that he, too, saw nothing. Gloom must have swooned, and sank deep as he slipped through the water. Perhaps the dog-fish were already darting about him.

Going behind the boat Mànus guided it back to the smack. It was not long before, with MacNeil's help, he righted the punt. One oar had drifted out of sight, but as there was a sculling-hole in the stern that did not matter.

"What shall we do with it?" he muttered, as he stood at last by the corpse of Marcus. "This is a bad night for us, Aulay!"

"Bad it is; but let us be seeing it is not worse. I'm thinking we should have left the boat."

"And for why that?"

"We could say that Marcus Achanna and Gloom Achanna left us again, and that we saw no more of them nor of our boat."

MacCodrum pondered a while. The sound of voices, borne faintly across the water, decided him. Probably Anne and the lad Donull were talking. He slipped into the boat, and with a sail-knife soon ripped it here and there. It filled, and then, heavy with the weight of a great ballast-stone which Aulay had first handed to his companion, and surging with a foot-thrust from the latter, it sank.

"We'll hide the—the man there—behind the windlass, below the spare sail, till we're out at sea, Aulay. Quick, give me a hand!"

It did not take the two men long to lift the corpse, and do as Mànus had suggested. They had scarce accomplished this, when Anne's voice came hailing silver-sweet across the water.

With death-white face and shaking limbs, MacCodrum stood holding the mast, while with a loud voice, so firm and strong that Aulay MacNeil smiled below his fear, he asked if the Achannas were back yet, and if so for Donull to row out at once, and she with him, if she would come.

It was nearly half an hour thereafter that Anne rowed out

towards the *Luath*. She had gone at last along the shore to a creek where one of Marcus's boats was moored, and returned with it. Having taken Donull on board, she made way with all speed, fearful lest Gloom or Marcus should intercept her.

It did not take long to explain how she had laughed at Seumas's vain efforts to detain her, and had come down to the haven. As she approached, she heard Mànus singing, and so had herself broken into a song she knew he loved. Then, by the water-edge, she had come upon Donull lying upon his back, bound and gagged. After she had released him they waited to see what would happen, but as in the moonlight they could not see any small boat come in, bound to or from the smack, she had hailed to know if Mànus were there.

On his side he said briefly that the two Achannas had come to persuade him to leave without her. On his refusal they had departed again, uttering threats against her as well as himself. He heard their quarrelling voices as they rowed into the gloom, but could not see them at last because of the obscured moonlight.

"And now, Ann-mochree," he added, "is it coming with me you are, and just as you are? Sure, you'll never repent it, and you'll have all you want that I can give. Dear of my heart, say that you will be coming away this night of the nights! By the Black Stone on Icolmkill I swear it, and by the Sun, and by the Moon, and by Himself!"

"I am trusting you, Mànus dear. Sure it is not for me to be going back to that house after what has been done and said. I go with you, now and always, God save us."

"Well, dear lass o'my heart, it's farewell to Eilanmore it is, for by the Blood on the Cross I'll never land on it again!"

"And that will be no sorrow to me, Mànus my home!"

And this was the way that my friend Anne Gillespie left Eilanmore to go to the isles of the west.

It was a fair sailing, in the white moonshine, with a whispering breeze astern. Anne leaned against Mànus, dreaming her dream. The lad Donull sat drowsing at the helm. Forward, Aulay

MacNeil, with his face set against the moonshine to the west, brooded dark.

Though no longer was land in sight, and there was peace among the deeps of the quiet stars and upon the sea, the shadow of fear was upon the face of Mànus MacCodrum.

This might well have been because of the as yet unburied dead that lay beneath the spare sail by the windlass. The dead man, however, did not affright him. What went moaning in his heart, and sighing and calling in his brain, was a faint falling echo he had heard, as the *Luath* glided slow out of the haven. Whether from the water or from the shore he could not tell, but he heard the wild, fantastic air of the "Dàn-nan-Ròn" as he had heard it that very night upon the feadan of Gloom Achanna.

It was his hope that his ears had played him false. When he glanced about him, and saw the sombre flame in the eyes of Aulay MacNeil, staring at him out of the dusk, he knew that which Oisìn the son of Fionn cried in his pain; "his soul swam in mist."

II

For all the evil omens, the marriage of Anne and Mànus MacCodrum went well. He was more silent than of yore, and men avoided rather than sought him; but he was happy with Anne, and content with his two mates, who were now Callum MacCodrum and Ranald MacRanald. The youth Donull had bettered himself by joining a Skye skipper who was a kinsman, and Aulay MacNeil had surprised every one, except Mànus, by going away as a seaman on board one of the *Loch* line of ships which sail for Australia from the Clyde.

Anne never knew what had happened, though it is possible she suspected somewhat. All that was known to her was that Marcus and Gloom Achanna had disappeared, and were supposed to have been drowned. There was now no Achanna upon Eilanmore, for Seamus had taken a horror of the place and his loneliness. As soon as it was commonly admitted that his two brothers must have drifted out to sea and been drowned, or at best picked up by some ocean-going ship, he disposed of the island-farm, and left Eilanmore for ever. All this confirmed the thing said among the islanders of the west, that old Robert Achanna had brought a curse with him. Blight and disaster had visited Eilanmore over and over in the many years he had held it, and death, sometimes tragic or mysterious, had overtaken six of his seven sons, while the youngest bore upon his brows the "dusk of the shadow." True, none knew for certain that three out of the six were dead, but few for a moment believed in the possibility that Alasdair and Marcus and Gloom were alive. On the night when Anne had left the island with Mànus MacCodrum, he, Seumas, had heard nothing to alarm him. Even when, an hour after she had gone down to the haven, neither she nor his brothers had returned, and the *Luath* had put out to sea, he was not in fear of any ill. Clearly, Marcus and Gloom had gone away in the smack, perhaps determined to see that the girl was duly married by priest or minister. He would have perturbed himself little for days to cóme, but for a strange thing that happened that night. He had returned to the house because of a chill that was upon him, and convinced too that all had sailed in the *Luath.* He was sitting brooding by the peat-fire, when he was startled by a sound at the window at the back of the room. A few bars of a familiar air struck painfully upon his ear, though played so low that they were just audible. What could it be but the "Dàn-nan-Ròn," and who would be playing that but Gloom? What did it mean? Perhaps, after all, it was fantasy only, and there was no feadan out there in the dark. He was pondering this when, still low but louder and sharper than before, there rose and fell the strain which he hated, and Gloom never played before him, that of the *Dànsa-na-mairv,* the "Dance of the Dead." Swiftly and silently he rose and crossed the room. In the dark shadows cast by the byre he could see nothing, but the music ceased. He went out, and searched everywhere, but found no one. So he returned, took down the Holy Book with awed heart, and read slowly till peace came upon him, soft and sweet as the warmth of the peat-glow.

But as for Anne, she had never even this hint that one of the supposed dead might be alive, or that, being dead, Gloom might yet touch a shadowy feadan into a wild, remote air of the grave.

When month after month went by, and no hint of ill came to break upon their peace, Mànus grew light-hearted again. Once more his songs were heard as he came back from the fishing, or loitered ashore mending his nets. A new happiness was nigh to them, for Anne was with child. True, there was fear also, for the girl was not well at the time when her labour was near, and grew weaker daily. There came a day when Mànus had to go to Loch Boisdale in South Uist, and it was with pain and something of foreboding that he sailed away from Berneray in the Sound of Harris, where he lived. It was on the third night that he returned. He was met by Katreen MacRanald, the wife of his mate, with the news that on the morrow after his going Anne had sent for the priest who was staying at Loch Maddy, for she had felt the coming of death. It was that very evening she died, and took the child with her.

Mànus heard as one in a dream. It seemed to him that the tide was ebbing in his heart, and a cold, sleety rain falling, falling through a mist in his brain.

Sorrow lay heavily upon him. After the earthing of her whom he loved, he went to and fro solitary: often crossing the Narrows and going to the old Pictish Towre under the shadow of Ban Breac. He would not go upon the sea, but let his kinsman Callum do as he liked with the *Luath.*

Now and again Father Allan MacNeil sailed northward to see him. Each time he departed sadder. "The man is going mad, I fear," he said to Callum, the last time he saw Mànus.

The long summer nights brought peace and beauty to the isles. It was a great herring year, and the moon-fishing was unusually good. All the Uist men who lived by the sea-harvest were in their boats whenever they could. The pollack, the dogfish, the otters, and the seals, with flocks of sea-fowl beyond number, shared in the common joy. Mànus MacCodrum alone paid no heed to herring or mackerel. He was often seen striding along the shore, and more than once had been heard laughing;

sometimes, too, he was come upon at low tide by the great Reef of Berneray, singing wild, strange runes and songs, or crouching upon a rock and brooding dark.

The midsummer moon found no man on Berneray except MacCodrum, the Rev. Mr. Black, the minister of the Free Kirk, and an old man named Anndra McIan. On the night before the last day of the middle month, Anndra was reproved by the minister for saying that he had seen a man rise out of one of the graves in the kirkyard, and steal down by the stone-dykes towards Balnahunnur-sa-mona,* where Mànus MacCodrum lived.

"The dead do not rise and walk, Anndra."

"That may be, maigstir, but it may have been the Watcher of the Dead. Sure it is not three weeks since Padruig McAlistair was laid beneath the green mound. He'll be wearying for another to take his place."

"Hoots, man, that is an old superstition. The dead do not rise and walk, I tell you."

"It is right you may be, maigstir, but I heard of this from my father, that was old before you were young, and from his father before him. When the last-buried is weary with being the Watcher of the Dead he goes about from place to place till he sees man, woman, or child with the death-shadow in the eyes, and then he goes back to his grave and lies down in peace, for his vigil it will be over now."

The minister laughed at the folly, and went into his house to make ready for the Sacrament that was to be on the morrow. Old Anndra, however, was uneasy. After the porridge, he went down through the gloaming to Balnahunnur-sa-mona. He meant to go in and warn Mànus MacCodrum. But when he got to the west wall, and stood near the open window, he heard Mànus speaking in a loud voice, though he was alone in the room.

"*B'ionganntach do ghràdh dhomhsa, a' toirt barrachd air gràdh nam ban!*" ...†

---

* *Baille-'na-aonar' sa mhonadh*, "the solitary farm on the hill-slope."
† "Thy love to me was wonderful, surpassing the love of women."

This, Mànus cried in a voice quivering with pain. Anndra stopped still, fearful to intrude, fearful also, perhaps, to see some one there beside MacCodrum whom eyes should not see. Then the voice rose into a cry of agony.

"*Aoram dhuit, ay an déigh dhomh fàs aosda!*"[*]

With that Anndra feared to stay. As he passed the byre he started, for he thought he saw the shadow of a man. When he looked closer he could see nought, so went his way, trembling and sore troubled.

It was dusk when Mànus came out. He saw that it was to be a cloudy night; and perhaps it was this that, after a brief while, made him turn in his aimless walk and go back to the house. He was sitting before the flaming heart of the peats, brooding in his pain, when suddenly he sprang to his feet.

Loud and clear, and close as though played under the very window of the room, came the cold, white notes of an oaten flute. Ah, too well he knew that wild, fantastic air. Who could it be but Gloom Achanna, playing upon his feadan; and what air of all airs could that be but the "Dàn-nan-Ròn"?

Was it the dead man, standing there unseen in the shadow of the Grave? Was Marcus beside him, Marcus with that knife still thrust up to the hilt, and the lung-foam upon his lips? Can the sea give up its dead? Can there be strain of any feadan that ever was made of man, there in the Silence?

In vain Mànus MacCodrum tortured himself thus. Too well he knew that he had heard the "Dàn-nan-Ròn," and that no other than Gloom Achanna was the player.

Suddenly an access of fury wrought him to madness. With an abrupt lilt the tune swung into the *Dansà-na-mairv,* and thence, after a few seconds, and in a moment, into that mysterious and horrible *Codhail-nan-Pairtean* which none but Gloom played.

There could be no mistake now, nor as to what was meant by the muttering, jerking air of the "Gathering of the Crabs."

With a savage cry Mànus snatched up a long dirk from its place by the chimney, and rushed out.

[*]"I shall worship thee, ay, even after I have become old."

There was not the shadow of a sea-gull even in front; so he sped round by the byre. Neither was anything unusual discoverable there.

"Sorrow upon me," he cried; "man or wraith, I will be putting it to the dirk!"

But there was no one; nothing; not a sound.

Then, at last, with a listless droop of his arms, MacCodrum turned and went into the house again. He remembered what Gloom Achanna had said: *"You'll hear the 'Dàn-nan-Ròn' the night before you die, Mànus MacCodrum, and lest you doubt it, you'll hear it in your death-hour."*

He did not stir from the fire for three hours; then he rose, and went over to his bed and lay down without undressing.

He did not sleep, but lay listening and watching. The peats burned low, and at last there was scarce a flicker along the floor. Outside he could hear the wind moaning upon the sea. By a strange rustling sound he knew that the tide was ebbing across the great reef that runs out from Berneray. By midnight the clouds had gone. The moon shone clear and full. When he heard the clock strike in its worm-eaten, rickety case, he sat up, and listened intently. He could hear nothing. No shadow stirred. Surely if the wraith of Gloom Achanna were waiting for him it would make some sign now, in the dead of night.

An hour passed. Mànus rose, crossed the room on tip-toe, and soundlessly opened the door. The salt wind blew fresh against his face. The smell of the shore, of wet sea-wrack and pungent bog-myrtle, of foam and moving water, came sweet to his nostrils. He heard a skua calling from the rocky promontory. From the slopes behind, the wail of a moon-restless lapwing rose and fell mournfully.

Crouching and with slow, stealthy step, he stole round by the seaward wall. At the dyke he stopped, and scrutinized it on each side. He could see for several hundred yards, and there was not even a sheltering sheep. Then, soundlessly as ever, he crept close to the byre. He put his ear to chink after chink: but not a stir of a shadow, even. As a shadow himself, he drifted lightly to the front, past the hayrick; then, with swift glances to right and left, opened the door and entered. As he did so, he stood as though frozen. Surely, he thought, that was a sound as of a step, out there by the hayrick. A terror was at his heart. In front, the darkness of the byre, with God knows what dread thing awaiting him; behind, a mysterious walker in the night, swift to take him unawares. The trembling that came upon him was nigh overmastering. At last, with a great effort, he moved towards the ledge, where he kept a candle. With shaking hand he struck a light. The empty byre looked ghostly and fearsome in the flickering gloom. But there was no one, nothing. He was about to turn, when a rat ran along a loose, hanging beam, and stared at him, or at the yellow shine. He saw its black eyes shining like peat-water in moonlight.

The creature was curious at first, then indifferent. At last, it began to squeak, and then make a swift scratching with its forepaws. Once or twice came an answering squeak; a faint rustling was audible here and there among the straw.

With a sudden spring Mànus seized the beast. Even in the second in which he raised it to his mouth and scrunched its back with his strong teeth, it bit him severely. He let his hands drop, and grope furtively in the darkness. With stooping head he shook the last breath out of the rat, holding it with his front teeth, with back-curled lips. The next moment he dropped the dead thing, trampled upon it, and burst out laughing. There was a scurrying of pattering feet, a rustling of straw. Then silence again. A draught from the door had caught the flame and extinguished it. In the silence and darkness MacCodrum stood, intent, but no longer afraid. He laughed again, because it was so easy to kill with the teeth. The noise of his laughter seemed to him to leap hither and thither like a shadowy ape. He could see it: a blackness within the darkness. Once more he laughed. It amused him to see the thing leaping about like that.

Suddenly he turned, and walked out into the moonlight. The lapwing was still circling and wailing. He mocked it, with loud, ، shrill *pee-weety, pee-weety, pee-weet*. The bird swung waywardly, alarmed: its abrupt cry and dancing flight aroused its fellows. The air was full of the lamentable crying of plovers.

A sough of the sea came inland. Mànus inhaled its breath with a sigh of delight. A passion for the running wave was upon him. He yearned to feel green water break against his breast. Thirst and hunger, too, he felt at last, though he had known neither all day. How cool and sweet, he thought, would be a silver haddock, or even a brown-backed liath, alive and gleaming, wet with the sea-water still bubbling in its gills. It would writhe, just like the rat; but then how he would throw his head back, and toss the glittering thing up into the moonlight, catch it on the downwhirl just as it neared the wave on whose crest he was, and then devour it with swift, voracious gulps!

With quick, jerky steps he made his way past the landward side of the small, thatch-roofed cottage. He was about to enter, when he noticed that the door, which he had left ajar, was closed. He stole to the window and glanced in.

A single, thin, wavering moonbeam flickered in the room. But the flame at the heart of the peats had worked its way through the ash, and there was now a dull glow, though that was within the "smooring," and threw scarce more than a glimmer into the room.

There was enough light, however, for Mànus MacCodrum to see that a man sat on the three-legged stool before the fire. His head was bent, as though he were listening. The face was away from the window. It was his own wraith, of course; of that Mànus felt convinced. What was it doing there? Perhaps it had eaten the Holy Book, so that it was beyond his putting a *rosad* on it! At the thought he laughed loud. The shadow-man leaped to his feet.

The next moment MacCodrum swung himself on to the thatched roof, and clambered from rope to rope, where these held down the big stones which acted as dead-weight for thatch against the fury of tempests. Stone after stone he tore from its fastenings, and hurled to the ground over beyond the door. Then with tearing hands he began to burrow an opening in the thatch. All the time he whined like a beast.

He was glad the moon shone full upon him. When he had made a big enough hole, he would see the evil thing out of the grave that sat in his room and would stone it to death.

57

Suddenly he became still. A cold sweat broke out upon him.
The thing, whether his own wraith, or the spirit of his dead foe,
or Gloom Achanna himself, had begun to play, low and slow, a
wild air. No piercing, cold music like that of the feadan! Too
well he knew it, and those cool, white notes that moved here and
there in the darkness like snowflakes. As for the air, though he
slept till Judgment Day and heard but a note of it amidst all the
clamour of heaven and hell, sure he would scream because of
the "Dàn-nan-Ròn."

The "Dàn-nan-Ròn": the *Roin*! the Seals! Ah, what was he
doing there, on the bitter-weary land? Out there was the sea. Safe
would he be in the green waves.

With a leap he was on the ground. Seizing a huge stone he
hurled it through the window. Then, laughing and screaming,
he fled towards the Great Reef, along whose sides the ebb-tide
gurgled and sobbed, with glistening white foam.

He ceased screaming or laughing as he heard the "Dàn-
nan-Ròn" behind him, faint, but following; sure, following.
Bending low, he raced towards the rock-ledges from which ran
the reef.

When at last he reached the extreme ledge he stopped
abruptly. Out on the reef he saw from ten to twenty seals, some
swimming to and fro, others clinging to the reef, one or two
making a curious barking sound, with round heads lifted against
the moon. In one place there was a surge and lashing of water.
Two bulls were fighting to the death.

With swift, stealthy movements Mànus unclothed himself.
The damp had clotted the leather thongs of his boots, and he
snarled with curled lip as he tore at them. He shone white in the
moonshine, but was sheltered from the sea by the ledge behind
which he crouched. "What did Gloom Achanna mean by that?"
he muttered savagely, as he heard the nearing air change into
the "Dance of the Dead." For a moment Mànus was a man again.
He was nigh upon turning to face his foe, corpse or wraith or
living body; to spring at this thing which followed him, and tear
it with hands and teeth. Then, once more, the hated "Song of
the Seals" stole mockingly through the night.

With a shiver he slipped into the dark water. Then with quick, powerful strokes he was in the moon-flood, and swimming hard against it out by the leeside of the reef.

So intent were the seals upon the fight of the two great bulls that they did not see the swimmer, or if they did, took him for one of their own people. A savage snarling and barking and half-human crying came from them. Mànus was almost within reach of the nearest, when one of the combatants sank dead, with torn throat. The victor clambered on the reef, and leaned high, swaying its great head and shoulders to and fro. In the moonlight its white fangs were like red coral. Its blinded eyes ran with gore.

There was a rush, a rapid leaping and swirling, as Mànus surged in among the seals, which were swimming round the place where the slain bull had sunk.

The laughter of this long, white seal terrified them.

When his knees struck against a rock, MacCodrum groped with his arms, and hauled himself out of the water.

From rock to rock and ledge to ledge he went, with a fantastic, dancing motion, his body gleaming foam-white in the moon-shine.

As he pranced and trampled along the weedy ledges, he sang snatches of an old rune—the lost rune of the MacCodrums of Uist. The seals on the rocks crouched spellbound; those slow-swimming in the water stared with brown, unwinking eyes, with their small ears strained against the sound:

It is I, Mànus MacCodrum,
I am telling you that, you, Anndra of my blood,
And you, Neil my grandfather, and you, and you, and you!
Ay, ay, Mànus my name is, Mànus MacMànus!
It is I myself and no other.
Your brother, O Seals of the Sea!
Give me blood of the red fish,
And a bite of the flying *sgadan*:
The green wave on my belly,
And the foam in my eyes!

I am your bull-brother, O Bulls of the Sea,
Bull— better than any of you, snarling bulls!
Come to me, mate, seal of the soft, furry womb,
White am I still, though red shall I be,
Red with the streaming red blood if any dispute me!
Aoh, aoh, aoh, arò, arò, ho-rò!
A man was I, a seal am I,
My fangs churn the yellow foam from my lips:
Give way to me, give way to me, Seals of the Sea;
Give way, for I am fey of the sea
And the sea-maiden I see there,
And my name, true, is Mànus MacCodrum,
The bull-seal that was a man, Arà! Arà!

By this time he was close upon the great black seal, which was still monotonously swaying its gory head, with its sightless eyes rolling this way and that. The sea-folk seemed fascinated. None moved, even when the dancer in the moonshine trampled upon them.

When he came within arm-reach he stopped. "Are you the Ceann-Cinnidh?" he cried. "Are you the head of this clan of the sea-folk?"

The huge beast ceased its swaying. Its curled lips moved from its fangs.

"Speak, Seal, if there's no curse upon you! Maybe, now, you'll be Anndra himself, the brother of my father! Speak! *H'st—are you hearing that music on the shore?* 'Tis the 'Dàn-nan-Ròn'! Death o' my soul, it's the 'Dàn-nan-Ròn'! Aha, 'tis Gloom Achanna out of the Grave. Back, beast, and let me move on!"

With that, seeing the great bull did not move, he struck it full in the face with clenched fist. There was a hoarse, strangling roar, and the seal-champion was upon him with lacerating fangs.

Mànus swayed this way and that. All he could hear now was the snarling and growling and choking cries of the maddened seals. As he fell, they closed in upon him. His screams wheeled through the night like mad birds. With desperate fury he struggled to free himself. The great bull pinned him to the rock; a dozen others tore at his white flesh, till his spouting blood made the rocks scarlet in the white shine of the moon.

For a few seconds he still fought savagely, tearing with teeth and hands. Once, a red irrecognisable mass, he staggered to his knees. A wild cry burst from his lips, when from the shore-end of the reef came loud and clear the lilt of the rune of his fate.

The next moment he was dragged down and swept from the reef into the sea. As the torn and mangled body disappeared from sight, it was amid a seething crowd of leaping and struggling seals, their eyes wild with affright and fury, their fangs red with human gore.

And Gloom Achanna, turning upon the reef, moved swiftly inland, playing low on his feadan as he went.

Six Celtic Sonnets

Thomas Samuel Jones, Jr

Thomas Samuel Jones (1882–1932) was born in Oneida County, near the Adirondack Mountains in New York State. He came of Welsh and Irish stock and was baptized in Welsh at the Bethel Meeting House in Boonville. Throughout his life he maintained a deep and abiding love for all things Celtic, a fact reflected in his poetry, which includes many fine poems on Celtic themes. As a young man he edited a journal called Pathfinder *in the pages of which he featured work by Fiona Macleod. From 1930 to 1934 he visited England several times, meeting Frederic Bligh Bond, the "psychic archaeologist" of Glastonbury, and hearing AE speak in Dublin, where he also became friends with Padraic Colum. Though never an important figure within the Celtic revival, his vision is every bit as rich as that of his fellows. The six sonnets which follow are from the volume* Aknahton and other Sonnets, *originally published in 1930. Each reflects a facet of Celtic tradition. "Caer Sidi" is one of the many names for the Otherworld: Taliesin is the name of the greatest of the old Welsh bards: and New Grange was a centre of the oldest spiritual activity in Ireland.*

From *Shadow of the Perfect Rose*. Farrar and Rinehart, New York and Toronto 1937.

Art O' Murnaghan

Six Celtic Sonnets

Caer Sidi

Alone, unarmed, the Dragon King must go
   To seek the Cauldron by a magic shore,
   For gleaming harness wrought of wizard ore
Is powerless against an unknown foe;
The lonely Caer, walled with the flaming Bow,
   Lifts dark enchanted horns where wild seas roar,
   And in the moon's white path a mystic door
Moves to strange music only Merlins know.

Within, vast shapes and awful shadows start,
   While deathless gods who hold the wave-worn stairs
     Do ghostly battle with a hero's soul;
But at his eagle cry their thonged shields part,
   And from the cloven fire the Chieftain bears
     High in his mighty grasp the star-rimmed Bowl.

Taliesin

On lonely shores where dreams are drifted sand
   He follows to the end a star's bright course,
   A ghostly hunter without hound or horse,
The warrior-bard, last of the Druid band;
But still his wizard harp rings in his hand
   Beside the Stream of Sorrow's hidden source,
   Still from a breaking heart his wild songs force
Their way into the god's mysterious land.

Dauntless he sings, and sees the drear wood turn
   To golden orchards by the river bed
      Where healing waters of the rainbow run;
And past the valley near great peaks that burn
   With beaconing fire, the hero-bard is led
      Up toward the Dragon City of the Sun.

New Grange

The golden hill where long-forgotten kings
   Keep lonely watch upon their feasting-floor
   Is silent now,— the Dagda's harp no more
Makes sun and moon move to its murmurous strings;
And never in the leafy star-led Springs
   Will Caer and Aengus haunt the river shore,
   For deep beneath an ogham-carven door
Dust dulls the dew-white wonder of their wings.

Yet one may linger loving the lost dream—
   The magic of the heart that cannot die,
      Although the Rood destroy the quicken rods;
To him through earth and air and hollow stream
   Wild music winds, as two swans wheeling cry
      Above the cromlech of the vanished gods.

May upon Ictis

Far out at sea beneath rich Tyrian sails
   The merchants watch a ghostly mountain spread
   Terrific dawn-wings fired with cloudy red,
And cease their barter over purple bales;
Wild headland flames to headland; in the dales
   Hushed warriors wait, for no torqued chief may tread
   That dim white forest where the vanished dead
Gather like birds before the spume-drenched gales.

Around the mount barbaric trumpets cry;
   Then Ictis thunders through her altar-stone,
     Long cloven by a god's mysterious rune;
And pinnacled between the earth and sky
   Her savage prophet stands, majestic, lone,
     Helmed with the sun and girdled with the moon.

A Druid Town

A sunless maze of tangled lanes enfold
   The magic dwellings of the forest race,
   Whose hidden shapes are flames that leave no trace
At mid-moon when the Druid's dream is told;
The shadows of enchanted orchards hold
   Red thatch of wings and woad-stained doors that face
   The wandering stars, and guard the secret place
Where faery women thread their warps with gold.

The dragon knight shall lose his strength of hand
   Nor ever raise his long leaf-shapen shield,
     If he but follow where the white deer roam;
And never will the mariner reach land
   When harps ring seaward as the dawn fires yield
     The golden caer upon the ninth wave's foam.

Arthur

Behind storm-fretted bastions gray and bare
  Flame-crested warriors of Cunedda's line
  Feast in a golden ring,—their targes shine
Along the wall and clang to gusts of air;
And in the shadow, torches blown aflare
  Reveal a chief, half human, half divine,
  With brooding head, starred by the Dragon Sign,
Hung motionless in some undreamed despair.

But when he starts, three torques of twisted gold
  Writhe on his breast, for voices all men fear
    Wail forth the battle-doom dead kings have borne;
And as the mead-hall fills with sudden cold,
  Above the wind-tossed sea his heart can hear
    The strange gods calling through their mystic horn.

The Druid and the Maiden

Edward Burne-Jones

Sir Edward Coley Burne-Jones (1833-1898) is best known as one of the foremost members of the Pre-Raphaelite Brotherhood whose numbers included William Morris, William Holman Hunt, and Dante Gabriel Rossetti. Founded by a group of young English painters in 1848, the Brotherhood deliberately turned its back on the academic style then in vogue and looked instead to the influence of the High Renaissance which they considered to predate the work of Raphael. Much of their work was of a narrative kind, describing stories of Biblical and mythological themes in vivid images. Burne-Jones drew upon many subjects of this kind for his paintings, and though not a Celt by blood, he was certainly inspirited both by Celtic myths and art styles. The story published here appeared originally in The Oxford and Cambridge Magazine of 1856, and does not seem to have been reprinted since. It is, however, an excellent story, and shows that Burne-Jones was a talented writer as well as artist. Its inclusion here will hopefully bring it to the attention of a wider audience.

From *The Oxford and Cambridge Magazine*, 1856.

The Druid and the Maiden

"It is a wild corner of earth, this Brittany. It lies like a dead branch on a green elm, or a burial-ground in the middle of a huge city, the great fossil of the past in the very lap of the civilized world. And how is it that Brittany seems scarcely to have altered since the days of Caesar? how is it that it has defied canals and railroads, that the vulgar slang of the nineteenth century—that paragon of progress!—has not polluted its hills and vales, that it is useless, manufactureless, unheeded in your exhibitions and annual reports, uncared for by the speculator, and spurned by the hack traveller? Is it not that the Present with all its achievements, its men turned to machines, and its machine-turned men—with all its powers of motion and creation, this newspaper present that sings its own praises till hoarse in the throat—blushes before the long-forgotten, unknown Past, which in one thing at least has outdone it? Is it not ashamed to bring its patent-leather boots over the ground, where a wondrous race once trod—a race which possessed a mighty secret we cannot solve, unless forsooth it was a race of giants, of Anakim—and has left its mighty works to stand, not for ages only, but as long as Earth shall last? Thank Heaven, there is at least one spot of Earth left, and that, too, no distant desert, but within a day's journey, where this vile, fresh-paint odour of the new age cannot reach us!"

Thus I mused, as with knapsack on my back, and a railing misanthropy in my heart, I wandered over the wild hills of Brittany. I had just left Carnac—wonderful Carnac!—that petrified army—those rows of a thousand stones, brought no one knows whence, no one knows how, no one now knows why, and set upright in long, straight ranks, by a people who flourished some two thousand years gone, of whose existence and glory nought now remains but a few wild legends and these huge unmeaning stones.

I had caught my first view of the Atlantic, that eternity of waves, the boundary of the ancient, the highway of the modern, world,—and stretching far away into it I had seen the long, bleak spit of Quiberon, where a little faithful band of Royalists had once landed, full of hope, full of courage, full of confidence in English protection, and little dreaming of English mismanagement, to be cut to pieces by a band of ruthless revolutionists. I passed on to Locmariaquer.

From the hill above the little desolate village, I looked down on the bright inland sea of Morbihan, rushing fiercely in from the Atlantic through a gate of rocks, and studded with a hundred islands. Nay, the fishermen declare that there are as many rocky isles within it as the days of the year. It was a bright sunset. The cloudlets circled golden around the sinking day-god, like angels round a dying man, and the last red beams purpled the cliffs of the foremost islands, with the breakers of the Atlantic dashing at their feet.

In a few minutes I rushed down the hill into the village of fishermen's huts, and ere long had hired a sailing boat to take me over to Gavr Inis, or the beautiful island.

Two honest Breton sailors were all the crew of the little bark.

"We must make the best of our time," said one of them to me; "for, fair as it is now, there will be a breeze up before the sun is down. We can run over in half an hour, for the wind is with us, but when you have seen the cave, we shall have barely time to weather back again."

I leapt into the boat, the broad sail was hoisted, and away we went, heaving and dashing through the blue waves. The men sat down and pulled out their pipes. I did the same, and offered them some English tobacco, which was much finer than their own, and thus paved the way to a lively conversation.

"It's a good country, is England, sir," said one of them in a large tarpaulin hat. "I spent a long time at Southampton, in the last war. I was on board a French corvette that was cruising in the Channel, and we all got taken prisoners. But I never spent a better time in my life. They treated me wondrous well, and I like your beer a deal better than our cider here."

He was a weather-beaten man of about sixty. The other, who was younger, listened to him with respect.

"Tell the gentleman," said he, "how it was you made friends over there."

"Ay, ay, that was a curious business. I was only a boy then, and we were being marched up to Southampton, and there were a couple of others from these parts with me. We were laughing and talking a good deal together in Gallic, and making a pretty good noise, when up comes the sergeant of the escort and calls out something to the soldiers who were with us, meaning to keep us quiet. 'Agh,' cried I in Breton, 'it's a shame that we should not be allowed the freedom of tongue, when every other kind of freedom is taken from us.' The sergeant turned round, and looked quite astonished: 'Arragh,' cries he, in my own language, 'you're not from Ireland, my lads, are ye?' 'That we're not, indeed, God be praised,' answered I; 'but it seems you're from Brittany, for you speak the same as we do.' And sure enough he turned in and had a long chat with us, and that's the first time I found out that the Irish people talked Gallic."

"But surely," said I, "there is a great difference between Breton and Irish."

"Not so much tho', sir. They have many words that we could not understand, and some of our words they pronounce differently, but we could understand each other well enough; and the sergeant, who was the only Irishman in the company, and was glad to talk a bit in his own tongue, was our friend ever afterwards, and many a good turn he served us."

"And what kind of a cave is this on Gavr Inis?" I asked.

"Well, sir, it's a wonderful place. It was cut, so they say, many a hundred year ago by our forefathers, who, I've heard tell, were once kings of France, and England too,—right into the living rock. You go in by a little hole, that a fox might make, and climb down into a long passage quite in the middle of the hill, where you could not see your hand before you without a light."

"Then you have brought lights with you, I suppose?"

"Oh yes, sir, a candle a-piece. You'll see a hole cut out in the stone of one of the sides, where they say they used to tie a man's hands behind his back, and sacrifice him to some of their gods, sir; for it seems they were not Christians at that time."

There was a short silence. I was thinking whether any reliance could be placed on this local legend, whether the nature-worship of the Druid had ever descended to human sacrifice, as their enemies indeed have averred, but which we have so little reliable authority for believing.

My train of thought was suddenly interrupted by a loud cry in Breton, and the next moment the sail swung round, the beam struck me on the back of the head and threw me into the bottom of the boat. When I had scrambled up again, I saw the two men anxiously labouring to manage the sail. We were in a whirlwind; the waves were rising higher and higher, and a huge cloud, which five minutes before had been scarcely noticed in the distance, was driving rapidly towards us, and covering the whole heavens with its black wings.

"We shall have a bit of a squall," cried one of the men to me. "But it will not last. Will you take the rudder, sir, a moment or two, while we manage to tack about?"

"Don't you think we could run back again to Locmariaquer?" I replied, going to the stern. "We can give up the attempt to reach the island to-night, and try again tomorrow morning."

"It's impossible, sir," answered the sailor. "We should only be running into the thick of the storm, and we can reach the island in five minutes, if we can only manage the wind. You see it there, sir? well, steer right at that white point, and—"

Whatever he might have said, was lost in the hurricane that came down upon us. The rain rushed pelting down; the whole air was black around us; in another minute the sail was down, and the two men were working lustily at the oars against wave and wind.

I could just see the white speck through the darkness, and I steered straight ahead towards it. We were making some way, and the white rock, for such it seemed to be, was nearer and nearer. But the waves broke in upon the boat, heavy tub though it was, and completed the wetting that the rain had already given me.

"Steer out, steer out, sir, a bit, not too much. Out, out, sir, quick. There are hidden rocks here: ah!—"

74

At this instant a huge wave broke right upon us. For a moment I was blinded by the water, and when I recovered my sight I saw that we were close in upon a shore, girt with a bed of low rocks, just peeping above the retiring waves. The next moment there was a crack, and the handle of the rudder was torn from my hand, while the boat nearly capsized. I got on my knees with the speed of lightning to try and recover my hold of the rudder, when to my utter discomfiture I saw it a yard or two behind us dashed about in the foam of a huge breaker.

"The rudder is gone," I cried, turning round, and saw the younger of the men leap from the boat upon the rocks with the painter in his hand, while the other was endeavouring to keep the boat clear with an oar.

The young man leapt fearlessly from rock to rock in the surge. He must have known the spot well, for it was quite dark, and by dragging the boat along, he at last brought the boat's head on to the bank. Two or three rapidly succeeding waves drove us with violent shocks up the stones. The old man leapt out into the shallow surge; I followed his example, and in a few minutes our united efforts had dragged the skiff high and dry up the shingle.

"Well, now," said I, when the boat was secured, "we must look out for a place of shelter, for this rain will last several hours yet, in spite of the wind. Which is the way up to the cave?"

The old man, to whom I put this question, looked confused.

"Monsieur does not wish to see the cave tonight?"

"Why not? I intend to sleep there for an hour or two, so as to be out of the wet."

The two men looked at one another oddly.

"Monsieur will not sleep much, I am thinking," said the younger one.

"Not sleep? what do you mean? I am sure I am tired enough."

The old man scratched his head and looked perplexed.

"There was never anybody slept in that cave yet," he resumed.

"Ah! I see, you have some stories about it, eh?"

The old fellow looked down obliquely.

"Well," I continued, "we shall be three together. We can't come to much harm. Come, a stout old fellow like you!"

The old man only looked foolish.

"No, sir," said the younger one, "I don't mind showing you the way up there, but I and my partner here will sleep outside, if you please. We shall get shelter enough under the shrubs about there."

"Move on, then," I said, internally grumbling at their obstinate superstitions, and rather gloating over the prospect of doing what they said nobody had ever done before, and so proving to them that they were wrong.

We had to climb a long way in the dark, up a steep, winding path, where my hands came into as frequent use as my feet. We were nearly half an hour getting up, and I was not a little torn and bruised, when we reached a kind of landing-place some yards below the top of the rocky hill.

Short, thick shrubs surrounded this place on every side. The sailors advanced slowly together towards a place where the gorse and the shrubs were thickest, and beckoned to me to follow them.

"Here, sir," said the old man, "put these in your pocket: you may want them." So saying, he gave me a short piece of a tallow candle, and a small iron box full of lucifers.

I crept in on hands and knees through the opening which they made by holding the shrubs back, and soon found I was able to stand upright on a hard pavement of stone.

I struck one of my lucifers and lit the candle. The light was dim and illumined a space of about a yard round me, not more. Beyond this, the darkness seemed even thicker than before. I was in a kind of passage, about six feet high and seven broad. The walls consisted of large flat stones, and as I passed the candle along them, I saw to my astonishment a series of the most elegant serpentine designs, graven in single lines over the whole surface. On each stone the pattern was different, but still in each there was a certain resemblance to the twisted form of the snake, which I remembered was an animal of deep symbolical import among the old Druids.

I sang out "*Bon soir*," before I passed on, imagining that the sailors would hear me. But my voice range like a bell from wall to wall with a hollow ding-dong noise, and I waited in vain for an answer.

I confess that this feeling of loneliness, and the terror of the two Bretons, had an effect on me as I groped along, and this increased when, after some yards of the passage, I found myself within a loftier hall. It was not large, it is true. There was room perhaps for some dozen people to stand, but the strange devices on the walls seemed to call up the Past to people it with shades.

I groped round it. The cave ended here, and the only thing that broke the monotony of the graven stones above, below, and around me, was a curious double niche cut out on one side. It was so managed as to leave a strong stone bar in the middle.

Here then was the place to which the sailor had referred. Here it was, to this stone bar, that the human victim was tied, and between those stones in the floor his blood must have flowed away.

I set my candle in this niche, took off my cloak, laid it upon the ground, and prepared to make myself as cozy as possible, by divesting my shivering limbs of their dripping nether garments. I kept the rest of my clothes on to guard again the cold, and lying down, covered my legs with my cloak.

The candle was already burning low, for there was not much of it, and the darkness grew closer and closer about me, as I thought dreamily on all the old tales I had ever heard of the Druids and the Celts in general. I was rather excited by the events of the evening, and it was evident that I could not sleep soundly.

From time to time I dozed a little, while the light still burned, and was annoyed with those funny dreams one has now and then, of being at a large party in my actual costume, and not discovering till I had waltzed once or twice, that my lower limbs were bereft of the garments which society requires to be worn. I would wake up at the moment of a desperate attempt to put on my trousers, which always proved futile.

At length the last flicker of the candle blazed up, and the next moment I was left to doze in utter darkness. Whether I was awake or not I knew not, but my ears, at least, were not shut, and the sound of a wild distant song came up the passage. It seemed to be the mingled voices of men and women. It grew nearer and nearer, and at last resounded in the passage itself. I remembered turning on my side, and then I felt cold drops of sweat rise at the roots of my hair, my flesh crept, my arm clung powerless to my side, and my legs bent up under me.

Two tapers were dimly glittering at the bottom of the passage, and behind them two shadowy figures, clothed in long white robes, slowly and solemnly moved towards me.

My heart stopped beating; my breath hovered in my throat. The figures moved on, and behind them I could see some dozen others, all in long white robes.

They came and came, nearer and nearer, and at last filled the chamber where I lay. Then the low wild music ceased, and one of the two foremost raised his lank arms and fell flat on his face before me. My eyes closed, and again all was dark.

When I opened them again the forms were gone.

For some minutes I scarcely dared to move. I am one of those strong-minded people who will never believe in "humbugs" of this kind. I had been accustomed to run down everything in which imagination seemed to play any prominent part. But this was the first trial my principles had received, and I must confess it converted me for the moment even in spite of myself. I knew not what to believe, but I perfectly knew what I felt. And yet, surely, I thought, it must be a dream, or an hallucination—of course it must. So I rubbed my eyes to see whether I was awake or not, and certainly believed that I was wide awake.

At last I summoned courage to turn my eyes round in their sockets, (for hitherto they had remained paralyzed with an unde-fined fear,) and as I did so I started to see almost close to my side something long and white upon the floor. This time I was less frightened, for I had got accustomed to unwonted sights.

But whatever the prostrate mass might be, it was not content to remain prostrate. It rose slowly and stood at last before me, by my side, almost over me. It was the form of a man in his thirtieth year, tall, majestic, handsome. A loose dress of white linen fell from his neck to his feet, and was girt at the waist with a band of twisted tender oak sprigs. The robe was sleeveless, and his bare arms were muscular, though white. His face was hand-some, with high intellectual, almost noble, features; but there was an expression about his eyes of cunning foiled and shamed, ambition disappointed, and selfish intrigue worked up to the crisis of crime.

The reader will be wondering—though, for my part, I had no wonder to spare on such a trifle *then*—how in the thick darkness of the cave I could manage to see all these details. This question would pose me. Gentle reader, have you ever seen a ghost? Have you ever passed a night with the shade of a reanimated Druid priest? No? well then, I cannot help it. I must wait till your turn comes, when you will perfectly appreciate the kind of invisible halo that surrounds an incorporeal being, and fully understand what I cannot, for the life of me, explain.

I have described the phantom's expression, that is, the expres-sion which his character had imprinted on his features; but I have not added, that at this moment he wore one of intense melancholy besides.

He was turned towards me, and was looking at me. This did not now disquiet me; but still my tongue refused to move and demand, as I longed to do, who it was that I spoke to. He saved me the trouble, however, by quietly sitting down beside me, which sent a new thrill of agitation through my body.

"Does he sleep?" he muttered low, though in what language I cannot say. I only know that I understood him very well, so that it must have been either French or English.

"And who," he continued, "is brave enough to break upon my solitude, to seek the Druid in his den, and bring the vulgar Present to the shadows of the Past? Is not the temple which my own father built, the shrine I hallowed with HIS blood"—here he buried his face in his hands, and was silent a moment—"is not this of right our own? Why then does the stranger, rather than our own descendants, who speak our tongue, seek our haunts to lay his head in? Stranger!"

I muttered a trembling "Yes."

"So you are come to see the famous Gavr Inis, the beautiful island? Well, you do well to come by night, for its glory is departed."

"Ichabod, Ichabod," I murmured instinctively.

"But," he continued, not heeding my little remark, "it once merited its name. It once was the beautiful island indeed, the loveliest of three hundred and sixty-five that spring within this inland sea. Here the oak forest was thicker, here the mistletoe more luxurious—"

"So that you might have had Christmas twice a year," I thought, with a little chuckle, but said nothing.

"—The wood-flowers bore a fresher bloom, the shepherd warriors were stouter and more terrible, and the shepherd maidens fairer to look upon than in all the land of the Celts. But now, alas! how changed!—"

By this time I had become quite myself again. But it was with a frightful effort that I brought my voice to my lips.

"May I ask"—again I paused—"are you—a—a Druid?"

"I was a Druid. I am now what you see me."

"And that is?—"

"A Spirit of the Past."

There was such a solemnity in the voice with which he uttered these words that a strong desire to laugh, which my "common sense" roused in me, was nipped in the bud.

I looked at the strange being with respect and awe.

"What brings you here to-night?" I asked, timidly.

"A crime committed on this day nineteen centuries ago. For twenty centuries I was condemned to revisit the spot where I had shed innocent blood, once a year, and to pass my night in the torture of memory. Every circumstance of my life on earth is now recalled; its neglected opportunities, its happiness too soon blighted, its—its—crimes—"

I raised myself on my elbow. I felt an interest in, almost a sympathy for, the man of so strange a fate.

"It might perhaps soften this pain of recollection, to tell your tale to an interested listener."

His eyes turned obliquely towards me, with a slight look of suspicion. Then he smiled a melancholy smile.

"There was a time," he said, "when I should have suspected some latent motive in your suggestion. Now, how can you, how can any mortal harm me? What are my confidences now—known as they are in heaven? It would relieve my sorrow. I will tell you my tale.

"My father was the Arch-Druid of the province. Carnac, even then, had passed into a mystery. The Dolar Marchant, as you now call it, was the great resort of the members of the college, because the great menhir—alas! alas! thrown down and shivered now into three huge pieces—was close to it. My father lived at yonder village, Cœr-Bhelen, we called it, and now 'tis named Locmariaquer. Yes, Bhelen, the great, the noble, had given place to a woman!

"At my birth, a wandering bard came from the south. He struck his lyre of the triple chord and sang:

'Woe to the child when the Eagle's wings
Shall darken the skies of the north;
Woe to the child when Venetan kings
To battle shall march forth.
An eaglet's blood shall stain his hand,
A woman lead the host,
A maiden's death-shriek fill the land,
And the Druid's rule be lost.'

"My father loved me none the less for the evil omen. I was his only child, and at an early age he taught me all the awful legends of the truth. I was a silent wondering boy, and I grasped eagerly after knowledge. The science of the stars, the science of the world, the science of the great invisible soul of nature,—such were my early studies.

"He sent me, at fifteen, to Alesia. At the Sacred College I was marked as the student who knew most, and learned most; and when I left it, proud in my honours, I stood before the whole college of Druids, and swore by Esus, by Bhelen and by Thiutath—what oath could have been greater?—that I would never forsake its cause, and that day and night I would strive to preserve the great religion.

"I returned home with the oak-wreath on my brows—a priest. I took ship at Wenedh (Venetum), to cross to Cœr-Bhelen. A storm arose, and we put in at this very island. From a child I knew it well. I had often sought it in my father's boat with its red sails of hide.

"The next day I learnt that the gathering of the Vervain was to take place on the island. I felt a natural pride to show the inhabitants my newly-won oak-wreath, and I stayed for it. For this ceremony a company of virgins is chosen, and the youngest maiden culls the little herb.

"Beneath the spreading oaks they came. A lovelier band was never gathered on green sward, and yet she who led them was lovelier than all the rest. She was a girl of fifteen summers, and still looked a child in form and bearing. She came on, timid as a young fawn, and blushing at every step. It was a lovely sight, such as I may never see again—alas! Each maiden wore a robe of flowing white linen, girt below the breast, and sweeping, not clinging, around her form. In their long locks were woven bands of spring flowers, and their hair, each one's silkier than the other's, each one's of another hue, flowed down their young shoulders, and courted the sunbeams with their gloss. Their white arms were bare, and a gold bracelet, pliable, and simple, clasped the tender flesh above the elbow.

"But she—ah! Dona!—she, lovelier in her childish form, lovelier in her modest face, lovelier in her timid gait—with the young knowledge struggling with the child's innocence in her tender bosom—than all the rest, came on through the thick wood, with the sunbeams gilding one leaf and forsaking another, brightening one lock of hair, and deepening the shade of the next, and chequering the briary ground beneath her bare feet, small and tender as young rosebuds—and looked from right to left to find the sacred herb. A young Druid, whom I knew well, bore the basket before the troop, and on either side the islanders accompanied them.

"Suddenly, she started from the path, and darting with the fire of heaven in her soul among the briars and brambles which tore her white feet, she burst out with the first note of the holy hymn. All the voices took it up. An old bard stepped from the crowd and struck his lyre to the air.

"Then, as they sang, she stooped. With her left hand she put back the long brown locks that fell across her shoulders, and curving the little finger of the right hand, she culled the sacred herb with it alone. No other finger touched it, as she rose and dropped it into the basket of the young Druid.

"The ceremony was over, and we returned to the village. As we went, I asked the Druid, my friend, who the maiden was.

" 'You,' he answered, 'you, newly come, pride-laden from Alesia, know all that the Roman is doing in the South. I need not tell you that Caesar is driving all before him, northwards. Well, this maid, who is indeed a gem of beauty, has fled from the neighbourhood of Bibracte with her aged mother. She tells how her life—her honour even—was saved by a Roman knight, and how she staid not till they reached these hills, whither the southron will find it hard to penetrate.'

"Need I tell you that I fell enamoured of this damsel? Need I say how often I spread the red hide-sail to the northern breeze, and sought Gavr Inis and the smile of the lovely Dona?

"But I found her cold. My honours seemed little in her sight—myself nothing. Still I hoped. She was young, and I had nought but a student's glory to recommend me. I was fired with the ambition of love. I resolved to win a name in the province, for I saw that she loved the great and noble.

"A year passed, and the Roman Eagle again darkened the land with his huge wings. Julius Caesar was a name which all had heard, and heard with horror. I became popular by my working. I laboured hard among the people. I kept up the falling faith. I incited them to prepare for war. I collected the priests and the chieftains, and we trained the people to the bow and the axe. Everywhere I exclaimed proudly, 'the Celt shall never be a slave.'

"But the sky was dark. Another year and Vercingetorix was the name which resounded louder than that of Caesar in our hills. The news came that Alesia was besieged. All trusted to the noble band of Vercingetorix. But how was it that a melancholy silence fell on Dona when she heard the tidings? What was she meditating in that maiden breast? These two years had altered her. She was no longer the timid girl, she was rising to ambitious womanhood; she was reserved and pensive.

"At last my ambition called me to Wenedh, and I was parted for many a month from Dona.

"One day a man rode headlong into Wenedh, covered from heel to head with dirt and dust. His horse dropped dead beneath him.

"The townsmen crowded round him, and then, with sad voice, he declared that Alesia was fallen, and Vercingetorix was lost.

"The news flew like wildfire. My father came among the first from Locmariaquer. In every quarter we sent for every bowman that could still fix an arrow. Wenedh was crowded. The capital of our hill country, it was always the trysting place in times of danger. And now the whole country poured into it; some to see their friends depart for the war, some from curiosity, some to hear the news, and some even to offer their arms in their country's cause.

"A motley crowd assembled in the little market-place. The wild wood-cutters from the hills, with their axes across their swarthy arms; the peasant from the plains, with nought but a hide to cover him; the priest and the Druid in his long flowing garment of white linen; and the herdsman from the island, in his rough breeks of sheep-skin. Some from the neighbourhood still held a yoke of oxen by the horns, in such haste had they come; and others from hunting the wolf, had rushed hurriedly in with the heavy hang-jawed hounds still prancing on before them. All were asking, all stupidly waiting to see what would happen, all thinking that, because the capital was taken, the Roman must of course be on their threshold. Poor things, they knew not whether Alesia were one or ten days' journey from them.

"But the market-place was thronged the day after the news had come. The noise of oxen, horses, dogs and men was terrific. A large body of Druids had assembled, and my father had consulted with them what was to be done, and had agreed to harangue the people.

"We formed in procession and walked slowly, and with the

sound of the mournful lyre, to the market-place. The crowd opened and knelt as we passed, and my father passed his thin white hands to and fro to bless them.

"He was very old, and his white hair danced about his temples like flakes of snow. Mounting a large stone in the middle of the place, he called on the folk to pray with him to Bhelen.

"He rose to address them, when the prayer was done, but, whether from age, or the excitement, his voice faltered and clung to his jaws. The people murmured, and looked down, and I was just going to come forward and lend the old man my voice, when I saw the farthermost of the crowd turning round, and looking up the road. The next moment I heard the hard rattle of hoof and stone. All the crowd turned to the quarter whence the noise came. A moment more, and the women were shrieking, and pulling back their children; the crowd opened and three horsemen dashed madly up to the stone where we stood.

"There was a moment's silence. Each man was straining his ears. Then the foremost of the three horsemen, standing up in his stirrups, took his lance in his hand and brandished it furiously over his head.

" 'Men of Wenedh,' he cried in a voice of thunder, 'the Roman is coming. A Roman legion has crossed the Sechen. Their van is even now only five days hence. The chieftains have fallen back on the hills, and they call on you in the name of Thiutath, of Bhelen, of Esus, to march out to their aid—ye and all the land. Men of Wenedh, arise!'

"A deathlike silence hung upon these words; they had taken the breath of all away. It lasted a minute, and then one wild shriek, one bitter wail from all the women, one mass of shouting, and loud defiant talking from the men filled the whole air.

" 'The Roman coming here? Caesar? the Eagle? the black Eagle with its talons and jaws streaming already with our blood? oh! terrible! terrible!'

"A panic had fallen on all. Alesia was gone, the country had lost its corner-stone. Still they had hoped to stand. They had thought that the Roman would have been sated with the pillage of the capital, and the autumn was coming on. Another month, and the careful Romans would have been gathering into winter-quarters. 'But, oh! oh! they are coming hither; death, slavery, pillage; our wives, our children slain or dishonoured before our eyes, our hearths polluted, our homes destroyed, ourselves in bondage!'

"Such was the thought of each, the thought that overpowered them, for they knew how terrible the Roman was, and shrank from the awful vision of Death.

"I saw that now was my moment. I rose upon the broad stone, flung my hands forward, and summoning all my voice, I cried, 'Celts, are ye ready to defend the land?'

"A murmur,—I had expected a loud reply of 'Yes,'—but only a murmur, low, grumbling, and wretched, followed my words. Then I know not what I said. I conjured them by all that was most holy, most dear, by their very name of Celt, to rise and strike for home, for life. But, oh! when fear possesses a whole crowd, there is no rousing them. I called them cowards. There was a low murmur, but nothing more. Just then my eyes fell on a distant corner, whither they had not wandered before.

"I saw a lovely face with blue eyes strained in anxious stare, the dark brown locks now hanging on the back, the slender neck stretching forward, the curved nostril of the high nose dilating with passion,—one hand resting on the stone on which she sat, the other seeming each moment to clutch at some visionary thing at her side, the little bosom heaving, throbbing, swelling quick and warm,—and this was Dona.

"Her eyes were on me, and seemed to call me. I gathered up my whole force and cried, 'Once more I call you, brothers—once more, and then your blood, your children's, wives' and mothers' blood be on your own heads,' and sank down, filled with the gaze of Dona. Oh! her eyes bright with ambition, glittering with her people's love, wild with suppressed indignation, called me, inspired me, pleaded to me—to *me*, whom she had almost scorned. I was drowning in my reverie, when I heard the deep vibration of the harp beside me. I turned, and Cervorix, the bard who had chanted the evil omen at my birth, was spreading his broad hand and branching fingers over the chords.

86

'Celt, is the war-axe whetted,
    Celt, is the arrow bright,
To pierce the Southern Eagle's heart?
    Rise, Celt, march on and fight.
Fight for thy land, thy home, thy wife;
    Wield strong the glittering glaive;
Shed the warm blood, fling down the life;
    But scorn to be a slave!
What! shall the Roman triumph,
    And trample on the name
Which echoed once from sea to sea,
    The Gallic warrior's fame?
Shall your sons curse the cowards
    That dared not meet the foe?
And bondsmen, rattling chains, mock out,
    "They fear'd to brace the bow?"
No! Celts, it never shall be, no!
    The Gaul shall turn the day;
Gird on the quiver, brace the bow;
    Up! Celts, strike home and slay.'

"The chords were strong and wild as the flight of the sea-gull, and the voice deep and rolling as the blue waves it skims o'er; but oh! for the coward heart of man, these shepherds and wood-cutters, even the armed men we had trained, were moved a moment, murmured a faint applause—one or two shouting for the bard, and crying 'to arms,'—and then sank back into their old fears.

" 'What can we do against the Romans?' cried one.

" 'We have no arms, no provisions,' shouted another.

" 'No discipline,' sneered a third.

" 'We shall go out to be cut to pieces,' murmured a shepherd.

" 'Like calves in the shambles,' cried a cowardly cowherd.

" 'And our hills are better defences than our arms.'

"So they went on, while we were quiet. I was trembling in every limb. The people were before me, still obstinate, still immoveable, and if they held out, if they still refused, then not our glory and honour only were gone, but our land, our freedom, all that we loved. I trembled, for the will of a whole people is a dire antagonist for one man. But I felt power in myself. I despised the illiterate mob. All I feared was the stubbornness of the mass, in which each clown supported his brother blockhead. Should I speak to them again, and in a tone of authority? Should I, if it were necessary, even invent some message from Heaven, some divine inspiration of Bhelen? I looked instinctively towards those blue eyes of Dona for an answer. But they were no longer turned towards me. She was looking indignantly, almost angrily around her. I could see her bosom heaving yet more rapidly, her eyes gliding continually from one to another, her hand nervously drawing the long brown tresses from her brow.

"For a moment there was another awful stillness. The crowd seemed still to hesitate; still to look for somebody to reassure them. I should have sprung up then, I should have caught them in the nick of time, but all my thought, all my soul was riveted on that lovely face, working with all the passion of indignant shame.

"Suddenly I saw her stretch her arm beside her, still looking forward, and grasp a battle-axe that lay neglected by her side. One second I saw her rise, proud, furious, carried away,—the next and she had mounted beside me, and was flourishing the glittering axe above her head, with all the strength of her woman's arm.

" 'Cowards,' she cried, throwing back her fine head, and gasping with emotion. 'Cowards, for I cannot call you men: a woman shall put you to shame, a woman shall do what no warrior amongst you dares. Cowards today, you were not so once. What shall your fathers say in the Heaven of Bhelen? Shall your dead mothers own that they have suckled dastards? Shame, shame. I have seen the Roman, and I fear him not. I will march on to meet him; with this axe, this woman's hand, I will strike the first blow for my country, and let him follow who dares.'

"She flung the axe once more round her head, and as she did so a thousand voices leapt up, 'We will, we will! lead us on!'

"Her beauty had done what all my eloquence had not done.

Her weakness, her woman's courage had shamed the young men. The older ones followed in the wake. She leapt down from the stone, and walked stately as a queen through the opening crowd. The young men clutched their weapons, and pushed forward after her. Shouting and shouting, they formed in rank. I pressed my father's hand, I called on the other Druids to follow me, and rushing on one with another, we closed behind her, and with one voice raised the war-chant of Bhelen.

" 'On! on!' she cried, in shrill accents, that rang above our hundred voices. The impulse was given. With one accord all closed behind her. Children and wives were greeted with hurried kisses; we turned with one accord, and with one voice bade adieu to the old and the feeble, and our own loved homes, and then marched rapidly from the town. The women followed us for a long way. Dona still marched at our head, waving us forward with her white arm, and her dark tresses floating in the air. On, on, with tears and cries and hopes all mingled around us, on, on, for half-an-hour across the hills, and then all again was silent. We marched steadily to death or victory.

"Three days we travelled onwards to meet the awful foe. Three nights we camped beneath the starry heaven, gathering our food from the villages we passed, and joined at every step by fresher hearts and stouter arms. Three days Dona still marched at our head, adored by all, our woman-general, stronger in her will and her ambition than any of us.

"The third night we camped behind a range of low hills, with the Roman, unconscious, in fancied security, in the valley on the other side.

"None slept. All knew that ere morning the fatal hour would come. All thought of their wives, their children, their sisters, their fathers, and their homes, that they had left. And amid all that throng, Dona was the only woman.

"Three hours after midnight the word passed in silence to prepare.

"Then there was a slight noise in the camp, if camp it could be called, with nought but bushes for our tents. The bowman was seeing to his lock and the buckle of his quiver; the woodcutter felt the edge of his axe, and sharpened it stealthily on the nearest stone; the trained warrior girded on his glaive, and took his buckler of hide on the left arm. And amid the stealthy business a light footstep woke me from thought, and Dona stood by my side.

" 'Friend,' she said to me, more warmly than she had ever spoken, 'Friend, *you* are to win the fight. To you the honour of rousing the Roman.'

"I looked in wonder at her. I, a Druid, to wield the sword?

" 'Yes,' she answered to my look. 'The frighted eagle soars not straight towards the sun, but flutters his huge pinions till the huntsman's aim is taken. Up, friend, take a Druid band with you, climb yon ridge, and wait in long line till the first beams of morning gild the hill-tops. Then with one throat pour out the war-hymn. I will do the rest.'

"I would have seized her hand, I would have fallen and worshipped her as a heroine worthy of Nehallenia's court,—but she was gone, and in silence I led my band up the heather.

"We had scarcely formed, when the first grey light twinkled in the east. In a minute or two we could see the sleeping camp beneath us, and hear the heavy footfalls of the nightwatch.

"Clothed all in white, and stretched along the ridge of the dark hill, we were a strange sight in that early morning.

"Then a long, low cry from behind was the signal. I raised my hand, and a hundred hill-trained throats poured out the wild hymn, while Cervorix, the bard, struck the ringing chords.

"A clatter in the valley; the night-guards moving rapidly, a trumpet call, a rush to arms, and the next moment the glitter of a brandished axe on a distant hill-top, the white robe of a maiden fluttering in the chill morning breeze, dark bands closing rapidly after it, and then, still in doubtful silence, a downward rush upon the foe.

"For one second we heard nothing but the clatter of arms down the distant hill, the next, a huge, wild shout that rent the air, the next, the din of close, bloody strife. We saw nothing but a huge black mass, moving unsteadily in the dark valley, but we heard the terrible cries, the axe shivering the helmet, the arrows rattling like hail upon the armour, the shouts of vengeance, hatred, wounds, death, all mingled.

"I understood it all. We had been placed there to divert attention, and our warriors had thus secured the flank attack.

"Wild with excitement, I could not endure our stillness. I bounded almost headlong from rock to rock, and rushed shouting and throwing up my arms into the fight. Everywhere the Roman, utterly surprised, was yielding ground, crying quarter, or being struck to the earth. Everywhere the axe of the Briton glittered above the invader, and everywhere I thought I saw the white robe of the warrior-maiden.

"That was my real lure. I thought fearfully of her danger, and dreamed wildly of saving her, and I rushed madly to where the white robe glittered. I saw her—saw her turn, followed her. A band of some twenty of my countrymen had surrounded three or four Southrons, who were fighting desperately with the sword. The tallest of them was cutting down his assailants right and left. I saw Dona pass her hand across her brow. I saw her waver a moment, and in that moment I saw an axe gleam above the head of the Roman knight. The next, and Dona had struck its bearer to the ground.

"The Roman stepped back at the sight of his deliverer. She swung her axe wildly round and cleared the space about him.

" 'Away, away!' she cried furiously. 'Go, Celts, and drive your foes down elsewhere. This man is my prisoner.'

"The assailants shrank back amazed, and Dona turned to the Roman and stretched her white hand to his arm.

" 'You saved me once,' she said, 'and now I save your life in quittance of my debt. That done, I am still your foe, and I claim you as my prisoner.'

"The Roman stooped. I bounded forward in my agony, and caught his words, 'Lady, your captive would I ever be.'

"Caesar recalled his forces into winter quarters. The war had ended that summer with his defeat, and the Roman soldier blushed to hear that a woman had been the general in his rout. Half the legion had been cut to pieces; the other half had either fled or been taken.

91

"The Roman warrior lay wounded and captive in the home of Dona's mother, and I,—I, who had hoped against hope itself, roamed, more deeply wounded in my love, pierced to the heart, and fostering yellow jealousy in my bosom.

"To Dona I never went—how could I?

"To the gods, to the temple, I went as a sneak. I felt that my heart was not with them. I shunned the mild gaze of my old father, I hated the honours that the people poured upon me. I was the most popular Druid in all the country. They coupled my name with Dona's as their deliverer. All said that the song of the Druids had saved the land. But I felt like a fiend at their praises, and when they praised Dona I rejoiced with a bitter joy.

"Over the wild hills of heather, through the thick, dark forests, I roamed half-mad. The image of my beloved one grew brighter and brighter, as I dwelt upon it. She was far more beautiful, far more a heroine—nay, she was scarcely a woman, she must be some goddess. And that *her* heart, hers, the deliverer of her race, should be given to its direst foe! Oh! it was terrible.

"But the dark night of the forest blackened my darkening soul. First came the thought of ambition. I was already a great man. I would be the greatest in the kingdom. I was a Druid—I would be a warrior too. I would take the sword and the field against the Roman, and rival Vercingetorix himself. She loved honour and glory. These would I gain. But the winter came apace. There was no fighting the Roman then; and in the frozen glades, and the deep snow, my jealous love was all that burned.

"Then it was that in despair I bethought me of slaying the southern knight. If he were once away, she might sorrow awhile, but her love would die with its object.

"Through the long, cold winter I cherished this thought. Scheme after scheme passed through my heated brain. I tutored myself to cruelty. I grew exacting and harsh to the people, who yet seemed to love me all the more. It was the business of the Arch-Druid to decide all the difficult points of quarrel between the people. He was the chief magistrate, and held the appeal from the petty chieftains.

"I became my father's adviser, and privily urged him to punishments of intense cruelty, which the old man abhorred in his soul, but in which he yielded to my stronger will. Thus I became a tyrant.

"Meanwhile my father was building this temple in which you lie. He had been about it for a year. The stones were graven with the mystic signs; the cave was dug out slowly. It was nearing its completion, and when the first spring sun turned the frosts to water, the work was recommenced.

"One day he begged me to go and see the first stones placed against the walls. I came to Gavr Inis, and when my work was done I strolled down the island, drawn by an irresistible impulse towards the cottage of Dona.

"As I trod the wet rotting leaves of the oak forest, I caught the sound of coming footsteps. Instinctively I hid myself in the hollow of an oak. On they came, and then from my lurking place I saw the Roman Knight circling his stout arm around Dona's gentle form. I felt my brows meet, I felt my breath choking me, I felt the hot blood rush into my head, as they passed. I longed to dart out and strangle him with these hands, but a spirit within me muttered, 'Wait.'

"They came, each pouring love into the other's lips; and Dona, she I loved and longed for, gazing into his eyes with burning passion. And thus they passed, and I held back my vengeance.

"The spring came, and again the land was roused. The Roman was alive again, and again his dreaded arms were turning to the west. All were mad with fear. They sought Dona, and implored her to lead them on again, and she only shook her head, and said nought. They sought me, and I assembled the people.

"My dreadful purpose was made up.

" 'Celts,' I cried to the assembly, 'the gods are wroth with us. Our faith is tottering, our temples are deserted, our sacrifices are not what they once were, and for this Bhelen sends the Roman upon our land. If you would be saved you must make one grand propitiation.'

" 'Speak, speak,' cried a hundred voices, 'we are ready to do anything. Our cattle, our flocks, are Bhelen's. Let the god command.'

93

" 'No,' I answered, smiling bitterly, 'the blood of oxen and the blood of sheep are stale to the offended god. Think you a common offering can appease him? No. Last night I stood beneath Bhelen's holy oak, and whispered my prayer in the bark. The leaves fluttered, and they answered me. 'A man, a man,' was the oracle. 'One man must die for the many.'

"The people and the chieftains, and the Druids, all stood aghast. How long had it been since a man had been slain in sacrifice? Never since the days of their grandsires.

" 'Yes,' I cried again, 'ye are fostering in your very bosom an enemy of our land and our gods. A Roman dwells among us in safety, and a Roman is an insult to the Holy Bhelen.'

"The assembly breathed again. All knew who was meant, and now none feared for himself.

" 'It is good,' they cried, 'the offering shall be made.'

"I turned to my father, who stood pale and trembling—not with age, but horror—at my side.

" 'Father,' I said, 'your new temple is all but finished. This will be fine blood to hallow it, better than that of bulls and goats.'

" 'Horrible, horrible,' muttered the old man, turning from me in disgust, 'and that Bhelen should have asked for human blood!'

" 'And yet,' I answered humbly, 'it is Bhelen's will, father; it must be done.'

"He said nothing, but hurried away.

"I passed a horrible night. My father's disgust at me—he, always so fond, so proud of his son,—had struck me deeply, and now set me thinking. I now saw that my last friend had been undeceived in me. One by one my links to life had dropped away. There seemed to be no hope of Dona's love, which had once been the constant companion of my mind. Though I dreamed at times of such a hope, though that was the excuse I made to my own conscience for the deed I was preparing to do, I knew well that there was really none. Then the people too had found me out. I had tyrannized, I had become brutal, and though they respected my talents, and the divine communications which I pretended were made to me, there was not one who loved me—not one. And now even my father seemed to loathe my cruelty, for this last act was dreadful.

"I confess that for a moment I was weak, when these thoughts oppressed me; for a moment I wavered. I said to myself, 'What right hast thou to this man's blood? Why shouldst thou hate him for an accident. He does not even dream that he has a rival. Thou hast no right even to be his rival, for thou hast never told thy love. What! wilt thou make these two wretched that are now so happy? Thou yearnest thyself for Love, for something on which to lean thy soul, as a head on the pillow. Thou yearnest for some soft beauty to rest thy cheek on her warm breast, that thou mayest gaze up into her eyes for sympathy, and feel her bosom heaving in her love. Thou longest for all this, and thou knowest that they have found it. Canst thou be so cruel, so remorseless as to tear them from this joy?'

"But then as I raised to myself this picture of perfect Love, that other picture which I had seen from the hollow of the oak flashed back upon me. It was a demon's doing, and I writhed with hatred, with wounded self-love.

" 'I will not only have his blood,' I cried, 'but I will make her—yes *her*, take it. He shall die by the white hand that fondles him.'

"The resolution was grand, and I spent a night of heat and fury, tossing on my bed of hide and straw, and planning the affair.

"I rose a little before the sun, and bent my steps in the direction of a distant village, called Cœr-Brachd. Once arrived there, I marched straight to the house of a Druid whom I knew.

" 'Friend,' I said, when the ordinary greetings were over, 'you have two Roman prisoners among your slaves; you find them troublesome, I hear, and difficult to bring to work. Say what value you put upon them and I will give it you.'

"The Druid clasped my hand.

" 'Last night,' he said hurriedly, 'the news came here from Cœr-Bhelen, that some Roman prisoner was to be sacrificed. These men heard it, and fearful lest the lot should fall on them, they attempted to escape for the ninth time this winter, but my trusty Britons again foiled their essay. But you see how I am troubled with them. Besides, they refuse to draw water or hew wood. I would far sooner have some dozen sheep, or a new set of arms for my men.'

" 'You shall have both,' I said.

"He called a witness, who brought a javelin, which I broke on my knee, as a sign of a firm contract.

"An hour after my Romans were receiving their lesson from me. I told them that the people had demanded the blood of the Roman Knight, and that I, for my own reasons, and for friendship's sake, was willing to save him; that I had bought them up for the purpose of aiding me, and that if they did my bidding their liberty was secure, but not otherwise.

"The night before had been very stormy, and the wind was still blowing furiously. It was very early too, and so I felt certain that the news of my assembly had not yet reached Gavr Inis. I therefore took my own boat, spread the red sail, and carried the two Romans privily over.

"I fixed a trysting place for them in the forest near Wenedh, and sent them to Dona herself. They were to tell her that the people had resolved to slay her lover in sacrifice, but that I—I whom she had always respected, who was ever her friend, had thus schemed to save the Knight and the man she was affianced to. I could not doubt that Dona would at once relinquish her prisoner.

"I landed them at Gavr Inis, and sped back in my bark to Cœr-Bhelen. Here I rushed madly along the street, calling loudly for help. The people poured from their houses in sad alarm.

" 'This morn,' I cried, 'I went to Cœr-Brachd, and bought two Roman slaves of the Druid Grosna. I wished that they too should be led in triumph to the sacrifice of propitiation, and be humbled by the sight of their Knight's slaughter. It seems that they had learnt our intention, and as we came along by the water's edge they saw my boat. Suddenly one of them seized me by the neck, threw me down, and held me there by the throat, while the other jumped into the skiff and spread the sail; then the first leapt up and jumped into the boat after his companion, before

I could prevent it, and I saw them steer their way to the forest of Wenedh. Up friends and after them, seek them in the forest and bring them back, for if they escape they will reveal all to the Romans, and we are lost. Meanwhile I will go and secure the other on Gavr Inis.'

"A score of stout forms sprang into their boats, and some five or six sails were soon wafting them across the sea.

"I stretched my hide towards Gavr Inis, for I knew that they would take much longer to reach the forest than I should to gain the island. Like a wild horse, I bounded through the oaken groves on the island, and when I reached Dona's hut the two Romans were just preparing the boat, and Dona and the Knight were standing on the shore.

" 'No,' I heard her cry from my hiding-place, 'no, I will not weep. It is better that you should go alone, without me, and yet I seem to fear some mishap. But what matter? you are fleeing from a frightful death here, and in the forest and across the hills you will have to meet, at worst, a foe that you can combat. Now I will bind on your sword, and for my sake use it nobly.'

"She stooped, took up his sword, which was lying beside him, and girt it round his hips.

" 'Yes,' she continued, 'I shall follow you. You will await me in the forest, and ere sundown I shall see you again—and then no longer a captive, but a free citizen of hateful Rome. Yes, for I do hate Rome—and love it too—for your sake. But you will remember your vow—you will turn the Roman from our land. You will tell them how barren, how wretched it is. But ah! I shall be with you then—and yet—'

"She threw her arms around his neck, and hung upon his lips, and I exulted in my awful secret, for I knew that that embrace was the last.

"He tore himself away, and leapt into the boat. And she stood with clasped hands upon the beach, and I could see that she was pressing down her tears.

"The boat dashed wildly over the foam, and was borne away farther and farther. Still she stood and watched it, till the red sail was but a speck between heaven and the ocean. Then she fell upon her knees, and threw her hands to heaven, and the hot tears rolled in a torrent down her pale, pale cheeks.

"She rose again, and looked in vain for the distant boat. Then, dashing her hand across her eyes, she turned into the hut, slowly and sorrowfully. At that moment my heart smote me. I longed to spring to her side, to tell her all—to bid her despise me—to rescue her lover, and to undo my wretched deed. But this time, the demon within me was stronger still, and I nestled in my own hatred.

"She came out again, with a large grey woollen cloak over her shoulders. I watched her set the sail of her little skiff; and then, bounding back through the forest, I steered my own towards the wood of Wenedh.

"I followed her at some distance for a time, and then turning the helm, reached another part of the mainland, and made for the trysting-place. I saw that she had steered round an island which was in the way, and that she could not reach the shore till some time after me.

"The forest of Wenedh was cut about with paths and ox-tracks in different directions, but all met at one spot. It was there that I had appointed the trysting-place. I mounted the wooded steeps rapidly, and turning, after a time, I saw, through an open glen, the distant sea, and the five sails of the pursuers spread towards Cœr-Bhelen. Was he among them?

"I sped on, and reached the trysting-place. I saw the marks of a skirmish. I traced them over the rotting leaves, and presently came upon the body of one of the Romans, lying dead in a pool of blood. A little farther on the other was pinioned to a tree by a javelin.

"In a moment my plans were formed. I carried both the bodies to a distance, and covered them with brushwood and dry leaves.

"Then I returned to the trysting-place and sat down.

"In a few minutes I heard a rustling behind me. Though I knew it was Dona, I started like a guilty thief. She was coming on quickly and hopefully. The moment she saw me, she rushed towards me.

" 'Where is he?' she cried, 'Oh! tell me where he is.'

"I looked up with a face of well-feigned grief. I exulted in this moment of triumph.

" 'Dona,' I said, 'sit down, while I tell you all.'

" 'Is he alive? is he safe? Tell me, tell me.'

" 'Patience,' I answered, 'Listen to me, and you shall hear where he is. You know my hopes of saving him. You know that I brought the two Romans to Gavr Inis—'

" 'Yes, yes, but tell me all.'

" 'I will. But listen. I sailed back when I had landed them. I found Cœr-Bhelen in an uproar. I was surrounded, threatened—'

" 'And you betrayed him?' She looked at me with eyes of hate.

" 'No, no, never. They had seen me leave the shore with the Romans. They accused me of a plot to release the knight. I denied all—everything. I told them that the two Romans had gone straight to Wenedh, for I thought to put them off the track, and I sailed hastily back to Gavr Inis, to stop the—the—your lover—Dona—'

" 'Yes, yes—my beloved—'

" 'From going to the forest. But they must have discovered all. I sailed once more from Gavr Inis to the forest, still hoping to warn the fugitives, and as I touched the shore I met their pursuers coming back with three bodies borne among them, which they threw into the sea. The knight was one of them.'

"Her expression had changed, as I spoke, from anxiety to a fearful calm. She looked me sternly in the face, as a lioness might look, and I could not meet her eyes.

" 'You lie,' she said, calmly and firmly. 'You lie, he cannot be dead.'

" 'Would to heaven I lied,' I answered, with tears in my voice—sham tears. 'Follow me and I will show you.'

"I broke through the brushwood, and she followed to the spot where I had found the first body.

" 'That is his blood,' I said, pointing to the red pool.

" '*His* blood?'

"She gathered herself together, her eyes turned up, then

99

closed, and with a long loud shriek, she threw herself into the pool of gore.

"I stood above her, laughing in my sleeve at her credulity, laughing at the pangs, which I had power to inflict, and did inflict. It was better this—than bullying peasants, or wringing the innocent with tortures. It was a keener, more intellectual pleasure. But still I feared I felt what did not amount to trembling, but had all the pain of a guilty horror.

"Then I sat down on a ledge of stone, and coolly watched her. The grey cloak had half slipt off, and left her white shoulders bare. I saw that their whiteness now was not that of healthful beauty, but a bloodless pallor. Once or twice I saw the flesh quiver, as she lay with her face on the ground, and seemed to kiss what she believed was his blood.

"I sat for at least half-an-hour, while she remained motionless.

"I did not care now to go after my other captive. This enjoyment was enough for the day, and I revelled in the imagination of what her thoughts must be as she lay there; if, at least, she did think, but perhaps she had swooned. I cared not, but I watched her till the setting sun reminded me of the evening chill, which I had not felt till then.

"Beyond her form the hill shelved rapidly down, and the pines, those sombre giants, who alone seemed to favour this gloomy spot, stretched up in tall, thin ranks, with leaves and brushwood crowding round their feet. Far, far behind them, I could catch a glimpse of the ocean, and the slant rays were gilding the alternate leaves, and now played fitfully on my victim at my feet.

"But dark clouds gathered round the sun, and the shadows seemed to close me in behind. I felt frightened at my own wickedness, I shuddered, got up, and touched Dona's arm.

" 'Dona.' I spoke in a tone of well-feigned sympathy.

"She did not move, nor answer. I circled her waist with my arm, and raised her up. The drops of blood fell off her face and bosom, and she stood up before me—changed—utterly changed; and yet she had not shed a single tear. Gently, almost imperceptibly, she glided from my grasp,—a grasp in which

100

there was no guilty longing—and turning her pale face, covered with the cold blood, from me, stretched me her hand.

" 'Thank you, thank you,' she said, in a hoarse low whisper. 'Thank you for all you have done, or wished to do. Now, leave me.'

" 'No, Dona,' I answered, still in a voice full of false tears, 'I may not leave you here. You know the Briton well. You know his vengeance, and his thirst of blood. Now, that they have slain the knight—'

"She trembled visibly.

" 'They will seek you. You must not return to Gavr Inis. They will devour you.'

" 'And what matter, if they do?' she said, calmly, and drew her hand across her brow.

" 'It must not be. You would not tempt these dogs to another murder.' She was silent, and again trembled slightly.

" 'I know your heart too well. Besides, remember your mother.' She uttered a bitter 'Ah!'

" 'I will secure her. I will secure you too. There is a hut at the border of the forest, far from Wenedh, far from Gavr Inis, where you must remain a day or two, till all is calm again, till these blood-lappers have forgotten the murder of your lover.'

"How I delighted to remind her of that! But this time she betrayed no feeling of it.

" 'I will lead you there now, and to-morrow I will come to you, give you news of your mother, and hopes for the future. There is an old woman at the hut, who will take good care of you. Come.'

"Still she did not move. She was looking down at the blood on the ground.

" 'Come,' I repeated, taking her arm in my hand, 'the sun is down. Ere long the night will come on, and the wolf will steal from his lair. Come, Dona.'

"She walked passively beside me, but still she turned her face away. Presently we passed a running stream. She stopped, and thought a moment. Then stooping down, she washed the blood from her face and robe, looked silently up to heaven, and then followed me.

"The old woman was a hag, who lived alone and watched the stars. I drew her aside, promised her two sheep, and told her to be kind to her charge, but never leave her side for a moment.

" 'Three days hence,' I said to her, 'a woodcutter will come to the house and ask for food. Give him some, and talk to him. He will tell you that the Romans have had a battle with some of the chieftains. That they are marching this way. That two or three prisoners have been taken and brought to Cœr-Bhelen, and that all the folk are in terror. It will be a lie, mother, but you must believe it, and take care that the maiden hears it.'

"I left them, and returned across the sea to Cœr-Bhelen.

"I found the people in high glee. They had had a fight for their prisoner, killed the two Romans and captured the knight.

" 'Good,' I said, 'in seven days he shall be offered to Bhelen.'

"I visited my prisoner, but only once. There was so deep a reproach to me in his quiet, contemptuous smile, that I could not triumph over him, if indeed my mind had been vulgar enough to do so. But it was not. My triumph was in my own heart. I exulted in causing misery where I could not myself enjoy. Besides these cruelties were grown a habit, at least in mind.

"The knight did not thank me. Probably he suspected me, knowing more of man's villainy than poor Dona did. On my side I took no trouble to explain anything. I came there simply to tell him that he was destined to replace the ox and the ram at the sacrifice, and to enjoy his horror at the news.

"He turned very pale for a moment, and then I noticed a kind of swallowing in his throat, as he said, 'Sir, a Roman citizen can always die.'

"I left him in his chains, and sailed again across to the opposite shore. Dona had lain upon the straw, so the hag told me, but had not seemed to sleep. In the morning she had refused all food, and sat at the door, looking at the forest near at hand.

"I was very kind to her in my mockery. I talked to her about becoming a Druidess, about dedicating her virgin form to Nehallenia. She seemed to listen, but said nothing.

"Day after day I went. I persuaded a wood-cutter to play the part I had arranged, and the same day I rushed breathless into the hut, to confirm the false news. I added that some prisoners had been taken, and that the people had decided on a human sacrifice.

"She only shuddered.

"The next day I came to tell her that the people were calling for her. That they protested she alone was fit to strike the blow; that Bhelen had revealed to me in the quivering of the oak-leaves that no sacrifice would be accepted, unless a warrior maiden slew the victim.

"Her fixed eyes turned to me for the first time, and looked through me, till I trembled beneath them. But I made a grand effort. I rose, still answering her gaze, and said, 'What Bhelen bids us, no one dare refuse.'

"Then for the first time she spoke.

" 'Will Bhelen save the Land if this is done?'

" 'He will.'

" 'Then I will do it. I am ready.'

"I was myself again. The next two days I passed in preparing the procession.

"On the night of the third day, a mighty crowd was brought together on Gavr Inis. The stars were bright and numberless. The sky was moonless and doubly blue.

"A wild air thrilled along the branches of the oaks; and three bards, with Cervorix at their head, trod slowly up towards this temple.

"They were followed by a band of maidens, and Dona led them, holding in her falling arm a bright, sharp dagger. The music thrilled again wild and melancholy, and voices caught it up behind. A hundred white-clad Druids, their brows wreathed with oak-leaves, and branches of the ash in their hands, chanted the hymn of penitence. Then came two figures. Over one was thrown a long white cloth, that covered his head, and hid his naked body. This was the victim, and I led him by the hand.

"My father followed, with his silvery locks bent down as if in shame. And last, a band of Druidesses bore the glittering torches, streaming in the light breeze, and glaring on the ghost-like trunks of the huge oaks. The warriors and the people followed in a motley crowd.

"At the foot of the hill the long train stopped and turned. All were at last assembled, and as I came up, I saw Dona, calm, white as death, but yet with a look of quiet contentment on her sunken face. I saw her turn a glance full of pity at my victim, but it was clear she suspected nothing, and I had so arranged that she arrived only at the moment of the procession setting off; and as it was forbidden to speak when once it had begun, she could scarcely have discovered who the victim really was. She seemed to be happy again for a moment in the hope of saving her people, for in this strange being the love of her country seemed stronger than even that other love.

"The whole mass knelt at the foot of the hill. Here at least was true grief; the Roman was coming, and they knelt in real fear, real prayer for their hearths and homes. The bards mounted to midway up the hill, and Cervorix, strange bard, sang again.

> 'An eaglet's blood shall stain his hand,
>   A woman lead the host,
> A maiden's death-shriek fill the land,
>   And the Druid's rule be lost.'

"I trembled as the words swam down clear and ringing into my very brain. I had counted for all this, but still I trembled.

"Then regaining my firmness in the strength of my hatred, I led the victim up the hill. Dona followed near, but now alone. Behind her came my father, stooping, sinking more than ever. One Druid bore the vase to catch his blood, another bore a torch, and that was all.

"My father turned midway and blessed the kneeling people. At last we entered the low mouth of the temple. The two Druids marched first, and I thanked the darkness that covered at last my guilty pallor. I passed behind the smoking torch, still holding the prisoner's hand. Dona was next, and my tottering father came slowly, last.

"In the temple all knelt, but my victim and I. I took a cord from the hand of one of the Druids, turned the knight's back to this hole that you see, and taking his hands, bound them firmly to this shaft. Then I drew the ends of the white cloth over his shoulders, laying bare his hairy chest, but not his head.

"I looked at Dona, as I did so. She was bowed in fervent prayer.

"Then my father rose, and in a smothered voice, and raising his hands to heaven, he murmured:—'Oh! wrathful God, Oh! mighty formless Bhelen, will this appease thee? Oh! wash our sins out with this Roman blood.'

"The knight was motionless still. Then the torch-bearer drew near. The other Druid came to the left of the victim, and held his vase beneath the heart. I stood at the right, holding with my hands the ends of the white cloth that covered him.

"Then I motioned to Dona to draw near. She rose, she sighed slightly, and stood before the victim. She raised the dagger, with the point to his heart. Again I motioned with my head. She cried,

" 'I strike for my people.'

"I felt the victim start, I heard him cry bitterly 'Dona,' as he caught her voice. I quivered, for I thought all was lost, but the same instant I saw the blood spurt from his heart, and jerked the cloth from his head.

"Dona had started back. She had seized the torch from the Druid's hand, she had passed it before the dead man's face, her eyes starting from their sockets, her hair streaming wildly behind. She had thrown the torch down again, she glared fearfully into the victim's face, she passed her thin hands across his brow, parted his hair asunder, and even while I looked at her with bitter exultation, snatched the dagger from his heart, and with a fierce, long, awful shriek that shook the very stones, plunged it reeking into her own. I fled."

"And what did you do?" I asked, when the terrible scene was over. "Whither did you flee?"

"To the Romans," he muttered. "I became their spy, and led them to devour my own father's house. Stay,—"

He laid his heavy hand on my shoulder. I started, for I knew it was a murderer's. I jumped up, and as I did so, a bluff harsh voice at my side, cried: "Monsieur must get up. This wind won't last, and we had better be off before it changes."

I rubbed my eyes. The old sailor of last night was before me. The daylight was struggling dimly into the cave, and I saw clearly that he was not a Druid. I also noticed that my nether garments lay just in the place where the Druid had thrown himself on his face, and that they now caught the stray beam of day, and looked white.

I rubbed my eyes again and looked round the temple.

"Come, sir," said the sailor, in a hurry, "my wife will be tired of waiting for me. Have you had a good night?"

"Pretty well," I answered, as I gazed round the strange place. "I must have dreamed a good deal."

"Perhaps it was not all dreaming, sir," replied the other, doubtfully.

"By the way," I said as we were getting into the boat, "I heard some strange music last night. Were you singing?"

The two sailors looked blank at one another. "We heard it too," said the younger one, rather pale, "and thought it was Monsieur."

The boat dashed over the waves, and I lay in the bottom, thinking of Dona and the Druid. At last the keel grated on the shingle.

"Already at Cœr-Bhelen?" I cried, jumping up.

"Cœr-Bhelen!" answered the sailors, staring at one another in amazement. "This is Locmariaquer."

"Ah," rejoined the elder one, "Monsieur *has* seen the man in white, then."

The Romance of the Echoing Wood

W J T Collins

*William John Townsend Collins (1868–1952) was born at
Stratford-on-Avon but chose to settle in Newport, Monmouth, where he
became a well-known and familiar figure. He worked on the South
Wales Argus from 1892, becoming its editor from 1917 until his
retirement in 1939. He published several volumes of humorous verse,
but is best remembered for his collection* Tales from the New
Mabinogion *(1923) and his* Romance of the Echoing Wood
*(1937), published here for the first time since its original appearance.
Collins was a friend of the mystic Arthur Machen (1863–1947) to
whose influence he shows an indebtedness in all his published work.
His love of Celtic mythology shines through every word of his writing;
no more so than here, in this romantic tale of long-ago Wales. Here,
in a simple-seeming tale of love, is a parable of the coming together of
two lands, of their slow recognition of each other's value, and finally
of their dawning trust. In Ceinwen, the gentle maid who finally shows
forth the warrior woman within, we have an unforgettable heroine
worthy of a longer tale which will one day perhaps be written.*

From *The Romance of the Echoing Wood* by W. J. T. Collins. R. H. Johns, Newport,
Monmouth 1937.

E. F. Powell

I

The Romance of the Echoing Wood

On the hearth the logs flamed fitfully. On a low bench, high backed and laid with skins, sat a grey-haired, grey-bearded man. With his elbows on his knees and his jaws on the balls of his thumbs he gazed steadily into the fire. By his side on the rush-strewn floor lay a wolfhound with his nose between his outstretched paws. The great hall was filled with the sound of the wind which roared outside, and a sudden gust of great fury blew to the floor the bundles of wool which had been stuffed into one of the narrow slits in the outer wall which in summer time admitted light and air. Into the hall came the sound of the wind charging through the treetops—a crashing sound as if a thousand men were plunging through the thickets of the wood. The hound raised his head and cocked his ears. The man remained crouched before the fire. Suddenly the hound barked sharply, and with that the chieftain straightened himself. Through the storm he heard the faint sound of a horn, the rattle of chains, the clang of the falling drawbridge. He sprang to his feet, and, with his face towards the arched doorway, waited with his arms folded across his breast. A giant in height and breadth of shoulder, he was thin, worn, hollow-cheeked, as if he had but newly dragged himself from the frontiers of death. As he waited, there came a knock at the door.

"Enter!" he cried, and a man muddied to the knees approached. With raised hand and bent knee he saluted, as his Chief asked: "What news?"

"Victory, master!"

"And—my son?"

"He is well. I was sent before him to give you news of success. At the head of our company he is marching through the wood, bringing with him captives and spoil."

"How went the fight?"

"Our spies reported that the Vikings were camped on the

headland above Solva creek, with their vessels moored in the harbour, and we surprised them in the grey of dawn. The main body of our men crept silently along the hollow of Gowny, while a small party made a sham attack on the Vikings' ships. As they moved to the defence, our men reached the ridge and drove them in swift flight to their boats. Ere they could escape half of them were slain. Eight of their ten ships were captured, one crashed upon the Black Rock, and only one escaped to the open sea. As it swept away we gathered together the arms, the gold, the garments and the stores of food they had left in their flight."

"What did my son?"

"Though so young, he led us with courage and judgment. He is his father's son. We would follow him to the end of the world—against any foe, upon any quest."

"It is well. If I cannot drive the fever from my bones and march again at the head of my men, thanks be there is one to take my place."

"If these robbers of the sea, who have harried us so sorely should return, may you and he, side by side, lead us in defence of our homes, our women, our children, our flocks and herds. But it is at great price that we have rid the land of these rovers. Of those who set out, ten in the hundred were stricken, even in victory. Howel and Griffith and Alun, Morgan and Rhys and David, will go no more to the Place of Mustering in the Echoing Wood. Many are dead; more are wounded. But honour to the brave. They have bought our peace with their lives."

"At a great price they have bought our liberty. Honour in our memories for those who come not again! And for the living victors let the feast be spread."

From the wall he took a sword, and with its flat blade he clashed upon a shield which hung above the chimney arch.

"Prepare the feast for our returning warriors," he cried to the servants who entered. "Pile the tables with food. Bring mead and meat; we will eat, drink, and rejoice, for, though the cost be high, we have driven the Vikings from our land."

Even as he spoke there came through the roaring wind the loud call of a horn, the tramp of feet, the shouts of victory, and

110

into the hall a youth advanced at the head of a force of armed men. He saluted with upraised hand. He sank upon one knee in reverence; but the next moment his hands were on his father's shoulders, and the moment after he was clasped to the old man's heart amid the joyous shouts of the men. Few words they spoke; brief was their embrace. David of the White Rock led the boy to the raised platform at the end of the hall, placed him in the great chair of state, and seated him beneath the canopy supported by the Dragons of Dyfed.

"Behold your Chief-to-be," he cried. "A boy in years, he has played a man's part. I name him Lord of the Severn Cantref of Dyfed. He has led you, he has saved our land; is it not fitting that the power should pass from my weak grasp to the strong hand of youth?"

There was silence in the hall, but in a moment Illtyd was kneeling.

"Father," he said, "I am your loving son and loyal subject till death." Then springing to his feet, and turning to the warriors who crowded the hall, his voice rang out: "Long live the King!"

"Long live the King! Long live the King!" came back the answer, and, moved by a common impulse, each man drew his sword, sank upon one knee, and, with their blades stretched high above their heads, they thundered out: "Long live the King!"

Illtyd sprang from the dais and knelt with them. The old man's eyes flashed. He straightened his body and squared his shoulders. Vigour for the moment returned to his fever-racked body, and once more he seemed to those who were his subjects and loving friend the Warrior King they had known in earlier years.

"Long live our King!" they cried.

"Long live Prince Illtyd," the King cried as he beckoned his son again to his side; and they echoed the words as Illtyd stood beside his father.

Waves of pride and affection swept over the men who had followed him so devotedly. Giant in height though the father was, he was not half a hand's breadth taller than his son and while the father's body was worn with fever, Illtyd was all sinew, strength, and youthful vigour. No one would have guessed from his well-knit figure that it was but fifteen years since, as a tottering baby of little more than a year, his little feet first danced among the brown beech leaves of the Echoing Wood. His hair was black and curly; his cheeks were ruddy, and when he smiled he won the hearts of men as well as of every woman who looked into his blue eyes, though the time had not come for him to love.

"If you permit," he said to his father, "I will lay before you the Vikings' treasure. Bring in the spoil," he cried, as his father nodded.

They laid before the dais rich garments of linen, cloth, and fur; the gold-hilted and richly-chased sword of the dead Viking Chief, cups of silver, jewelled rings, and chains of gold.

"There yet remains treasure of price," said Illtyd.

He clapped his hands, and six soldiers entered. Four of them bore a shield; the others each held the hand of a little maid who stood lightly poised upon it. Her feet were shod in gold-buckled sandals; her straight and graceful body was clothed in a silk gown, the colour of the primrose; her dainty head was crowned with golden curls, and her face had the beauty of a daughter of the gods. The men paused before the King. Illtyd gave his hand to the child, and she stepped lightly to the dais.

"This, father, is my gift to you. Too long has the Palace in the Echoing Wood lacked a child's sweet laughter and a girl's bright song."

The child held out her hand. The King's eyes filled suddenly with tears (for he was weak and overwrought, and memory was tugging at his heart). With great tenderness he stooped and took the hand. He turned it over, kissed the palm, and closed the fingers, saying, "That is a kiss for you to keep."

Then Illtyd told his father how three days before the attack on the Vikings one of his spies found the child a mile outside their camp, and brought her to the secret valley where his men lay hidden. By her speech he knew she was of their own stock, but whence she came she could not tell. All she knew was that she once lived in a great house by the ford of a tidal river. There was fighting; she was taken by the Vikings and carried to a ship.

112

When she looked back she saw her home in flames. They brought her with them to the camp at Solva, and while they were busy overhauling their ships she ran away, and was glad once more to be among those who spoke her own tongue.

"This is a gift indeed," said the old King. "She shall be Queen of the Homecoming. Let the feast begin." And, seated between Illtyd and his father, Ceinwen with the hair of gold ate the first of many meals in the Palace in the Echoing Wood, and paused at intervals to listen to the wind in the trees which was like the mustering of men among the thickets.

II

The Minstrel's Song

The storms of four furious winters beat upon the grey walls of the Palace in the Echoing Wood; but though there was tumult without there was peace within. Spring saw the daffodils dancing in the shelter of the grassy bank which fell away from the edge of the wood to the pastures; summer brought heat and brooding silence in which the orchards came to fruitage and the corn grew waist-high in the fields; autumn saw misty mornings and days of sunny harvest.

Within the stronghold there was springtime perpetually, for Ceinwen of the hair like gold grew in grace and joyous beauty, and at the end of four years was as beautiful as a young apple tree in bloom. A child of quick movements, ready words, and easy laughter, there were times when her presence seemed to fill the Palace. She had freedom within the bounds of safety. She was seldom still, and as she flitted through the castle her low laugh was heard everywhere—now in the great hall, now in the courtyard; then in the kitchen (for she early sought initiation into the mysteries); and sometimes the woodmen in the forest saw her golden hair shining on the battlements, or Illtyd, riding to the drawbridge, heard her welcoming voice from the gate tower. She knew every corner of the castle, amused herself by wandering through its rooms and passages, and climbed the winding stair to the tower, even as a child of seven, to look down over the tree-tops and listen to the voices of the wood.

For four years the Land of Dyfed was free from raids, and there was peace among the Kings of Wales. With peace came the return of minstrelsy. Every great house had its bard, who told in verse the great deeds of his chief and chanted stories of the heroes of old. Alun the Harper, who sat at the table of David of the White Rock, made a song of the defeat of the Vikings and the coming of Ceinwen to the Palace in the Echoing Wood. He knew all the old tales of the Mabinogion, and he chanted them to the guests as he touched the strings of the harp; but no song had power to move the followers of Illtyd like the story of the victory they had shared. Sometimes Alun asked the leave of his lord to go to other parts, there to engage in friendly contest with rival bards or to entertain courts whose minstrels were travelling on like errands, and often David and Illtyd made welcome bards who came from afar—singers of songs, tellers of tales, bearers of news.

Most of the minstrels were known throughout the land, but there came a day when a stranger sought the hospitality of the Palace in the Echoing Wood. He was made welcome, and when the evening feast was over he was asked to sing.

"I cannot tell a merry tale," he said; "nor do I sing of young men's love; but listen if you will to a tale of loss and sorrow—of surprise, defeat, and ruin; of a homeless man who lost his all and seeks it still."

Silence fell upon the company as he played the sad strains of his prelude. He described a castle by the ford of a tidal river which ran swiftly to the sea, foaming over the stones at low water, rising high about the castle walls with the return of the tide. He told of a beautiful and gracious woman, of a warrior husband who loved her, and of the little maid who, dear to them, was worshipped by the bard who sang his songs to her and carried her on his shoulder. But the coming of the sea rovers brought defeat to the chieftain, death to the lady, and the disappearance of the child.

114

The minstrel's song was a dirge for the loss of the matchless three—the bravest man, the fairest woman, the sweetest child in the fair land of Gwent.

> Then through the morning mist
>   (he chanted)
> Came the sea rovers;
> Borne by the drifting tide
> Reached they Casnewydd,—
> Beat at the water gate,
> Burst through unguarded halls,
> Slew man and wife and maid,
> Pillaged and broke and burnt
> And, while the castle roof
> Flamed like a blazing torch,
> Over the water dark
> Carried away the child
> Ceinwen, the golden-haired,
> Flower of the land of Gwent,
> Crown of the singer's song.

No sooner had the stranger finished this summing up of the story he had told at length than Alun rose and sang the song he had made of the defeat of the Vikings and the coming of Ceinwen.

The visiting singer listened in wonder.

"Surely," he said, "the Ceinwen of whom you sing is the Lily of Gwent—the child I seek?"

Now it chanced that Ceinwen was not at the evening feast. "I will send for her," said David. Silence fell upon the company, and all eyes were turned towards the door when a servant drew aside the curtains for the child to enter. She came smilingly, lovingly, and she carried herself as if she were a queen. The stranger bowed before her. "Lily of Gwent," he said, "to find you is to have an answer to many prayers." Then he told his tale. "When the Vikings carried you aboard the vessel which waited at the water gate—the last of the long ships to be lighted on its way by the flames of the burning castle—I followed and tried to snatch you from the deck, but was struck on the head and thrown overboard into the falling tide. The next thing I knew was that I was lying upon the mud of the river bank a few feet below the level of the gate. The Vikings were gone; the castle was in ruins. It was reported by a watcher from the shore at the mouth of the river that he had seen the Vikings sweep out to sea, and we thought they had returned to the Northland. The castle by the ford is still in ruins, for the dead lord's nephew, who has claimed the title and the lands, has his own home on the ridge which looks down upon the Valley of the Winding River. He has declared that the child must be dead or lost for ever, for there was news that the Vikings had suffered defeat and lost their ships, but no news of the child. This is indeed the Ceinwen whom I knew and mourned."

"Your quest is crowned," said David. "Welcome to the Palace of the Echoing Wood. Make this your home, free to come and go."

On his knees at Ceinwen's feet, looking up into her blue eyes, the minstrel said: "Where the Lily of Gwent is, there would I be."

So he sat at David's table, and wrote his song of the finding of Ceinwen.

III

Springtime in the Wood

Years passed, and David grew feeble, but Illtyd reached lusty manhood, and the Lily of Gwent grew fairer with every day that fled. In the main the land had peace. Sometimes the fires of tribal strife were kindled, but the flames were quenched before they could spread from the thickets to the corn; and the sea rovers made no serious attempt to press inland, though a long ship would dart into the harbour or drift in with the tide to a village on the banks of a river, make a sudden raid, and fly with

116

such spoil as could be gathered before the countryside was roused.

Through all the years the Echoing Wood was a power in Ceinwen's mind and heart. As a child she looked down from battlement or tower upon the tree-tops which seemed to her unending. When she looked from the edge of the moat across the narrow space of green between the castle and the wood the multitude of the trees seemed to her an army with banners—another hostile host—besieging her home. When she returned from cornfield or pasture—from the level fruitful land between the forest and the sea—the edge of the wood, with its glimpses of winding ways and tangled undergrowth, shadowed her with a fear to which she refused to give place. She saw breaks in the forest fence, the beginning of paths. Whither did they lead? What lay hidden in the black heart of the wood? In early childhood she was under the shadow of the days of blood and fire when she lost home and kindred; and, though a child cannot consciously define her thought, she felt that in the wood there might be enemies—that out of the wood there might come doom. She fought her fear, and conquered; yet never could she wholly put from her the thought that the wood was haunted by powers whose voices she heard—the kindly: whispering, singing, shouting; the angry: hostile, snarling, shrieking and roaring like wild beasts. One day of storm she climbed the winding stair which led to the battlements of the south-west tower, and, crouching there, looked down upon the swaying tree-tops and listened to the voices of the wind. And thereafter, by day and night, they spoke to something in her blood, answered an unexpressed desire and need, and called her aside—to solitude, to quiet in the midst of strife, to acceptance of whatever came on the wings of the wind. There were windless days when she looked out on the tree-tops spread before her, a carpet of misty green, and not a whisper reached her. There were nights of moonlight and starlight when the wood was full of soft and wooing voices—voices of cheer, comfort, promise, love. But on nights of utter darkness, when the south-west gale crashed through the bending tree-tops and rumbled and whistled round the castle, she would stand bareheaded on the tower, rejoicing that she had mastered fear—calm at the heart of the storm, confident, exultant, expectant. For she felt that spiritually she was come to the edge of the wood, that new paths were opening before her, that voices were calling her—and calling her to good.

Springtime was in the wood. The windflowers and the daffodils had faded, but primroses still lingered in the dim hollows, and in the glades bluebells were blooming, while on the edge of the wood a hawthorn put forth its first white blossom. Into the wood came Ceinwen. She was tall and slim and graceful as a birch tree; her hair was living gold, her face pure beauty, her eyes blue as the sky when summer stars are shining in the darkest hour. Kindness looked from those eyes, and sometimes her perfect lips drooped with pity, for she loved all living creatures and felt for their pains and griefs. But more often her eyes shone with joy and mirth, and laughter opened her mouth to show her little teeth. The wild roses which trailed their briars in the wood were not more delicately flushed with pink than her cheeks, and the tiny white rose which stars the sandhills by the sea was not more purely white than her throat. She was light and swift of foot, and, walking or running (few men could run farther, and only Illtyd faster), she moved with easy grace. She was strong, too, and could draw a bow, wield an axe, or use a sickle along the edge of the corn in a long day of reaping (for there were late harvests when it was a race between the reapers and the autumn storms, and she was not too proud to share the field toil of David's folk). Tall as she was, she was so perfectly proportioned that it was only when she stood beside a woman of common height that her stature seemed to be unusual. But Illtyd towered above her, for, with a man's height and strength in youth, in manhood he was a giant who on level ground could look over the bare head of any man in his father's land.

To this black-haired giant love came with another spring, though at first he did not know it. The windflowers were gleaming white in the wood, and for the first time Illtyd was conscious of their pure beauty. Something stirred within him. Was it joy or

118

sorrow, hope or fear, satisfaction or unsatisfied longing? He did not know—he could not understand his own feeling, but only knew that the pale beauty of the fragile anemone somehow spoke to him of Ceinwen—of a quality in her which in its unconscious perfection set her apart from all the world. And, looking at her as she walked beside him down the broad path which was the main road through the wood, he blunderingly told her that she was as wonderful as a windflower. She was tempted to turn to the protective mockery with which women so often seek to hide their hearts; and she laughed: "It is a tiny flower with which to compare one so tall and strong, but"—and she sighed—"it is very beautiful."

"And you are very beautiful," said Illtyd.

When daffodils were blooming Illtyd found in them symbols of her tallness and her upright bearing ; primroses spoke to him of the delicate fragrance of her character; the tall bluebells dancing in the wind reminded him of her grace and ease of movement; and as he tried to tell her these things he found that she listened with pleasure (for she was a woman, and loved praise from his lips). He made progress in the arts of compliment and in knowledge of his own heart and hers. She was young—not yet nineteen—but she was not a child in years or experience, and she awoke with joy to a realization of the fact that Illtyd was daily falling more deeply in love. Her thought was swifter than his: it flew ahead down the unknown path of marriage which strikes into the unexplored forest of life. Something of the adventures of those who took the path she knew: some rumour had reached her of joys and disasters in the unknown wood. She knew that for most women there were flowers by the wayside—love, and the joy of motherhood; that for others the thorns in summer were trailed with the purple flowers of the deadly nightshade and in the autumn by its poisonous scarlet berries. But she had no doubts for herself and for Illtyd, and almost passively she watched the development of his love, certain that the day was near when he would declare it, and just as certain that she would give him love for love. She was one with Nature, and was content that the flowers and love should come in their season and grow

119

without forcing. She did not with mockery kill the budding poet in Illtyd ; she did not discourage his love-making, but she did not play the wooer.

Upon Illtyd's shoulders, as his father faded, were laid the cares of the kingdom, and often he was far afield. On a stormy night of March he returned from a journey, and as he approached the palace he heard the voices of the Echoing Wood. He listened to the booming of the wind, and once more, as on the night of the coming of Ceinwen, it was as if a host of armed men were crashing through the undergrowth. In a moment of swift fear he thought of danger to Ceinwen from unseen and unknown enemies. Overhead there was a swaying and thrashing of the bare branches. It was like the dash and drag of waves on a shingle beach, and with the thought of the hostile sea came memories of the sea rovers. For himself he had no fear; but he feared for Ceinwen, and the night and the wood seemed full of threatening and warning voices. His heart was heavy till the drawbridge fell behind him—till in the warmth and light of the great hall he took the lady's outstretched hands and looked long into her calm and fearless eyes. In the morning—the March sky blown clear of clouds, the sun shining, the wind no more than a happy whisper to the daffodils that decked the glades—the fears of the night seemed foolish.

So days and nights went by, and Illtyd and Ceinwen lived their lives in happy comradeship. But always in their ears were the warning voices of the Echoing Wood.

They paced the woodland paths together, and sometimes from the high ground looked out over the sea—for memories of the sea rovers were never long out of their minds. They were so happy in each other's company, and Illtyd was so content with the joy of the hour, that he held back the word of love. In his heart was the sense of a need which only Ceinwen could satisfy, and slowly his mind shaped out the way of wooing and avowal.

But before he had told his love he all but lost her. They were two hundred yards away from the landward skirts of the wood near sundown when from the darkening depths there ran a small band of the Northmen. Taken by surprise Illtyd hardly had time to know their numbers before the leader was at arm's length, spear in hand. Barely had Illtyd drawn his sword when the Northman thrust at his throat. With his feet firm on the earth Illtyd swayed swiftly to the left, and the spear head passed harmlessly over his shoulder while the running Northman took the point of the sword in his throat.

"Run!" cried Illtyd to Ceinwen. But she stooped, caught up a stone, and threw it with all her strength into the face of the nearest of their enemies, who went down for the moment, blinded and insensible. Fortunately for Illtyd and his love, the Northmen in the effort to take them unawares and to gain the glory of capture, had raced each other out of the wood up the steep slope, and not only were they breathless but they came in a straggling line. Their leader was mortally wounded, another lay insensible, but the others—five in number—came on. "Run!" repeated Illtyd.

"I stay!" said Ceinwen, as she stooped to pick up the fallen spear. "Take this! Give me your sword!"

"Give me space!" cried Illtyd.

She moved a few yards away, and for a moment the Northmen hesitated, doubtful whether to follow and capture her or to attack Illtyd. But he gave them no choice. He charged, and, thrusting and withdrawing quickly, he wounded one man in the thigh and another in the right arm. The other three bore down on him. As he gave ground, beating aside their spear points, but hard pressed, Ceinwen dashed forward on the flank, and with all her strength drove the sword into the arm of the man on the right who was pressing Illtyd hardest. So the fight was two to two, but before it had proceeded two minutes the invaders surrendered, and a party of soldiers from the castle took them and the wounded away as prisoners. They confessed that their object was to capture and carry away Ceinwen, the fame of whose beauty had been carried far and wide on the lips of wandering bards.

The thought of how near he had been to losing the light of his life and the desire of his heart stirred Illtyd to speech. They stood at the edge of the Echoing Wood, and as they listened Illtyd said:

121

"From the mountain and the sea come the voices of the wind, and in the night-time, at dawn, at noon, and twilight they carry your name to me. 'Ceinwen, Ceinwen, Ceinwen,' they say, and my heart answers 'I love you.' "

"I know you love me—as I love you," said Ceinwen.

"I would be as a tree of the forest to shelter you from the wind and the sun," said Illtyd, "and if the storm should break me and the sun should scorch, the wreck of my life should be fuel to give you warmth in the winter of your years."

"Saviour and shelter and shield you have been," said Ceinwen; "and whether we walk in the wood in springtime, with the flowers at our feet and the birds in song, or crouch in a hollow beneath the roots of a fallen tree, while the storm rushes over us and the night comes down, it will be your hand I shall reach for, your love to which I shall turn."

The Return of Lugh Lamh-Fada

Alice Milligan

Alice Milligan (1866–1953) was a gifted poet, novelist and writer for the stage. She was born at Omagh, Co. Tyrone in Ireland and after studying history at Dublin University travelled the country under the auspices of the Gaelic League. She became active in the Nationalist cause and edited their journal The Shan Van Vocht *from 1896 to 1899. Her play* The Last Feast of the Fianna, *based on ancient Irish myths, was one of the first dramatic products of the Celtic revival to be performed (in 1900) by the Irish Literary Theatre. The poem printed here captures the sinewy lines of medieval Irish hero poems, and celebrates one of Ireland's greatest heroes, in whom it finds an expression of a more archetypal heroic cause—that of Nationalism. As with several of the writers represented in this collection, Alice Milligan was a passionate believer in the rebirth of an Ireland which would reflect the glory of the past. After the horror of the 1916 uprising she lost faith in this vision and wrote little or nothing more until her death in 1953.*

From *Hero Lays* by Alice Milligan. Maunsel & Co Ltd, Dublin 1908.

Beatrice Elvery

The Return of Lugh Lamh-Fada

Lugh Lamh-Fada, mighty and immortal,
Lordliest of the fosterlings of Mananaan mac Lir,
Far out of Erin, behind a fairy portal,
Tarried in bliss till his boyhood's ending year.
  The whole world held no gladder place to dream in,
  With honey of the heather fed and milk of magic cows,
  Where flowers round the towers of apple-blossomed
      Eman
  Were mingled with the burdens of heavy-fruited boughs.

And the green leaves of spring, with the gold
      of autumn weather,
Were lit by the light of unending eve and morn;
For the sun and the moon stood o'er the hills together,
And looked upon the snowy vales, thick-sheafed
      with yellow corn.
  There, in those fair, far-off, sea-sundered places,
  The islands of the kingdom of the Ocean-ruler's son,
  He tarried many days among the bright De Danaan races,
  And all the wisdom of the world invisible he won.

Hosts came down from the future's misty regions,
Ghosts of buried heroes from rath and barrow flew;
And the world's long dead, with her yet unbodied legions,
Walked and talked on Aran shore with Lugh.

And they led him up to a peak upon the highland,
And bade him look unto Ocean's utmost rim,
Where the faint and lovely phantom of an island,
The dwelling of his father's race, was beckoning to him.

And they told how of old that island had been taken,
And made the prey of plunderers—the mockery of hate,
The poor of the land by their rightful lords forsaken,
Appalled by giant tyranny, oppressed by witching fate.
    And the torture of the day and the darkening
        of the morrow;
    The woe endured in Erin's isle through all his absent
        years;
    Lugh heard of till his godlike heart was touched
        with human sorrow,
    And his glad immortal eyes were for the first time
        wet with tears.

And the sun on high was powerless to hold him,
The moon in heaven had no might to make him stay,
So the bright De-Danaan people flocked beachward
    to behold him
Mount upon his magic steed and ride upon his way,
    O'er the high-flung wind-swung, emerald and amber
    Over-arching, onward marching billows of the main,
    That the light, bright hoof was powerful to clamber
    As swiftly as it swept the sod on Aran's smoothest plain.

And all the while, in Erin's isle, the clouds
    of sorrow darken;
The champion hand lets fall the brand,
    the lips of song are dumb,
Or sing in wildernesses lone, since no man
    cares to hearken
To wonder-chimes of long-gone times or tales
    of years to come.

And the music-strings, like human things, mourn
        when their masters sound them,
In lamentation wild and shrill, bewailing glories past;
And the fetters of the captives have the rust of years
        around them,
And the latest-buried champion by all lips
        is called "the last."

So patient necks are bowed beneath the yoke
        of servile labour,
Till lo! What shining on the land? What light along the
        main?
The glitter of a burnished shield, the glancing of a sabre,
And Lugh Lamh-Fada rides in glory back again.
    On the light, bright steed that was powerful to clamber
    Without breaking any bubble of the swiftly-trodden
        foam;
    O'er the high-flung, wind-swung emerald and amber,
    Onward-sweeping, shoreward-leaping billows to his
        home.

And the land is lit with a strange unearthly beauty,
And patriot strength and courage are to every heart
        restored;
And boyhood leaps impatient at the trumpet-call of duty,
While maiden hands are hastening to gird him with a
        sword;
    For Lugh has come from the beach, where bards have
        hailed him,
    While cliff and rock re-echo to the sound of battle-song;
    And the latest-buried warrior stands up where many
        wailed him,
    Arisen from the sepulchre to see them ride along.

And the world's long dead, in cairns of hill and hollow,
Have left their bones among the stones to hasten after
        Lugh;

127

While myriads of the yet unborn the march of freedom
    follow,
And the mighty lords invisible are thronging out at Brugh.
    And Lugh Lamh-Fada, the child of an immortal,
    Who came with the flame of the sunburst over sea,
    Leads on the host, both man and ghost, against the
        tyrant's portal.
    The stronghold shakes! the barrier breaks! his fatherland
        is free.

The Cave of Lilith

"AE"

George William Russell (1869–1935) who wrote under the name of "AE" (a contraction of 'aeon') was a talented poet, painter and playwright. But it is for his remarkable visionary writings that he is best remembered. These include The Candle of Vision *(1918) which he described as "the autobiography of a mystic";* The Earth Breath *(1897),* The Avatars *"A fantasy of the future"; and* The House of the Titans *(1934). His poetic drama* Deirdrie *was performed in 1901 at the Abbey Theatre in Dublin, which he helped to found with his lifelong friend W. B. Yeats. All of his work is coloured by a seemingly constant awareness of the presence of inner worlds, the faery race and the ancient gods of Ireland, which he also strove to paint. Towards the end of his life he sought to discover a visionary and symbolic language—"The Language of the Gods," a goal to which all his writings seemed to be leading. He was active, with Yeats, in the founding of the Dublin Lodge of the Theosophical Society, to which both Ella Young and Kenneth Morris were, for a time, attached.*

From *Imaginations and Reveries* by "AE." Maunsell & Co. Ltd, Dublin 1915.

The Cave of Lilith

Out of her cave came the ancient Lilith; Lilith the wise; Lilith the enchantress. There ran a little path outside her dwelling; it wound away among the mountains and glittering peaks, and before the door one of the Wise Ones walked to and fro. Out of her cave came Lilith, scornful of his solitude, exultant in her wisdom, flaunting her shining and magical beauty.

"Still alone, star gazer! Is thy wisdom of no avail? Thou hast yet to learn that I am more powerful, knowing the ways of error, than you who know the ways of truth."

The Wise One heeded her not, but walked to and fro. His eyes were turned to the distant peaks, the abode of his brothers. The starlight fell about him; a sweet air came down the mountain path, fluttering his white robe; he did not cease from his steady musing. Lilith wavered in her cave like a mist rising between rocks. Her raiment was violet, with silvery gleams. Her face was dim, and over her head rayed a shadowy diadem, like that which a man imagines over the head of his beloved: and one looking closer at her face would have seen that this was the crown he reached out to; that the eyes burnt with his own longing; that the lips were parted to yield to the secret wishes of his heart.

"Tell me, for I would know, why do you wait so long? I, here in my cave between the valley and the height, blind the eyes of all who would pass. Those who by chance go forth to you, come back to me again, and but one in ten thousand passes on. My illusions are sweeter to them than truth. I offer every soul its own shadow. I pay them their own price. I have grown rich, though the simple shepherds of old gave me birth. Men have made me; the mortals have made me immortal. I rose up like a vapour from their first dreams, and every sigh since then and every laugh remains with me. I am made up of hopes and fears. The subtle princes lay out their plans of conquest in my cave, and there the hero dreams, and there the lovers of all time write in flame their history. I am wise, holding all experience, to tempt, to blind, to terrify. None shall pass by. Why, therefore, dost thou wait?"

The Wise One looked at her, and she shrank back a little, and a little her silver and violet faded, but out of her cave her voice still sounded:

"The stars and the starry crown are not yours alone to offer, and every promise you make I make also. I offer the good and the bad indifferently. The lover, the poet, the mystic, and all who would drink of the first fountain, I delude with my mirage. I was the Beatrice who led Dante upwards: the gloom was in me, and the glory was mine also, and he went not out of my cave. The stars and the shining of heaven were illusions of the infinite I wove about him. I captured his soul with the shadow of space; a nutshell would have contained the film. I smote on the dim heart-chords the manifold music of being. God is sweeter in the human than the human in God. Therefore he rested in me."

She paused a little, and then went on: "There is that fantastic fellow who slipped by me. Could your wisdom not retain him? He returned to me full of anguish, and I wound my arms round him like a fair melancholy; and now his sadness is as sweet to him as hope was before his fall. Listen to his song!" She paused again. A voice came up from the depths chanting a sad knowledge:

> What of all the will to do?
>   It has vanished long ago,
> For a dream-shaft pierced it through
>   From the Unknown Archer's bow.
>
> What of all the soul to think?
>   Some one offered it a cup
> Filled with a diviner drink,
>   And the flame has burned it up.
>
> What of all the hope to climb?
>   Only in the self we grope
> To the misty end of time,
>   Truth has put an end to hope.

132

   What of all the heart to love?
     Sadder than for will or soul,
   No light lured it on above:
     Love has found itself the whole.

"Is it not pitiful? I pity only those who pity themselves. Yet he is mine more surely than ever. This is the end of human wisdom. How shall he now escape? What shall draw him up?"

"His will shall awaken," said the Wise One. "I do not sorrow over him, for long is the darkness before the spirit is born. He learns in your caves not to see, not to hear, not to think, for very anguish flying your illusions."

"Sorrow is a great bond," Lilith said.

"It is a bond to the object of sorrow. He weeps what thou canst never give him, a life never breathed in thee. He shall come forth, and thou shalt not see him at the time of passing. When desire dies the swift and invisible will awakens. He shall go forth; and one by one the dwellers in your caves will awaken and pass onward. This small old path will be trodden by generation after generation. Thou, too, O shining Lilith, shalt follow, not as mistress, but as handmaiden."

"I will weave spells," Lilith cried. "They shall never pass me. I will drug them with the sweetest poison. They shall rest drowsily and content as of old. Were they not giants long ago, mighty men and heroes? I overcame them with young enchantment. Shall they pass by feeble and longing for bygone joys, for the sins of their proud exultant youth, while I have grown into a myriad wisdom?"

The Wise One walked to and fro as before, and there was silence; and I saw that with steady will he pierced the tumultuous gloom of the cave, and a spirit awoke here and there from its dream. And I thought I saw that Sad Singer become filled with a new longing for true being, and that the illusions of good and evil fell from him, and that he came at last to the knees of the Wise One to learn the supreme truth. In the misty midnight I heard these three voices—the Sad Singer, the Enchantress Lilith, and the Wise One. From the Sad Singer I learned that thought of itself leads nowhere, but blows the perfume from every flower, and cuts the flower from every tree, and hews down every tree from the valley, and in the end goes to and fro in waste places—gnawing itself in a last hunger. I learned from Lilith that we weave our own enchantment, and bind ourselves with our own imagination. To think of the true as beyond us or to love the symbol of being is to darken the path to wisdom, and to debar us from eternal beauty. From the Wise One I learned that the truest wisdom is to wait, to work, and to will in secret. Those who are voiceless today, tomorrow shall be eloquent, and the earth shall hear them and her children salute them. Of these three truths the hardest to learn is the silent will. Let us seek for the highest truth.

The Song of the Salmon-God

W P Ryan

William Patrick Ryan (1869–1942) was born in Templemore, County Tipperary. A prolific journalist, he worked initially for The Irish Peasant, *an organ of the Irish Labour Movement. Ryan became its editor in 1906—the same year in which the paper was suppressed by the Catholic Church. Undaunted, Ryan re-instated it as* The Peasant *and continued to edit it until 1908 when it changed its name again, becoming* The Irish Nation—*under which title it continues to be published today. Ryan returned to London in 1910 and became involved in the Labour movement in Britain. Later he was to edit the journal of the Gaelic League, and during this busy career still found time to write a number of books and essays, including* The Celt and the Cosmos *(1914) and* King Arthur in Avalon *(1934). He was deeply committed to the cause of Nationalism in Ireland, and as with several of the writers whose work is featured here he also possessed a visionary sense of the spirituality underlying his country's history. The dramatic poem reprinted here is one of his most colourful expressions of this fascination with both history and myth. Based in part on the story of Fionn, the great Irish hero and poet, its theme is really that of rejuvenation and initiation—one feels, not only of the hero, but also of Ireland herself. Ryan was a follower of Rudolf Steiner for many years and published at least one work with the Theosophical Publishing House.*

From *The Song of the Salmon-God* by W. P. Ryan. J M Watkins, London *c.* 1934.

135

The Song of the Salmon-God

THE CHARACTERS
Fionn Eigeas, an aged sage.
Sorcha, an old woman.
Deimne, a student of the art of poetry.
MacReeva, an official Shanachee, or story-teller, at Tara.
Conal, a young friend and pupil of MacReeva.

I

Fionn Eigeas on May morning at the door of his shieling by the deep pool of Fec in the Boyne.

FIONN EIGEAS.
    Fionn Eigeas, Fionn the learned, Fionn the bard,
    One with the pool of stillness have I grown,
    Here in my shieling by the sacred Boyne,
    Through seven lean years of vigil and of dream,
    Of fasting, hoping, yearning, ecstasy,
    Fired by the prophecy from druids old,
    Whose every word was in my night a star:
    "Supreme the wisdom that shall come to Fionn
    When he the holy salmon takes and eats,
    The salmon-god that one day swims the Boyne."

    How have I watched the waters at the dawn!
    How have I peered in the still waves at noon!
    How have I scanned them spent and pale at eve!
    Started at sudden splash in deep of night!
    Waiting the salmon-god that never comes.

Now I am old of frame as men count years,
Knowing no joy save in the pool of thought.
A sage of Tara, passing yester eve,
Said: "Still this ancient ghost braves out the light!"…
But when the sacred feast is ended, age
Shall be no greater burden than a breeze
That flutters, pleases, passes, and is not.
All-open wisdom shall reveal the power
To conquer time and trouble and grey death,
Shall lead me as an equal 'mid the hosts
Who weave their spells behind all forms and hues,
Whose play is spring, whose joy is summer's gleam,
Who bring us autumn in their bounteous moods,
And winter when their thought is wild and weird,
Whose deeper homes are other planes than ours.

       (*Sorcha, bent and grey, approaches.*)

SORCHA.

Ah, foolish Fionn, still dreaming by the pool!
Ah, witless Fionn, who turned from love and me
When in our young veins fire and music ran.
Now we are withered as the winter trees,
Our tale brings smiles to lusty youths and maids
Who come to Tara, though the wise are grave
When they remember how my beauty paled
And how an age-long vigil sered my heart,
Waiting for one whose life grew frozen thought
And then was haunted by the crazy dream
A god could be a salmon in the Boyne.

FIONN EIGEAS.

Peace, woman, we shall have our youth again,
And love shall be no frenzy, but a bliss
Such as the gods feel on their hallowed hills,
Flaming in song and deed past dreams of men.
When I have fed on wisdom salmon-shrined
And know the secrets that renew the world
My foremost thought-deed shall your youth restore.

138

SORCHA.

    Poor withered Fionn, who yet enchanter's robes
    Can don in fancy by the heedless Boyne!
    Poor sapless Fionn, you are a winter tree
    Too bent and wasted for new-weaving spring.

FIONN EIGEAS.

    O wandering woman! talking, walking wind!
    Your soul, long fed on surface-mind, is starved.
    Gaze in the pool of Fec as I have gazed,
    Peer in the pool of thought ten thousand days,
    And curb your wilfulness and see my goal.

SORCHA.

    I go betimes to Tara's May-day feast.
    I still can dream when music wakes the past.

                     (*She wanders onward.*)

FIONN EIGEAS.

    Light love of woman and the wandering mind
    Were ever worst distractions of the seer.
    One have I conquered, one torments me yet
    Whene'er I turn a moment from the pool.

          (*He gazes intently into the waters of Fec.*)

II

*By the Boyne, a league below the pool of Fec, young Conal, handsome,
eager, thoughtful, meets the genial old Shanachee, MacReeva.*

CONAL.

    A while agone I sought to say farewell
    To Fionn at Slánya by the pool of Fec;
    But in the calm of morn my words were vain
    As though he were upon the further bank,
    Not nigh me, and a tempest raged between.

He peered so deeply waveward that it seemed
The solemn waters and his soul were one.

MacReeva.

None wakes him when that wizard mood is come
Save Sorcha, she who charmed young manhood's years,
Or Deimne, whom he taught the poet's art,
And loved as son—still loves, when he awakes
Awhile to feelings of our humankind.

Conal.

Wild is his dream: to think a godly power
Would take a salmon's form and he could eat
Rare knowledge with its flesh.

MacReeva.

         Is it more strange
That power eternal with a salmon's form
Should in the waters of the Boyne be linked
Than that all ages in rude forms of men
Immortal souls are fastened and constrained?

Conal.

Men are far higher on what druids call
The cyclic Path, the planetary round.

MacReeva.

Yet oft I think, alone by woods and streams,
The birds and fishes have some sweeter traits;
And then I wish I were a lusty trout
Or songster trilling in the jocund noon.

Conal.

You read your story-laden self in birds
And with your mind-adventures dower the beasts.

MacReeva.

> The secret powers, since old Atlantean days,
> When they would commerce hold with humankind
> Have often taken form of bird or beast—
> Bull, dragon, eagle. Thus, in guise we knew
> They bridged the vastness 'twixt ourselves and them.
> And still in Tara does the bright god Fál
> Loom o'er his servants as divine horse-man.

Conal.

> Oh, leave in these last moments that we spend
> Together by the long-loved banks of Boyne
> Speech of our wasted island's rites and tales.
> Her brightest life is as an ebbing tide,
> Her drearest—we have seen it symbolized
> In crazed Fionn Eigeas peering in the pool.
> All Inis Alga but a relic seems;
> Stonehenge and Carnac are as Tara cold,
> The fossils of an ended world; their spells
> Have no relation to my life of thought.
> And so—though Deimne like yourself I love,
> And cannot take my whole self leaving ye—
> I fare far eastward, to the heights of Hind,
> Land of the mighty lore our druids laud,
> Land of the wonders that our travellers maze.
> Long have I dreamed of sacred Angkôr-Tôm.

MacReeva.

> Yours is the dreaming pride of student-youth,
> Athirst for newest learning, losing ours,
> Unloving listeners to our primal tales,
> And seeing scarce the surface of our rites.
> Yet luck I wish you with your eastern quest!
> The hints I've heard of that strange lore of Hind
> Have brought a sleepy spinning in my brain:
> It wrinkles even Tara's druids' brows!
> I shrink from eastward gazing, but my heart

Turns often westward to its ancient home,
To great Atlantis and the long ago.
Ah, many a life of tale and play was mine
Within her City of the Golden Gates.

CONAL

Yet druids hint of long Atlantean years
When cloud and vapour gloomed, and day was night.
So seldom did a sun-gleam cross a life
Whole ages deemed the sun no more than dream,
A legend, or a sheen of passing god.
And when the end came and the favoured hosts
Escaped and eastward fled to fair new lands
And saw the daily splendour of that sun
They thought it God and gave it worship sweet—
And soon it set aglow their deeps of mind
That long all fallow in Atlantis lay.

MACREEVA.

No, for a million years Atlantis turned
To regal destinies her sequent dreams.
And if she fell on days of cloud and wrath
(The fruit of power abused and vision lost)
When storms abroad were as the storms within,
Forget them—on the primal wonder dwell.

CONAL.

E'en if Atlantis glowed a million years
It left no lore, no golden fruit of mind.
And Alga's but a stage whose day is done,
A place of spells and peering in a pool.
Life's fair fruition needs the sun of Hind,
And Hind's new lore that suns the seeking soul.
I tire of wonders that ye weave in tales
Of lost Atlantis and our own weird isle.
Thought makes true Wonder, as the sun the day.

142

MacReeva.

    We have our own bright round of wonders here.
    Come with me: wait a day for Tara's feast
    Of Maytime, long the charm of all the West.

Conal.

    No; story-tellers spoil all feasts of ours.
    At Tara, once a shrine, they crowd so much
    The druids shrink or seem ashamed of thought
    Or grown too proud to teach a folk so fallen.
    The best, whose frames are still unaged, have gone
    Before me Hindward, glad to leave our pools
    And spells and drones who dream of salmon-gods—
    The East draws home the thinkers like a tide.

MacReeva *(smiling.)*

    Proud youth will break its brain on mysteries,
    On life's enigmas, harder than the rocks.
    No more I seek to hold you. With a song
    I take the path to Tara where I tell
    New-garnished tales of old Atlantean times.

Conal (*looking inward from the Boyne.*)

    I want dear Deimne, for the parting word.
    I know he muses somewhere in the fields.
    'Tis sad so bright a soul should e'er be bound
    To mad Fionn Eigeas, peering in the pool.

MacReeva.

    His glad reward will come the fated day
    His master feasts upon the salmon-god
    And wins the wisdom that outshines your East.
  (*Conal laughs lightly. They turn and walk inward from the Boyne.*)

III

Deimne, a tall, strong, fair-featured youth, rests by the waters a few hundred steps from the shieling of Fionn Eigeas.

DEIMNE.
> I sigh for Conal,
> No more my comrade,
> This hour gone eastward,
> Allured from Alga
> By shrines, by sages,
> By tales of mind-feats
> That make the brain reel.
> Ah, Conal, Conal,
> Our trees, our grasses,
> Our shining waters,
> Our birds on branches—
> Wee wonder-songsters—
> Our flowers, all summer
> In silence smiling:
> Hold sweeter secrets
> Than Hind's thought-mazes,
> Could we but read them… .

> > > > (*He muses pensively for a while.*)

> My loved old master,
> The lone Fionn Eigeas,
> Has long left living,
> Though death still comes not
> To lead him homeward.

> Like mindless murmurs
> The morning lessons
> That still he gives me
> In rules of song-craft
> That pass like shadows
> And leave me craving

The light that comes not,
The spell deep-hidden:
That straight would open
The heart to secrets
Of mead and tree-life,
Bird-rapture, wave-lore,
And true song-weaving... .

E'en as I leave him
He turns and faces
The heedless waters
For day-long brooding:
Poor heart, awaiting
The salmon's coming,
And endless wisdom!
O mazed Fionn Eigeas,
Not thus comes vision... .

(*His face grows thoughtful*)

And shrunken Sorcha,
His love of old days,
In dreams I've seen her
A flower-sweet maiden
As fair and blithesome
As ancients tell me
She glowed in girlhood.
Her dream-shape haunts me,
And brings me love-pangs,
And leaves me heart-cold
To maids of Tara.
O gaunt, grey Sorcha,
What weird love-story!
O crazed Fionn Eigeas,
As crazed your pupil.
For ne'er till Boyne brings
Your sacred salmon
Shall gods of Alga
Give me my dream-love!

(*Strange cries from the direction of the shieling. Deimne arises
and returns. Sorcha comes out as he approaches the door.*)

SORCHA.
The final madness has o'ertaken Fionn.
He bids you haste. His hands so tremble now
And all his nature such a frenzy feels
He cannot roast the salmon he has caught—
He calls it sacred salmon in his maze.

(*Deimne starts and looks strangely at Sorcha. Cries of Fionn
Eigeas from the shieling. Deimne hurries in.*)

FIONN EIGEAS. (*coming forward with the salmon.*)
So flowed at last the wonder to my feet.
The salmon to his waiting servant came,
And leaves me trembling for the joy fulfilled.
Yet strange my fever: like a flower he rests,
And seems as light as hazel in my hand.
Come, you shall roast him while I calm my heart.
"Supreme the wisdom that shall come to Fionn
When he the holy salmon takes and eats,
The salmon-god that one day swims the Boyne."

IV

*Deimne rushes to the door of the shieling with a cry of pain. Suddenly he
presses the tips of the fingers of his right hand to his mouth. After a
moment or two the expression of pain leaves his face, and one of intense
joy comes over it. He gazes ecstatically on the waters, then on the trees
and fields, lastly on the heights. Fionn Eigeas comes out, followed by
Sorcha.*

DEIMNE (*rapturously*).
Hear the music of the May-time!
Whence have come the myriad singers?
Oh, the harping of the forest,
And the piping of the grasses,

And the lilting of the green leaves,
And the joy-talk of the rushes,
And the choirs adown the waters!

Whence have come the dazzling colours?
Not from sun but hidden star-sphere
In the earth's heart underneath us.
Oh, the colours talk like sages
In a tongue of seven-fold meaning.
Every gleam sings, every tone gleams,
And the tones and gleams are wisdom.
>   (*Waving his hands and still chanting, he dances onward.*)

FIONN EIGEAS.
>   Some madness took him, but it turns to joy.

SORCHA.
>   While you were brooding on your fancied bliss
>   I saw him touch the salmon with his hand.
>   He burned himself, and cried, and sought the door,
>   Then in his mouth the pricking fingers pressed
>   That kept a little of the salmon's flesh.
>   The taste has given him vision: strange at last
>   How comes the druid prophecy to pass.

FIONN EIGEAS.
>   Hush, woman, mine the feast, not his: he touched
>   The flesh—no more. Lo, what a touch has done!
>   But when I eat my fill!—
>
>   (*He turns to go in.*)
>
>   Approach and see
>   The wonder-working by the banks of Boyne.
>   "Supreme the wisdom that shall come to Fionn
>   When he the holy salmon takes and eats,
>   The salmon-god that one day swims the Boyne."

SORCHA.
>   (*Half to herself, as she looks down where Deimne has gone.*)

Friends have called Deimne *fionn,* since he is fair.
Now I remember—did the druids know?

FIONN EIGEAS.

Woman, you rave! Your wits are worn with years,
But when I feast, as now to feast I go,
And win the wisdom that renews the world
My foremost thought-deed brings your youth again.
(*He enters the shieling. Sorcha looks sadly to the waters. After a
few moments Fionn Eigeas comes out distracted.*)

FIONN EIGEAS. (*wildly*)

No salmon! Not a trace. It might be dream
From which I wake—my bliss made agony!
(*He stops suddenly and turns to the waters.*)
Hush! Listen! All the tide is song and flame.
The salmon-god back to the waters leaps;
The salmon-god is singing in the Boyne.
And I shall follow, there shall do his will
While he rewards my wisdom-quest at last.
(*He leaps into the waters.*)

SORCHA.

And by the Boyne is one lone woman left—
Nay, not a woman but a gaunt old tree
That lost its bloom and all its leaves for love.
A dreaming man of its renewal raved,
And now he drowns for yet a wilder dream.
(*Deimne comes back.*)

DEIMNE.

No, you the dreamer are. The Boyne is path
To life and beauty far beyond his thought.
List, how he sings, one with the salmon-god!
(*The voice of Fionn Eigeas rises in ecstasy.*)

SORCHA.

Do men dream after death?

FIONN EIGEAS. (*from the waters*)
> They wake! They wake!

V

The night succeeding the passing of Fionn Eigeas. Sorcha sleeps wearily on a couch of leaves in a corner of the shieling. Suddenly she is half awakened by a sound as of a roaring waters. She starts to her feet.

SORCHA.
> The Boyne has burst its bank; the waters roar;
> They overwhelm me, yet they drown me not,
> But gleam about me like unearthly light—
> > > (*She is now fully conscious.*)
> And all the singing light is as myself.
> (*She stands forth, a fair aura.* * *Apart from her lies her body on
> > the couch of leaves. She gazes upon it wonderingly while it
> > > gradually grows dimmer in the new light.*)
> Lo, what a garb I wore in outer life!
> Yet was it garb? So small, so mean, and *I*
> Am lofty, lustrous: 'tis like kernel crude
> Cast from a thing of splendour and delight.
> *Inside* the soul the body dwelt, meseems.
> Ah, here comes Fionn, all wisdom; he will solve
> The beauteous mysteries that encompass me.
> > (*Fionn Eigeas, a stately and radiant aura, appears.*)

FIONN EIGEAS.
> My last earth-body drifts upon the Boyne,
> Like some old robe I cast at night away,
> And, waking, take another, new and fair.
> Forget old bodies, like earth's fallen leaves.
> Here is renewal-time for tasks of souls.

---

*The luminous, somewhat oval-shaped "body" enveloping and raying out beyond the dense physical frame. Its colours and tones indicate to the seer the inner life and development of the individual. Apart from the physical body it expresses the permanent and supersensible being.

SORCHA.

My soul exults, yet wildered still am I
With fantasies and fears of weary days.
I dreamt I was a woman old and grey,
And you, my lordly lover, sought a fish,
A salmon in the Boyne or some old sea—

FIONN EIGEAS.

Ah, still you dream—upon this plane of light,
Or else the thought beyond the salmon's form
Eludes your waking nature. Think and gaze!
(*As she thinks and gazes, multitudinous beings are seen at work
in the waters, the meads, the trees, the heights. Concentrating her
thought, she senses a definite order and beauty in the work; when
her thought wanders the order and beauty are lost.*)

SORCHA.

Those lightsome beings were too far from me
In that last clouded life now half a dream.
I crave the kind affinities I knew.
Ah, where is Deimne who song-secrets sought?
(*The aura of Deimne appears. He is chanting a May-song.*)

DEIMNE.

I sang a May-song by the Boyne at noon.
It charmed the throng at Tara, chanted there
Again and yet again through eve and night.
Now in that song I sense an inner lay,
And in that lay another inner yet.
The ultimate entrancing inwardness
'Tis mine to seek through æons and through orbs
Far from the sun the seers of Tara praise.
(*Sorcha's thought tries to follow that of Deimne, but wanders,
and Deimne passes.*)

SORCHA.

Where is young Conal? Eastern lore he craved.
(*Conal's aura gleams before her.*)

150

CONAL.

My last earth-body goes the way to Hind,
My last earth-brain is busy with the lore
The brooding sages weave in Angkôr-Tôm.
Here flows it all, a fountain in myself.
List how I make it clear as inner Boyne.
*(Sorcha tries in vain to grasp his rendering of
the lore, and Conal passes.)*

SORCHA.

Haply MacReeva, man of endless tales,
Were nearer to my nature. Would he came !
(MacReeva's aura shines before her.)

MACREEVA.

Here am I living in Atlantean times
That well I love, that never pass away.
For each old life is now a living thought,
Part of my nature, and like spring and sun
Brimmed ever with new magic.

(To Sorcha)

Read in me
Till your own dimmed Atlantean lives shine out.
*(Looking into MacReeva's mind Sorcha is fascinated and
bewildered. She cannot grasp the sequence and relation of her
former lives which have become present in thought. MacReeva
passes. Sorcha knows not what else to seek. As she pauses she feels
drawn by innumerable forces to the body on the slowly
reappearing couch of leaves.)*

SORCHA.

Fionn Eigeas, save me, save me! Hold me back
From the dark dream and coils of outer earth!

FIONN EIGEAS.

Here in this light-sphere ever one are we,
And ever wakeful, in our Selves eterne.

151

But, still life's debtor, you must bear again
The body's burden and the dreaming state
Beside the outer Boyne. Yet through the dream
Will flower a sweeter fate.
Control your will,
Peer often deep within the pool of Fec,
Peer often deep within the pool of thought,
And you will harmonize the wandering mind,
Recover sunken secrets of yourself,
Find love and light without you, as within,
And wake new wonder by the banks of Boyne—
(*Many-moded music.*)
I hear the call of choir on choir beyond
The primal singing of the salmon-god.
(*He passes. Sorcha is joined to the body, and sleeps.*)

Taliessin Pen Beirdd

John Cowper Powys

John Cowper Powys (1872–1963) was born in Derbyshire, the eldest of eleven children, of Anglo-Welsh stock. Together with his brothers, Theodore and Littleton, he is among the giants of Celtic literature. Throughout his long life he maintained a steady and unwavering devotion to his homeland and its traditions, despite long periods in exile as a peripatetic lecturer. His work ranges from historical novels like Owen Glendower *(1940) and* The Brazen Head *(1956) to fantastic and visionary works like* Morwyn *(1937),* Atlantis *(1954) and* All or Nothing *(1960). As well as these, and a truly vast output of essays, critical works, poetry and philosophy, Powys contributed two novels of extraordinary power and scope:* A Glastonbury Romance *(1932) and* Porius *(1951). It is from the latter, a mighty and sprawling novel of the Celtic-Arthurian mythos, yet to be published in its entire form, that the following poem comes. It is based upon an ancient bardic song attributed to the poet Taliessin, the sixth century bard whose works became a repository of national wisdom in the Middle Ages, and whose writings (many attributed to him with little authority) embody the last vestiges of a Bardic-Shamanic tradition. Powys' version is faithful to the original vision of the old bard, but is as "Powysian" as any of his works. It can be seen as a kind of encapsulation of his belief in the power of nature and the magical forces of creation. Towards the end of his life Powys retreated to the mountains of North Wales, where he continued to pour forth an extraordinary torrent of strange and marvellous works into his ninetieth year.*

From *Porius.* Macdonald & Co, London 1951, by permission of the estate of John Cowper Powys and Laurence Pollinger Ltd.

Dorothea Braby

Taliessin Pen Beirdd

With the roots of a thousand worlds dangling beneath me,
With the mouths of a thousand worlds sucking the nipples
Of Nothingness round me, I've fled from the Mothers
To ride on the life-winds that whirl round Annwfyn!
Take the grey from the dawn, take the red from the sunset,
Take the purple-black bloom from the vine-press of thunder,
And pour them all out in the swine-troughs of Annwn!
I had darkened those beaches with the shadow of my
       main sail—
Sea-drift and sea-wreck and sea-weeds and sea-shells!—
Ere another ship's keel on Caer Sidi had grounded
Or another ship anchored by Carbonek's dank wharf.
I was the blood-bubble in the throat of the Kraken
When the spout of its bursting engulfed Lost Atlantis:
I was the last thought in the mind of Tithonus
Ere he turned to cold stone on the breast of the morning;
I was the first word on the lips of Tiresias
When he lapped at the blood between Ocean and Hades:
Have I herded the worms of the earth in their millions
Have I followed the eels in their ocean-migrations
Have I crouched with the curving of the wave-crests that
       covered
The gulf-swallowed coast-cliffs of continents sunken
Not to share with the cliffs and the waves and the whirlpools
Not to share with the eels in their twists and their turnings
Not to share with the swine at the troughs of Annwfyn
Not to share with the spout from the throat of the Kraken
Not to share with the worms of the earth in their gropings
Not to share with the roots of the worlds in their fumblings
Not to share with the life-winds that whirl round Annwfyn
Not to share with the last thought that came to Tithonus
Not to share with the first word that came to Tiresias
The thing none can utter, the thing inexpressible,

155

That bird-wing and man-skin and fish-scale conniving
Convey to all lost souls curled up in their prisons,
Like Mabon ap Modron in his prison at Caerloyw,
The thing that was known from before the beginning,
And will be still known when the end is forgotten,
Known to star-fish and sun-fish and sea-worms and
        earth-worms
Known to sky-gods and earth-men and all living creatures!
He knew it, Pelagius, and I, Taliessin,
Who praise till I perish the Lord of Yr Echwydd
Who serve, while strength's in me, the feast-giving Cynan,
I know it from pond-slime and frog-spawn and grub-spit,
From bracken's green coral, white lichen, yellow mosses,
Newts sinking with their arms out to reedy pools' bottoms,
Swords rusting in their oak-stumps, wrapped in the long rains,
Eggs rotting in their lost nests, enjoying the wild mists,
I know it from all these, and to men I proclaim it:
The ending forever of the Guilt-sense and God-sense,
The ending forever of the Sin-sense and Shame-sense,
The ending forever of the Love-sense and Loss-sense,
The beginning forever of the Peace paradisic,
The 'I feel' without question, the 'I am' without purpose,
The 'It is' that leads nowhere, the life with no climax,
The 'Enough' that leads forward to no consummation,
The answer to all things, that yet answers nothing,
The centre of all things, yet all on the surface,
The secret of Nature, yet Nature goes blabbing it
With all of her voices from earth, fire, air, water!
Whence comes it? Whither goes it? It is nameless; it is
        shameless;
It is Time free at last from its Ghostly Accuser,
Time haunted no more by a Phantom Eternal;
It is Godless; but its gods are as sea-sands in number;
It's the Square with four sides that encloses all circles;
Four horizons hath this Tetrad that swallows all Triads;
It includes every creature that Nature can summon.
It excludes from Annwfyn nor man, beast, nor woman!

156

The Sorrow of Search

Lord Dunsany

Edward John Morton Drax Plunkett, Lord Dunsany (1878–1957), was born into the Anglo-Irish aristocracy and was educated at Eton. After serving in the Boer War (1899–1902) he became active in the work of the newly founded Abbey Theatre in Dublin, along with both W B Yeats and George Russell. He produced a number of brilliant verse dramas, including The Glittering Gates *(1909) and* The Laughter of the Gods *(1916) but is best known and remembered for his volumes of fantastic and visionary stories of which the one included here is among his finest. His best known books are* The Gods of Pagana *(1905),* Tales of the Three Hemispheres *(1919) and* The King of Elfland's Daughter *(1924). He was a literary magician who conjured scenes and characters from a mythic world which was, none the less, rooted firmly in the real world. Dunsany maintained that the seeds from which his stories and poems sprang, were sown in childhood memories, when one is closer to the world of the imaginal. In each of his books, this child-like view of the natural world shines through, making him among the finest and most enduring stylists and visionaries of this or any age.*

From *Time and the Gods*. J.W. Luce & Co, Boston, 1905.

Beatrice Elvery

The Sorrow of Search

It is told also of King Khanazar how he bowed very low unto the gods of Old. None bowed so low unto the gods of Old as did King Khanazar.

One day the King returning from the worship of the gods of Old and from bowing before them in the temple of the gods commanded their prophets to appear before him, saying:

"I would know somewhat concerning the gods."

Then came the prophets before King Khanazar, burdened with many books, to whom the King said:

"It is not in books."

Thereat the prophets departed, bearing away with them a thousand methods well devised in books whereby men may gain wisdom of the gods. One alone remained, a master prophet, who had forgotten books, to whom the King said:

"The gods of Old are mighty."

And answered the master prophet:

"Very mighty are the gods of Old."

Then said the King:

"There are no gods but the gods of Old."

And answered the prophet:

"There are none other."

And they two being alone within the palace the King said:

"Tell me aught concerning gods or men if aught of truth be known."

Then said the master prophet:

"Far and white and straight lieth the road to Knowing, and down it in the heat and dust go all wise people of the earth, but in the fields before they come to it the very wise lie down or pluck the flowers. By the side of the road to Knowing—O King, it is hard and hot—stand many temples, and in the doorway of every temple stand many priests, and they cry to the travellers that weary of the road, crying to them:

" 'This is the End.'

"And in the temples are the sounds of music, and from each roof arises the savour of pleasant burning; and all that look at a cool temple, whichever temple they look at, or hear the hidden music, turn in to see whether it be indeed the End. And such as find that their temple is not indeed the End set forth again upon the dusty road, stopping at each temple as they pass for fear they miss the End, or striving onwards on the road, and see nothing in the dust, till they can walk no longer and are taken worn and weary of their journey into some other temple by a kindly priest who shall tell them that this also is the End. Neither on that road may a man gain any guiding from his fellows, for only one thing that they say is surely true, when they say:

" 'Friend, we can see nothing for the dust.'

"And of the dust that hides the way much has been there since ever that road began, and some is stirred up by the feet of all that travel upon it, and more arises from the temple doors.

"And, O King, it were better for thee, travelling upon that road, to rest when thou hearest one calling: 'This is the End,' with the sounds of music behind him. And if in the dust and darkness thou pass by Lo and Mush and the pleasant Temple of Kynash, or Sheenath with his opal smile, or Sho with his eyes of agate, yet Shilo and Mynarthitep, Gazo and Amurund and Slig are still before thee and the priests of their temples will not forget to call thee.

"And, O King, it is told that only one discerned the End and passed by three thousand temples, and the priests of the last were like the priests of the first, and all said that their temple was at the end of the road, and the dark of the dust lay over them all, and all were very pleasant and only the road was weary. And in some were many gods, and in a few only one, and in some the shrine was empty, and all had many priests, and in all the travellers were happy as they rested. And into some his fellow travellers tried to force him, and when he said:

" 'I will travel further,' many said:

" 'This man lies, for the road ends here.'

"And he that travelled to the End hath told that when the

thunder was heard upon the road there arose the sound of the voices of all the priests as far as he could hear, crying:

" 'Hearken to Shilo'—'Hear Mush'—'Lo! Kynash'—'The voice of Sho'—'Mynarthitep is angry'—'Hear the word of Slig!'

"And far away along the road one cried to the traveller that Sheenath stirred in his sleep.

"O King, this is very doleful. It is told that that traveller came at last to the utter End and there was a mighty gulf, and in the darkness at the bottom of the gulf one small god crept, no bigger than a hare, whose voice came crying in the cold:

" 'I know not.'

"And beyond the gulf was nought, only the small god crying.

"And he that travelled to the End fled backwards for a great distance till he came to temples again, and entering one where a priest cried:

" 'This is the End,' lay down and rested on a couch. There Yush sat silent, carved with an emerald tongue and two great eyes of sapphire, and there many rested and were happy. And an old priest, coming from comforting a child, came over to that traveller who had seen the End and said to him:

" 'This is Yush and this is the End of wisdom.'

"And the traveller answered:

" 'Yush is very peaceful and this indeed the End.'

"O King, wouldst thou hear more?"

And the King said: ·

"I would hear all."

And the master prophet answered:

"There was also another prophet and his name was Shaun, who had such reverence for the gods of Old that he became able to discern their forms by starlight as they strode, unseen by others, among men. Each night did Shaun discern the forms of the gods and every day he taught concerning them, till men in Averon knew how the gods appeared all grey against the mountains, and how Rhoog was higher than Mount Scagadon, and how Skun was smaller, and how Asgool leaned forward as he strode, and how Trodath peered about him with small eyes. But one night as Shaun watched the gods of Old by starlight, he faintly discerned some other gods that sat far up the slopes of the mountains in the stillness behind the gods of Old. And the next day he hurled his robe away that he wore as Averon's prophet and said to his people:

" 'There be gods greater than the gods of Old, three gods seen faintly on the hills by starlight looking on Averon.'

"And Shaun set out and travelled many days and many people followed him. And every night he saw more clearly the shapes of the three new gods who sat silent when the gods of Old were striding among men. On the higher slopes of the mountain Shaun stopped with all his people, and there they built a city and worshipped the gods, whom only Shaun could see, seated above them on the mountain. And Shaun taught how the gods were like grey streaks of light seen before dawn, and how the god on the right pointed upward toward the sky, and how the god on the left pointed downward toward the ground, but the god in the middle slept.

"And in the city Shaun's followers built three temples. The one on the right was a temple for the young, and the one on the left a temple for the old, and the third was a temple with doors closed and barred—therein none ever entered. One night as Shaun watched before the three gods sitting like pale light against the mountain, he saw on the mountain's summit two gods that spake together and pointed, mocking the gods of the hill, only he heard no sound. The next day Shaun set out and a few followed him to climb to the mountain's summit in the cold, to find the gods who were so great that they mocked at the silent three. And near the two gods they halted and built for themselves huts. Also they built a temple wherein the Two were carved by the hand of Shaun with their heads turned towards each other, with mockery on Their faces and Their fingers pointing, and beneath Them were carved the three gods of the hill as actors making sport. None remembered now Asgool, Trodath, Skun, and Rhoog, the gods of Old.

"For many years Shaun and his few followers lived in their huts upon the mountain's summit worshipping gods that mocked, and every night Shaun saw the two gods by starlight as they laughed to one another in the silence. And Shaun grew old.

"One night as his eyes were turned towards the Two, he saw across the mountains in the distance a great god seated in the plain and looming enormous to the sky, who looked with angry eyes towards the Two as they sat and mocked. Then said Shaun to his people, the few that had followed him thither:

" 'Alas that we may not rest, but beyond us in the plain sitteth the one true god and he is wrath with mocking. Let us therefore leave these two that sit and mock and let us find the truth in the worship of that greater god, who even though he kill shall yet not mock us.'

"But the people answered:

" 'Thou hast taken us from many gods and taught us now to worship gods that mock, and if there is laughter on their faces as we die, lo! thou alone canst see it, and we would rest.'

"But three men who had grown old with following followed still.

"And down the steep mountain on the further side Shaun led them, saying: 'Now we shall surely know.'

"And the three old men answered:

" 'We shall know indeed, O last of all the prophets.'

"That night the two gods mocking at their worshippers mocked not at Shaun nor his three followers, who coming to the plain still travelled on till they came at last to a place where the eyes of Shaun at night could closely see the vast form of their god. And beyond them as far as the sky there lay a marsh. There they rested, building such shelters as they could, and said to one another:

" 'This is the End, for Shaun discerneth that there are no more gods, and before us lieth the marsh and old age hath come upon us.'

"And since they could not labour to build a temple, Shaun carved upon a rock all that he saw by starlight of the great god of the plain; so that if ever others forsook the gods of Old because they saw beyond them the Greater Three, and should thence come to knowledge of the Twain that mocked, and should yet persevere in wisdom till they saw by starlight him whom Shaun named the Ultimate god, they should still find there upon the rock what one had written concerning the end of search. For three years Shaun carved upon the rock, and rising one night from carving, saying:

" 'Now is my labour done,' saw in the distance four greater gods beyond the Ultimate god. Proudly in the distance beyond the marsh these gods were tramping together, taking no heed of the god upon the plain. Then said Shaun to his three followers:

" 'Alas that we know not yet, for there be gods beyond the marsh.'

"None would follow Shaun, for they said that old age must end all quests, and that they would rather wait there in the plain for Death than that he should pursue them across the marsh.

"Then Shaun said farewell to his followers, saying:

" 'You have followed me well since ever we forsook the gods of Old to worship greater gods. Farewell. It may be that your prayers at evening shall avail when you pray to the god of the plain, but I must go onward, for there be gods beyond.'

"So Shaun went down into the marsh, and for three days struggled through it, and on the third night saw the four gods not very far away, yet could not discern Their faces. All the next day Shaun toiled on to see Their faces by starlight, but ere the night came up or one star shone, at set of sun, Shaun fell down before the feet of his four gods. The stars came out, and the faces of the four shone bright and clear, but Shaun saw them not, for the labour of toiling and seeing was over for Shaun; and lo! They were Asgool, Trodath, Skun and Rhoog—The gods of Old."

Then said the King:

"It is well that the sorrow of search cometh only to the wise, for the wise are very few."

Also the King said:

"Tell me this thing, O prophet. Who are the true gods?"

The master prophet answered:

"Let the King command."

A Lay of Ossian and Patrick

Stephen Gwynn

Stephen Lucius Gwynn (1864–1950) had a remarkable career as a journalist, man of letters, soldier and statesman. He wrote novels, poems, plays, biographies and essays, while pursuing an active political career as the Nationalist Member of Parliament for Galway City. He served with honour in the 1914–18 war. His writing is rich in details drawn from Irish myth and tradition. In the poem printed here he deals with the story which tells of a meeting between St Patrick and the great hero-poet Ossian, who is supposed to have returned from the Otherworld in order to tell the stories of the Fianna to the Saint. Surprisingly enough, Patrick ordered a full account to be made of the stories, despite their pagan origins, and seems to have been well disposed to the ancient hero.

From *Collected poems of Stephen Gwynn*. Blackwood, London & Edinburgh 1923.

A Lay of Ossian and Patrick

I tell you an ancient story
    Learnt of an Irish strand,
Of lonely Ossian returning
    Belated from fairyland

To a land grown meek and holy,
    To a land of mass and bell,
Under the hope of heaven,
    Under the dread of hell.

It tells how the bard and warrior,
    Last of a giant race,
Wrestled a year with Patrick,
    Answering face to face,

Mating the praise of meekness
    With vaunt of the warrior school,
And the glory of God the Father
    With the glory of Finn Mac Cool

Until at the last the hero,
    Through fasting and through prayer,
Came to the faith of Christians,
    And turned from the things that were.

When the holy bread was broken,
    And the water wet on his brow,
And the last of the fierce Fianna
    Had spoken the Christian vow.

In a sudden glory Patrick,
    Seeing the fierce grown mild,

Laughed with joy on his convert,
   Like father on first-born child.

"Well was for you, O Ossian,
   You came to the light," he said;
"And now I will show you the torment
   From which to our God you fled."

Then with a pass of his crozier
   He put a spell on the air
And there fell a mist on the eyeballs
   Of Ossian standing there.

Shapes loomed up through the darkness,
   And "Now," says the saint, "look well:
See your friends the Fianna,
   And all their trouble in hell."

Ossian stared through the darkness,
   Saw, as the mist grew clear,
Legions of swarth-hued warriors
   Raging with sword and spear:

Footmen, huge and misshapen,
   Stiffened with snarling ire;
Chariots with hell-black stallions
   Champing a spume of fire,

And all of the grim-faced battle
   With clash and yell and neigh
Dashed on a knot of warriors
   Set in a rank at bay.

Ossian looked, and he knew them,
   Knew each man of them well,
Knew his friends, the Fianna,
   There in the pit of hell.

167

There was his very father,
  Leader of all their bands,
Finn, the terrible wrestler,
  Gripping with giant hands:

Oscar with edged blade smiting,
  Caoilté with charging lance,
And Diarmuid poising his javelin,
  Nimble as in the dance:

Conan, the crop-eared stabber,
  Aiming a slant-way stroke,
And the fiery Lugach leaping
  Where the brunt of battle broke.

But in front of all by a furlong,
  There in the hell-light pale,
Was the champion, Gull Mac Morna,
  Winding a monstrous flail.

And still the flail as he swung it
  Sang through the maddened air,
Singing the deeds of heroes,
  A song of the days that were.

It swung with the shrilling of pipers,
  It smote with a thud of drums,
It leapt and it whirled in battle,
  Crying, "Gull Mac Morna comes."

It leapt and it smote, and the devils
  Shrieked under every blow;
With the very wind of its whistling
  Warriors were stricken low.

It swept a path through the army
  Wide as a winter flood,

And down that lane the Fianna
  Charged in a wash of blood.

Patrick gazed upon Ossian:
  But Ossian watched to descry
The surf and the tide of battle
  Turn, as in days gone by.

And lo! at the sudden onslaught
  The fighters of Eire made,
And under the flail of Mac Morna,
  The host of the foemen swayed,

Broke; and Ossian, breathless,
  Heard the exultant yell
Of his comrades hurling the devils
  Back to the wall of hell.

And the sword-blades reaped like sickles,
  And the javelins hissed like hail,
And louder and ever louder
  Rose the song of the flail,

As whirling in air the striker
  Sang clear, or thudded dull,—
When, woe! the tug on a sudden
  Snapped in the grasp of Gull.

Hand-staff and striker parted;
  The song of the flail was dumb—
On the heart of Ossian, listening,
  Fell that silence numb.

And oh! for a time uncounted
  He watched with straining eyes
The tide of the devils' battle
  Quicken and turn and rise.

He watched the Fianna's onset
    Waver and hang in doubt,
He watched his leaderless comrades
    Swept in a struggling rout.

But Gull, with a shield before him,
    Crouched on the battle ground,
And there in the track of slaughter
    Tore at what he found,

Until in the crash and tumult,
    And dashed with a bloody rain,
He had knotted his flail together
    With sinews torn from the slain.

Then, as the gasping Fianna
    Felt their endeavour fail,
Chanting their ancient valour
    Rose the voice of the flail.

And again in the stagnant ebbing
    Of their blood began to flow
The flood of a surging courage,
    The hope of a crowning blow

And the heart of their comrade watching
    Stirred with joy to behold
Feats of his bygone manhood,
    Strokes that he knew of old.

Again he beheld the stubborn
    Setting of targe to targe,
Again he beheld the rally
    Swell to a shattering charge:

And surely now the Fianna
    Must slaughter and whelm the foe

In a fierce and final triumph,
   Lords of the realm below.

As they leapt in a loosened phalanx,
   Climbing on heaps of slain:
—And again Gull's wizard weapon
   Flew on a stroke in twain.

For a time and times uncounted
   Ossian endured the sight
Of the endless swaying tumult,
   The ebb and flow of the fight.

His face grew lean with sorrow,
   And hunger stared from his eyes,
And the labouring breath from his bosom
   Broke in heavy sighs.

Patrick watched, and he wondered,
   And at last in pity spoke:
"Vexed is your look, O Ossian,
   As your very heart were broke.

"Courage, O new-made Christian:
   Great is my joy in you:
I would like it ill on a day of grace
   My son should have aught to rue.

"Therefore for these your comrades
   I give you a wish today
That shall lift them out of their torment
   Into some better way.

"Speak! be bold in your asking,
   Christ is strong to redeem."
—Ossian turned to him sudden,
   Like one awaked from a dream.

171

His eye was fierce as an eagle's,
 And his voice had a trumpet's ring,
As when at the Fenian banquets
 He lifted his harp to sing.

"I ask no help of the Father,
 I ask no help of the Son,
Nor of the Holy Spirit,
 Ever Three in One.

"This for my only asking,
 And then let might prevail,—
Patrick, give Gull Mac Morna
 An iron tug to his flail."

Patrick is dead, and Ossian;
 Gull to his place is gone;
But the words and the deeds of heroes
 Linger in twilight on,

In a twilight of fireside tellings
 Lit by the poet's lay,
Lighting the gloom of hardship,
 The night of a needy day.

And still the Gael, as he listens
 In a land of mass and bell
Under the hope of heaven,
 Under the dread of hell,

Thinks long, like age-spent Ossian,
 For the things that are no more,
For the clash of meeting weapons,
 And the mad delight of war.

Sion ap Siencyn

Kenneth Morris

Kenneth Morris (1847–1937) was born in Wales, grew up and was educated in London, and in the 1890s found his way to Dublin and to the Theosophical circles frequented by AE and Ella Young. Subsequently he became a follower of Katherine Tingley (1847–1929) and when she moved to the USA to set up a Theosophical community at Point Loma in California, Morris went with her. His first book The Fates of the Princes of Dyfed *(1914) was dedicated to her. It was a deeply mystical reworking of tales from* The Mabinogion *and was published from the community under the name Cenydd Morus—the Welsh form of his name. It was to be followed in 1930 by* The Book of the Three Dragons *in which once again Morris turned to his Celtic roots for inspiration. He met Ella Young again in the late 1920s, when she travelled to Point Loma, and she was subsequently active in getting his second book into print with her own publisher, who had considerable success with it. Morris returned to Wales in 1930 where he continued to work in the cause of Theosophy until his death. His stories are still among the most lyrical and evocative of all the Celtic revivalists, with the possible exception of Fiona Macleod. The one printed here originally appeared in a collection of stories called* The Secret Mountain *published originally in 1926.*

From *The Secret Mountain and Other Tales.* Faber & Gwyer, London 1926.

R. Machell

Sion ap Siencyn

It was on a Thursday, and the day of the full moon; and the whitethorn was in bloom, and the birds were singing on the mountainside; and it was towards evening by that time, and the sunlight lying mellow-golden on the long green fields.

Sion ap Siencyn stood by the farmyard gate; and thinking he was—was there something in that sunlight now, and was there a tune in the air with the birds, or something, that he could make a l'l song of them whatever? Then the pigs set up a squealing and a pother, meaning to say dinner-time it was with them; and out from the old yellow-washed farm-house came Gwenno his wife with the pail in her hand to fill their trough.

"Sioni," said she, "for shame upon you loafing there, and me toiling all day, and slaving all night, to keep a loaf on the board and the dirt from the floor here!"

"Yes, sure," said he; "what is on you now?"

"What is on me?" said she; "and the pigs themselves crying out that but for me they shouldn't have bite nor sup nor support for their lawful ambitions!"

They were certainly crying out something; and Sion ap Siencyn was all for a bit of peace, with that l'l song in the air and all; and he wasn't going to argue, with his wife *and* the pigs against him.

"What is it, indeed now?" said he.

"You do know very well what it is. Bronwen Cow is after her meandering up the mountain, and in the Field of the Pool of Stars she will be; and she knowing well that I will be waiting to milk her. Such spiteful ways you do teach the creatures, woe is me!"

"Well, well; not much for me to go and fetch her, after all," said Sion; and with that, off with him.

In the farm kitchen old Catrin, Sion's mother, was in her chair by the hearth. "Where is Sion *bach*?" said she, when Gwen came in.

"Fetching Bronwen from the Field of the Pool of Stars he is," said Gwen.

"Uneasy is my heart for that news you are telling me; and this the Eve of May, and the faery night of all the nights in the year."

Sion went up through the long Field of the Stream; and the beauty of the world was delighting him; and the song in the air was coming nearer to him, but he was not catching it yet. And he went up through the green Field of the Hollow; and the way the light lay on the rushes, he had never seen the equal of it before. And he went through the gate in the hedge, and into the Field of the Pool of Stars; and there, in his deed, was Bronwen Cow out before him. He called her; but perverse she was, and walking on, and he must go after her; and the more he called, the more she went, and the more he must follow; and she put seven hedges between herself and the farm before he could even come near her;—and all the while the song was coming nearer to him; and it the loveliest song in the world or Wales, he was thinking.

And just as he came up with her, lo, there was the root and source and fountain of the song out before him and plain for his vision: it was a bird on the blossoming hawthorn tree; it no bigger than the druid wren, but its feathers aglimmer whitely like sunlight on the mountain snow; and with every flirt of its wings shaking out a ripple of song to steal and travel over the world till you could know the mountains were laughing in their deep hearts for pleasure of it; and in his deed to God he must stop a minute and listen to that.

Stop he did, and listen; and every sorrow he had ever known, he made nothing of it: converted it was, in his memory, into joy; with the richness and the pleasantness of that singing.

But there, wonder was on the world that day, certainly it was. As he listened, he was aware of a song on his south that was better than the other one; and turning, saw a bird among the rushes there, crested and crowned, and as blue as the heavens, and shining like a jewel, and making song to bring the stars leaning out of the sky to listen. Never could he turn to go back while that song might be there for his hearing. And wondering he saw what

176

the power of the song was: for the earth and the sky were changed about him, and the mountains that he saw were better than any he had seen before; and the population roaming on them and in the valley were beautiful—lovelier than human, flame-bodied, and with delicate plumes of flame over their heads. And lovely lights were rising out of the mountains; and it was a greater joy to him to be alive than any joy he had known formerly; and he had little thought for Bronwen Cow, or for Gwenno his wife, or for the farm. And then came a third bird, coloured like the rainbow; with a better song than either of the others had; and in the sweetness of her discoursing it seemed to him that he heard all the wisdom of the deep world. And it seemed to him that the ancient and flame-robed Kings of Wonder were about him; and that the vast mountains were their palaces; and he on a footing with them, as it were; and an inhabitant of the Ancient World, with wisdom and stature to him, and the dignity of the cloud-hidden peaks; and if there was anyone called Sion ap Siencyn, he was not remembering that one; instead, he was remembering the ages of the world and antiquity, and delighting in the beauty beyond time... .

Then the three of the birds flew away, and the stars were shining: an hour or more he must have been listening, though not five minutes it seemed. In the dimness he could see Bronwen Cow descending towards the farm before him; and happy he was as he turned to follow her, knowing that now the world of song was open to him, and that never again would he be at a loss for the words of beauty to sing. "It was as if I had listened to the Birds of Rhianon," said he. They were three faery birds that were in Wales at one time; you could be hearing them for a hundred years, and think it was an hour or less you had listened... .

There was firelight and candlelight in the farm kitchen, and the door was open; and when he had but looked in through the door, he stopped, there on the threshold; for what he saw and heard was not what he expected. A very old man was on the settle by the fire; and opposite him a young man that might be his grandson; and there were three children on the hearth between them; and moving about the kitchen a woman that had the voice and the look of Gwen with her, only there was something strange with her too.

"Indeed" she was saying "for shame that you don't go out after Bronwen Cow; and she in her meandering out upon the mountain!"

"Let you him be," said the old man. "Were you never hearing what befell the great-grandfather of my grandfather?"

"Ah, tell us the story!" cried the children all at once.

"Three hundred years ago it was," said the old man, "and the Eve of May it was; and a cow from this farm strayed out upon the mountain; and the great-grandfather of my grandfather —"

"What was his name?" cried the children.

"Sion ap Siencyn was his name," said the old man.

"There's somebody at the door," said the woman. "Come you in, and welcome to you!" said she.

No one came, and no one was there when they looked. "It was the wind sighing," said the young man. Then the grandfather went forward and told them the story of Sion ap Siencyn. "They say it was the Birds of Rhianon sang to him," said he.

The Revenge of Neumenoiou

Edith Wingate Rinder

Edith Wingate Rinder has proved to be the most elusive of all the writers whose works are represented in this collection. Despite a prolonged search through reference works, even her dates have eluded me! She contributed an introduction to Elizabeth Barret Browning's Aurora Leigh *in 1899, and her published works apart from this were published between 1887 and 1923. There were* Poems and Lyrics of Nature, *an anthology of nature writings to which she contributed an essay on the treatment of nature in poetry. This was followed by* The Shadow of Arvor *from which the following story is taken, and* The Massacre of the Innocents, *a collection of stories by Belgian writers translated by Edith Rinder. This appears to have been the sum and limit of her literary output. She was married to the art-historian Frank Rinder, whose interests seem to have been primarily in the mythology of Japan. Her Celtic stories, drawing on the less familiar Breton traditions are set forth in a rich and evocative prose and are more than simple retellings. "The Revenge of Neumenoiou," included here, is a dark little tale, which has its origins in the writings of the Breton story-teller, Hersart de la Villemarque.*

From *The Shadow of Arvor*. Patrick Geddes & Co, Edinburgh, n.d.

D. Mackay

The Revenge of Neumenoiou

Lo, as in a vision, I see the ancient land of Arvor, as it was in the days after the last white-robed Druids had chanted forgotten hymns under the oaks, and a new faith had come. I see it as a land shrouded in mist. It is autumn, and the golden ears are reaped: and as in a dream I see another reaping, that of the golden head of a Breton prince, reaped by the sickle of a Frankish sword.

Near the town of Huelgoat, on a barren perpendicular rock, stands the old dismantled tower of Kastel-Guibel. On the opposite side of the valley are the remains of an entrenched camp, the camp of Arthur.

Fortress and camp belonged to the mighty count whose lands stretched from the wooded slopes of Huelgoat to the steep arid flanks of the Arhez mountains. And this is what I saw, and that which follows is what I learned out of my seeing, and out of the lore of my fathers.

Day by day, for many days, the old grey-haired count of Arhez had sought to pierce the mist which wrapped valley and hill towards the land of the Franks. Denser and denser it had grown; not once had it lifted for a moment to reveal the face of his son.

On one of the noons of his longing, he beheld a wayfarer and hailed him eagerly.

"Tell me, good pedlar," he cried, "you who roam over our country, have you news of my son, Karo?"

"By what token might I recognize your son, my noble count; for I know not even whither he is gone?"

"My son is a man of honour, and he is gone to Roazon with the chariots which bear to the king of the Franks the full weight of the tribute of Armorica."

"At the gates of Roazon, whence I come, I met a procession of chariots, each drawn by three horses abreast: before these, on a white charger, rode a youth; fair as the yellowing corn was his hair. He and his company entered the town, making towards the palace of the Governor.

" 'My Lord Governor,' cried the man who would be your son, 'my master, the Duke Neumenoiou charges me to place in your hands the annual tribute which the Bretons pay to their over-lords, the Franks.'

"The bags containing the money were brought forward and weighed. The first and the second were of just weight, but, when the third was placed on the scales, it lacked three pounds to the hundred. Karo, wondering at the strange thing which he saw, leaned forward over the scales. A sullen silence reigned. The Breton stood humiliated; the Frank smiled contemptuously.

" 'Weight is wanting,' said the Governor, 'let thy head, vassal, supply that weight.'

"As the words were spoken, a sword flashed, and the head fell bleeding on the ground. The governor seized it by the long fair hair and threw it into the scales."

But at that, the count of Arhez could hear no more. With a cry of agony, he fell fainting to the earth. For long he lay on the rock where he had fallen, groaning and hiding his face in the white hair which fell about his shoulders.

"Karo! my son, my son!" he muttered. "The hope of our race, the comfort of my age! Ah, sorrow upon me, thou art gone, thou art slain, who wast so fair! Thou hast fallen by the hands of a cowardly assassin, Karo, my son; but ah, Karo, Karo, I will avenge thee. Tooth for tooth, eye for eye, shall I avenge thee. The heads of ten thousand Franks shall fall for thy head; the blood of ten thousand Franks shall be shed to wipe out thy blood-stains!"

As the old man rose, his eyes flamed like the eyes of a she-wolf robbed of her cubs.

The count was one of the well-loved princes of the country. He had but to speak a word, and that word would be as a flame amid dry stubble. So was it now, indeed; for when his call to war went forth a host of brave mountaineers rallied round his standard.

It was in his mind to make a sudden descent upon Roazon, there to seek vengeance for the death of his son. But even were victory his, he knew that, unsupported, it could be but short-lived. Therefore it was that he set out for Gwened to seek aid from Neumenoiou.

Though a Breton born, with a heart that throbbed for his own people, Neumenoiou governed, in the name of the king of the Franks, all that part of Brittany known as Browerech, the country of Gwened. He dreamed of independence; but, cunning in statecraft as well as brave in war, he sought to let his country recover from the long series of defeats sustained at the hands of its enemies. Now the moment to throw off the hated yoke appeared to be come. The murder of Karo had been as a trumpet-call throughout the land.

It was in the month of October that the count of Arhez, followed by his kindred and his mountaineers, set out from the fortress of Kastel-Guibel. As the sun climbed the heights of noon, they came to Ker-Ahez, and thence took the Roman road which led to Gwened. On their way, tidings reached them that Neumenoiou was at Elven, taking part in the chase; so thitherward, and with all speed, they fared.

The ancient fortress of Argoet, where Neumenoiou lived, stood on a height, scarce two miles from Elven, at the farther end of a little swampy valley, surrounded by great forests. Deep, wide moats encircled the outer walls, guarded here and there by circular towers, whence the eye might travel over a vast reach of wood and heather-clad plains, amid which rose ever and again the grey head of menhir or dolmen.

At nightfall, the count of Arhez and his suite reached Argoet. As the drawbridge was about to be lowered, a hunter emerged from the forest. A pack of hounds gambolled around him. In his hand he held a bow, and across his shoulder was slung a mighty boar. The head of the animal hung over the stalwart breast of the hunter, and the red blood dripped down his white hand.

"Greeting to you, worthy mountaineers: greeting first to you, revered chief of Huelgoat. What news bring you, and what would you of me?"

"We would learn of you, my lord, if there be a God in heaven, if there is justice in Brittany, if there is a chief in our land?"

183

"For sure, there is a God in heaven; and a chief in Brittany, if I can avail aught," made answer Neumenoiou.

"He who wills is powerful; he who is powerful will defend and avenge his people. He will drive out the Frank, he will avenge living and dead, even Karo, my son, he whose head, yellow as the honey of the bee, was severed by the accursed Frank and thrown in the balance to make up the weight."

As the old count finished, he was overcome by grief, and fell, sobbing, upon his knees. The tears flowed down his long, white beard, and shone like the dew on a lily at sunrise.

Thereupon Neumenoiou threw aside the boar. Raising to Heaven his blood-stained hand, and holding out his bow, he vowed a terrible, a bloody vow:

"By the head of this boar, and by the arrow which pierced it, I swear that ere I wash the blood from my right hand, I will cleanse the country of this evil."

"We will conquer with thee, or die with thee, so help us God," shouted the mountaineers.

"It is well said, my friends. Pass the night here, and to-morrow we will hold counsel to the end that we may deliver our land."

A year had passed since the death of Karo, a year wherein Neumenoiou did three things which never prince had done before. He went to the shore to gather white stones, stones to offer as tribute to the king of the Franks: he shod his own horse the reverse way with bright silver: he went in person to carry the tribute to Roazon.

With a large escort, among whom were the old count of Arhez and all the bravest warriors of Armorica, Neumenoiou set out. A chariot drawn by three horses abreast followed, bearing the tribute: not this time the gold coin of the land, but white stones from the shores of Morbihan.

It was at the wane of the day, when Neumenoiou, seated on his white charger, made his entry into Roazon. Trumpets blew in his honour, and, as he reached the palace, the Governor came. forth to meet him. Neumenoiou alighted and threw his horse's rein over his arm.

"Be welcome to my castle," said the Frankish lord. "My men

184

will care for your horse. I would have you sup with me. Come, wash first; there is the horn,* water is ready."

"I will wash, my lord, but first I would deal with matters of State. I bring you the tribute of Armorica. When once that has been weighed, nothing shall mar my feasting."

The Governor yielded, and orders were given to proceed to the court. The first two sacks were of just weight; but when the third was placed on the scales, it lacked three pounds to the hundred.

"Even so it was last year," said the Frank to Neumenoiou, with a malignant smile. "Let us seek the reason."

At that he bent forward, seized the bands which fastened the sack, and sought to untie them.

"Wait, my lord," cried Neumenoiou, " I will cut them."

The words were scarce uttered before a sword flashed from its sheath and fell on the bending form of the Frank. With one blow the head was severed from the body, and a scale-chain cut through. The head fell into the weighing dish, and now there was weight and to spare!

When the Franks saw their ruler fall at the hands of a Breton, they uttered a wild cry of vengeance, and threw themselves on their enemies. An indescribable tumult reigned in the court-yard. "Battle! Battle! Argad!" cried the Bretons, and the curses of the combatants mingled with the clank of arms, the clashing of swords, and the resounding shocks from smitten armour.

Crowded in that small space, the foes fought hand to hand with deadly fury, and in darkness, save for the flicker of one or two torches. At last the mighty voice of Neumenoiou called to his men to rally around him. Shoulder to shoulder, and behind a hedge of swords and spears, they left the fighting place, thence, under cover of the night, small as was their number, they reached safely one of the gates of the town. There the Franks made a last unsuccessful effort to cut off their retreat: but the Bretons, once outside the gates, galloped at full speed in the direction of Gwened.

"Stop! stop!" cried the following Franks. "Torches here, torches! the night is dark and the road slippery."

* It was the custom to blow a horn to invite guests to wash before a meal.

But in vain from that day might the Frank wear out his blue-embroidered slipper in hope to overtake the Breton. As for his golden scales, never again did they weigh, false or true, either the golden tribute of Armorica or the white stones of Neumenoiou.

Mesgedra

Samuel Ferguson

*Retelling the primal myths was a major part of the revival of interest
in the ancient traditions of the Celts. Sir Samuel Ferguson
(1810–1886) was a noted archaeologist as well as a poet in his own
right. He combined these two abilities in several popular books,
including the epic poem* Congal *(1872) and* Lays of the Western
Gael *(1865). The following poem, which originally appeared in* Lays
of the Red Branch *(1897) draws upon the stories of the Ulster
Cycle, which relates the adventures of the greatest of the ancient Irish
heroes, Cuchulainn. Here Ferguson concentrates on Mesgedra, a
semi-divine King of Leinster, and in particular on the hero Conal
Carnach. Both embody the qualities of greater hero-figures: courage,
indomitable will, and a visionary awareness of the Celtic spirit.
Though seeming old-fashioned in style and metre to the ears of today's
reader, it yet contrives to capture something of the old and powerful
rhythms of bardic utterance from which it draws its inspiration.*

From *Lays of the Red Branch*. T Fisher Unwin, London, and Sealy Bryers & Walker,
Dublin 1897.

187

Mesgedra

When glades were green where Dublin stands today,
  And limpid Liffey, fresh from wood and wold,
Bridgeless and fordless, in the lonely Bay
  Sank to her rest on sands of stainless gold;

Came Bard Atharna with his spoils of song
  From rich, reluctant lords of Leinster wrung;
Flocks and fat herds, a far-extending throng,
  Bondsmen and handmaids beautiful and young:

And,—for the dusky deeps might ill be pass'd,
  And he impatient to secure his store,—
A hurdle-causeway o'er the river cast,
  And bore his booty to the further shore:

Which ill-enduring, Leinster's king, the brave
  Mesgedra, following in an angry quest,
On Tolka bank of damsel and of slave
  Despoiled the spoiler now no more a guest;

Who, being bard and ministering priest
  Of those vain demons then esteemed divine,
Invoked a curse on Leinster, man and beast,
  With rites of sacrifice and rhymes malign;

And sang so loud his clamorous call to war
  That all the chiefs of bard-protecting fame
Throughout Ulidia, arming near and far,
  Came, and, to aid him, Conall Carnach came;

And, where the city now sends up her vows
  From holy Patrick's renovated fane,

(Small surmise then that one of Conall's house
    Should there, thereafter, such a work ordain),

Joined Leinster battle: till the southern lords,
    Their bravest slain or into bondage led,
At sunset broke before the Red Branch swords,
    And, last, Mesgedra climbed his car and fled.

Alone, in darkness, of one hand forlorn,
    Naas-ward all night he held his journey back
Through wood and fen, till ill-befriending morn
    Showed him fell Conall following on his track.

So chanced it, as the doleful daylight broke,
    That, wandering devious with disordered rein,
His steeds had reached beside the Sacred Oak
    On Liffey's bank, above the fords of Clane.

Glad to the Tree-God made he grateful vows
    Who deigned that green asylum to bestow;
Kissed the brown earth beneath the moss-green boughs,
    And waited, calm, the coming of his foe.

He, as a hawk, that, in a housewife's coop
    Spying his quarry, stoops upon the wing,
Came on apace, and, when in middle swoop,
    Declining sidelong from the sacred ring,

Wheeled, swerving past the consecrated bounds:—
    Then thus, between him and the asylum'd man,
While nearer brush'd he still in narrowing rounds,
    The grave, unfriendly parle of death began.

"Come forth, Mesgedra, from the sheltering tree,
    And render fight: 'tis northern Conall calls."
"Not from an equal combat do I flee,
    O Conall, to these green, protecting halls;

190

"But, mutilated, weak from many wounds,
   Here take I sanctuary, where none will dare
With impious wheel o'erdrive my measured bounds,
   Or cast a weapon through the spell-wall'd air."

"No impious man am I; I fear the Gods;
   My wheels thy sacred precinct do but graze;
Nor, in the strife I challenge, ask I odds,
   But lot alike to each of death or praise."

"See, then, one arm hangs idly by my side:
   Let, now, one answering arm put also by
From share of battle, to thy belt be tied;
   So shall thy challenge soon have meet reply."

Then Conall loosed his war-belt's leathern band;
   Buckle and belt above his arm he closed;
And, single-handed, to the single hand
   Of maimed Mesgedra, stood in fight opposed.

They fought, with clashing intermixture keen
   Of rapid sword-strokes, till Mesgedra's blade,
Belt and brass corslet glancing sheer between,
   Wide open all the trammelling closure laid.

"Respect my plight: two-handed chief, forbear!"
   "Behold, I spare; I yield to thy appeal;
And bind this hand again; but, well beware
   Again it owe not freedom to thy steel!"

Again they fought, with close-commingling hail
   Of swifter sword-strokes, till the fated brand
Of doom'd Mesgedra, glancing from the mail,
   Again cut loose the dread, man-slaughtering hand.

No prayer might now hot Conall's fire assuage;
   No prayer was uttered; from his scattered toils

Bounding in headlong homicidal rage,
   He flew, he threw, he slew, and took the spoils:

Then up, all glorying, all imbrued in gore,
   Sprang to the chariot-seat, and north amain
Chariots and steeds and ghastly trophy bore
   Through murmuring Liffey, o'er the fords of Clane.

There, softly glancing down the hawthorn glades,
   Like phantom of the dawn and dewy air,
There met him, with a troop of dames and maids,
   A lovely woman delicate and fair.

They, at their vision of the man of blood,
   Rightward and left fled fluttering in alarm;
She in his pathway innocently stood
   As one who thinks not, and who fears not, harm.

"Who thou, and whence, and who the woman-train?"
   "Buäna, King Mesgedra's wife, am I,
From vows returning sped at Tclacta's fane:
   These dames and maids my serving company.

"And, one moon absent, long the time appears
   Till back in Naas's halls I lay at rest
My dreams ill-omening and my woman's fears
   That daily haunt me, on my husband's breast."

"Mount here. Thy husband speaks his will through me."
   "Through thee! Thy token of my husband's will?"
"The royal car, the royal coursers see:
   Perchance there rests a surer token still."

"My king Mesgedra is a bounteous lord,
   And many a war-car doth his chariot-pen,
And many a swift steed do his stalls afford
   For oft bestowal upon divers men."

192

"See then," he said, "my certain warrant here."
    Ah, what a deed! and showed the severed head.
She paled, she sickened with a mortal fear,
    Reached her white arms and sank before him, dead.

No passing swoon was hers: he saw her die;
    Saw death's pale signet set on cheek and brow:—
Up through his raging breast there rose a sigh;
    And, "Sure," he said, "a loving wife wast thou!

"And I—my deeds today shall live in song:
    Bards in the ears of feasting kings shall tell
How keen Mesgedra cut the trammelling thong,
    And unbound Conall used his freedom well.

"For, what I've done, by rule of warrior-law
    Well was I justified and bound to do;
And poets hence a precedent shall draw
    For future champion-compacts just and true.

"Done, not because I love the sight of blood,
    Or, uninstructed, rather would destroy
Than cherish; or prefer the whirling mood
    Of battle's turbulent and dreadful joy

"To peaceful life's mild temper; but because
    Things hideous, which the natural sense would shun,
Are, by the sanction of religious laws,
    Made clean, and pure, and righteous to be done.

"Ye, in whose name these awful laws are given,
    Forgive the thought this woman's looks have raised;—
Are broken hearts acceptable to Heaven?
    Is God by groans of anguish rightly praised?

"I, at your law's commandment, slew her lord,
    And, at your law's commandment, would have borne

Herself, a captive, to a land abhorr'd,
    To spend her widowhood in pain and scorn.

"But now, since friendlier death has shut her eyes
    From sight of bondage in an alien home,
No law forbids to yield her obsequies,
    Or o'er her raise the green sepulchral dome.

"Or—for her love was stronger than her life—
    To place beside her, in her narrow bed,
Its lawful tribute rendered to my knife—
    The much-loved, life-lamented, kingly head.

"No law forbids—all sanguinary dues
    Paid justly—that the heart-wrung human vow
Your sterner rites, dread Deities, refuse,
    Some gentler Demon's ritual may allow:

"That yet, ere Time of Mankind make an end,
    Some mightier Druid of our race may rise;
Some milder Messenger from Heaven descend;
    And Earth, with nearer knowledge of the Skies,

"See, past your sacrificers' grisly bands,
    Past all the shapes that servile souls appal,
With fearless vision, from a thousand lands,
    One great, good God behind and over all.

"Raise, then, her mound": the gathering hosts he spake
    That, thronging to o'ertake their venturous king,
Poured from the ford through fen and crackling brake,
    And hailed their hero in acclaiming ring:—

"Raise, too, her stone, conspicuous far and near;
    And let a legend on the long stone tell,
'Behold, there lies a tender woman here,
    Who, surely, loved a valiant husband well.'

194

"And let the earth-heap'd, grass-renewing tomb
    A time-long token eloquent remain
Of Pity and of Love for all who come
    By murmuring Liffey and the banks of Clane."

Delicious Liffey! from thy bosoming hills
    What man who sees thee issuing strong and pure,
But with some wistful, fresh emotion fills,
    Akin to Nature's own clear temperature?

And, haply, thinks:—on this green bank 'twere sweet
    To make one's mansion, sometime of the year;
For Health and Pleasure on these uplands meet,
    And all the isle's amenities are here.

Hither the merry music of the chase
    Floats up the festive borders of Kildare;
And slim-bright steeds extending in the race
    Are yonder seen, and camping legions there.

These coverts hold the wary-gallant fox;
    There the park'd stag waits his enlarging day;
And there, triumphant o'er opposing rocks,
    The shooting salmon quivers through thy spray.

The heath, the fern, the honey-fragrant furze
    Carpet thy cradling steeps: thy middle flow
Laves lawn and oak-wood: o'er thy downward course
    Laburnums nod and terraced roses blow.

To ride the race, to hunt, to fowl, to fish,
    To do and dare whate'er brave youth would do,
A fair fine country as the heart could wish,
    And fair the brown-clear river running through.

Such seemest thou to Dublin's youth today,
    Oh clear-dark Liffey, mid the pleasant land;

With life's delights abounding, brave and gay,
    The song, the dance, the softly yielded hand,

The exulting leap, the backward-flying fence,
    The whirling reel, the steady-levelled gun;—
With all attractions for the youthful sense,
    All charms to please the manly mind, but one,

For, thou, for them, alas! nor History hast
    Nor even Tradition; and the Man aspires
To link his present with his Country's past,
    And live anew in knowledge of his sires;

No rootless colonist of alien earth,
    Proud·but of patient lungs and pliant limb,
A stranger in the land that gave him birth,
    The land a stranger to itself and him.

Yet, though in History's page thou may'st not claim
    High places set apart for deeds sublime
That hinge the turnings of the gates of Fame
    And give to view the avenues of Time;

Not all inglorious in thy elder day
    Art thou, Moy-Liffey; and the loving mind
Might round thy borders many a gracious lay
    And many a tale not unheroic find.

Sir Almeric's deeds might fire a youthful heart
    To brave contention mid illustrious peers;
Tears into eyes as beautiful might start
    At tender record of Isolda's tears;

Virtue herself uplift a loftier head,
    Linked through the years with Ormond's constancy,
And airs from Runnymede around us spread,—
    Yea, all the fragrance of the Charter Tree

196

Wafted down time, refresh the conscious soul
    With Freedom's balms, when, firm in patriot zeal,
Dublin's De Londres, to Pandolfo's scroll
    Alone of all refused to set his seal;

Or when her other Henry's happier eyes
    Up-glancing from his field of victory won,
Beheld, one moment, 'neath adoring skies,
    The lifted isle lie nearer to the sun.—

For others, these. I, from the twilight waste
    Where pale Tradition sits by Memory's grave,
Gather this wreath, and, ere the nightfall, haste
    To fling my votive garland on thy wave.

Wave, waft it softly: and when lovers stray
    At summer eve by stream and dimpling pool,
Gather thy murmurs into voice and say,
    With liquid utterance passionate and full,

Scorn not, sweet maiden, scorn not, vigorous youth,
    The lay, though breathing of an Irish home,
That tells of woman-love and warrior-ruth
    And old expectancy of Christ to come.

The Castle: A Parable

George MacDonald

George MacDonald (1824–1905) is probably best remembered for his children's books: At the Back of the North Wind, *(1871),* The Princess and the Goblin *(1872), and* The Princess and Curdie *(1883), and for his two adult fantasies* Phantastes *(1858) and* Lilith *(1895). His deeply mystical brand of Christianity caught hold of the imagination of many hundreds of readers, and his striking appearance and grandiloquent delivery made him a popular success during his lecture tour of America in 1873–8. He was a fine historical novelist, contributing nearly a dozen volumes in this field—but apart from this he also wrote a number of dazzling short stories, of which that printed here, "The Castle," is among the best, though least known. MacDonald influenced C.S.Lewis, who named him among his three favourite writers, and many of the contemporary school of fantasists can trace their literary ancestry to him. His works are shot through with extraordinary glimpses into a detailed symbolic world of the imagination. For the symbolism of "The Castle," Macdonald seems to draw extensively on that of the Spanish mystic St Teresa of Avila, whose own work* The Interior Castle *is imbued with a visionary outlook which seems to derive ultimately from the Celtic traditions—perhaps through Celto-Iberian roots.*

From *Adela Cathcart.* Hurst and Blackett, 1864.

R. Machell

The Castle: A Parable

On the top of a high cliff, forming part of the base of a great mountain, stood a lofty castle. When or how it was built, no man knew; nor could any one pretend to understand its architecture. Every one who looked upon it felt that it was lordly and noble; and where one part seemed not to agree with another, the wise and modest dared not to call them incongruous, but presumed that the whole might be constructed on some higher principle of architecture than they yet understood. What helped them to this conclusion was, that no one had ever seen the whole of the edifice; that, even of the portion best known, some part or other was always wrapt in thick folds of mist from the mountain; and that, when the sun shone upon this mist, the parts of the building that appeared through the vaporous veil, were strangely glorified in their indistinctness, so that they seemed to belong to some aerial abode in the land of the sunset; and the beholders could hardly tell whether they had ever seen them before, or whether they were now for the first time partially revealed.

Nor, although it was inhabited, could certain information be procured as to its internal construction. Those who dwelt in it often discovered rooms they had never entered before; yea, once or twice, whole suites of apartments, of which only dim legends had been handed down from former times. Some of them expected to find, one day, secret places, filled with treasures of wondrous jewels, amongst which they hoped to light upon Solomon's ring, which had for ages disappeared from the earth, but which had controlled the spirits, and the possession of which made a man simply what a man should be, the king of the world. Now and then, a narrow, winding stair, hitherto untrodden, would bring them forth on a new turret, whence new prospects of the circumjacent country were spread out before them. How many more of these there might be, or how much loftier, no one could tell. Nor could the foundations of the castle in the rock on which it was built be determined with the smallest approach

201

to precision. Those of the family who had given themselves to exploring in that direction, found such a labyrinth of vaults and passages, and endless successions of down-going stairs, out of one underground space into a yet lower, that they came to the conclusion that at least the whole mountain was perforated and honeycombed in this fashion. They had a dim consciousness, too, of the presence, in those awful regions, of beings whom they could not comprehend. Once, they came upon the brink of a great black gulf, in which the eye could see nothing but darkness: they recoiled in horror; for the conviction flashed upon them that that gulf went down into the very central spaces of the earth, of which they had hitherto been wandering only in the upper crust; nay, that the seething blackness before them had relations mysterious, and beyond human comprehension, with the far-off voids of space, into which the stars dare not enter.

At the foot of the cliff whereon the castle stood, lay a deep lake, inaccessible save by a few avenues, being surrounded on all sides with precipices, which made the water look very black, although it was as pure as the night-sky. From a door in the castle, which was not to be otherwise entered, a broad flight of steps, cut in the rock, went down to the lake, and disappeared below its surface. Some thought the steps went to the very bottom of the water.

Now in this castle there dwelt a large family of brothers and sisters. They had never seen their father or mother. The younger had been educated by the elder, and these by an unseen care and ministration, about the sources of which they had, somehow or other, troubled themselves very little, for what people are accustomed to, they regard as coming from nobody; as if help and progress and joy and love were the natural crops of Chaos or old Night. But Tradition said that one day—it was utterly uncertain *when*—their father would come, and leave them no more; for he was still alive, though where he lived nobody knew. In the meantime all the rest had to obey their eldest brother, and listen to his counsels.

But almost all the family was very fond of liberty, as they called it; and liked to run up and down, hither and thither, roving about, with neither law nor order, just as they pleased. So they could not endure their brother's tyranny, as they called it. At one time they said that he was only one of themselves, and therefore they would not obey him; at another, that he was not like them, and could not understand them, and *therefore* they would not obey him. Yet, sometimes, when he came and looked them full in the face, they were terrified, and dared not disobey, for he was stately, and stern and strong. Not one of them loved him heartily, except the eldest sister, who was very beautiful and silent, and whose eyes shone as if light lay somewhere deep behind them. Even she, although she loved him, thought him very hard sometimes; for when he had once said a thing plainly, he could not be persuaded to think it over again. So even she forgot him sometimes, and went her own ways, and enjoyed herself without him. Most of them regarded him as a sort of watchman, whose business it was to keep them in order; and so they were indignant and disliked him. Yet they all had a secret feeling that they ought to be subject to him; and after any particular act of disregard, none of them could think, with any peace, of the old story about the return of their father to his house. But indeed they never thought much about it, or about their father at all; for how could those who cared so little for their brother, whom they saw every day, care for their father whom they had never seen?—One chief cause of complaint against him was, that he interfered with their favourite studies and pursuits; whereas he only sought to make them give up trifling with earnest things, and seek for truth, and not for amusement, from the many wonders around them. He did not want them to turn to other studies, or to eschew pleasures; but, in those studies, to seek the highest things most, and other things in proportion to their true worth and nobleness. This could not fail to be distasteful to those who did not care for what was higher than they. And so matters went on for a time. They thought they could do better without their brother; and their brother knew they could not do at all without him, and tried to fulfil the charge committed into his hands.

At length, one day, for the thought seemed to strike them

simultaneously, they conferred together about giving a great entertainment in their grandest rooms to any of their neighbours who chose to come, or indeed to any inhabitants of the earth or air who would visit them. They were too proud to reflect that some company might defile even the dwellers in what was undoubtedly the finest palace on the face of the earth. But what made the thing worse, was, that the old tradition said that these rooms were to be kept entirely for the use of the owner of the castle. And, indeed, whenever they entered them, such was the effect of their loftiness and grandeur upon their minds, that they always thought of the old story, and could not help believing it. Nor would the brother permit them to forget it now; but, appearing suddenly amongst them, when they had no expectation of being interrupted by him, he rebuked them, both for the indiscriminate nature of their invitation, and for the intention of introducing any one, not to speak of some who would doubtless make their appearance on the evening in question, into the rooms kept sacred for the use of the unknown father. But by this time their talk with each other had so excited their expectations of enjoyment, which had previously been strong enough, that anger sprung up within them at the thought of being deprived of their hopes, and they looked each other in the eyes; and the look said: "We are many, and he is one—let us get rid of him, for he is always finding fault, and thwarting us in the most innocent pleasures;—as if we would wish to do anything wrong!" So without a word spoken, they rushed upon him; and although he was stronger than any of them, and struggled hard at first; yet they overcame him at last. Indeed some of them thought he yielded to their violence long before they had the mastery of him; and this very submission terrified the more tender-hearted among them. However, they bound him; carried him down many stairs, and, having remembered an iron staple in the wall of a certain vault, with a thick rusty chain attached to it, they bore him thither, and made the chain fast around him. There they left him, shutting the great gnarring brazen door of the vault, as they departed for the upper regions of the castle.

Now all was in a tumult of preparation. Every one was talking of the coming festivity; but no one spoke of the deed they had done. A sudden paleness overspread the face, now of one, and now of another; but it passed away, and no one took any notice of it; they only plied the task of the moment the more energetically. Messengers were sent far and near, not to individuals or families, but publishing in all places of concourse a general invitation to any who chose to come on a certain day, and partake for certain succeeding days, of the hospitality of the dwellers in the castle. Many were the preparations immediately begun for complying with the invitation. But the noblest of their neighbours refused to appear; not from pride, but because of the unsuitableness and carelessness of such a mode. With some of them it was an old condition in the tenure of their estates, that they should go to no one's dwelling except visited in person, and expressly solicited. Others, knowing what sorts of persons would be there, and that, from a certain physical antipathy, they could scarcely breathe in their company, made up their minds at once not to go. Yet multitudes, many of them beautiful and innocent as well as gay, resolved to appear.

Meanwhile the great rooms of the castle were got in readiness—that is, they proceeded to deface them with decorations; for there was a solemnity and stateliness about them in their ordinary condition, which was at once felt to be unsuitable for the light-hearted company so soon to move about in them with the self-same carelessness with which men walk abroad within the great heavens and hills and clouds. One day, while the workmen were busy, the eldest sister, of whom I have already spoken, happened to enter, she knew not why. Suddenly the great idea of the mighty halls dawned upon her, and filled her soul. The so-called decorations vanished from her view, and she felt as if she stood in her father's presence. She was at once elevated and humbled. As suddenly the idea faded and fled, and she beheld but the gaudy festoons and draperies and paintings which disfigured the grandeur. She wept and sped away. Now it was too late to interfere, and things must take their course. She would have been but a Cassandra-prophetess to those who saw but the pleasure before them. She had not been present when her brother was imprisoned; and indeed for some days had been so wrapt in her own business, that she had taken but little heed of anything that was going on. But they all expected her to show herself when the company was gathered; and they had applied to her for advice at various times during their operations.

At length the expected hour arrived, and the company began to assemble. It was a warm summer evening. The dark lake reflected the rose-coloured clouds in the west, and through the flush rowed many gaily-painted boats, with various coloured flags, towards the massy rock on which the castle stood. The trees and flowers seemed already asleep, and breathing forth their sweet dream-breath. Laughter and low voices rose from the breast of the lake to the ears of the youths and maidens looking forth expectant from the lofty windows. They went down to the broad platform at the top of the stairs in front of the door to receive their visitors. By degrees the festivities of the evening commenced. The same smiles flew forth both at eyes and lips, darting like beams through the gathering crowd. Music, from unseen sources, now rolled in billows, now crept in ripples through the sea of air that filled the lofty rooms. And in the dancing halls, when hand took hand, and form and motion were moulded and swayed by the indwelling music, it governed not these alone, but, as the ruling spirit of the place, every new burst of music for a new dance swept before it a new and accordant odour, and dyed the flames that glowed in the lofty lamps with a new and accordant stain. The floors bent beneath the feet of the time-keeping dancers. But twice in the evening some of the inmates started, and the pallor occasionally common to the household over-spread their faces, for they felt underneath them a counter-motion to the dance, as if the floor rose slightly to answer their feet. And all the time their brother lay below in the dungeon, like John the Baptist in the castle of Herod, when the lords and captains sat around, and the daughter of Herodias danced before them. Outside, all around the castle, brooded the dark night unheeded; for the clouds had come up from all sides, and were crowding together overhead. In the unfrequent pauses of the music, they might have heard, now and then, the gusty rush of a lonely wind, coming and going no one could know whence or whither, born and dying unexpected and unregarded.

But when the festivities were at their height, when the external and passing confidence which is produced between superficial natures by a common pleasure, was at the full, a sudden crash of thunder quelled the music, as the thunder quells the noise of the uplifted sea. The windows were driven in, and torrents of rain, carried in the folds of a rushing wind, poured into the halls. The lights were swept away; and the great rooms, now dark within, were darkened yet more by the dazzling shoots of flame from the vault of blackness overhead. Those that ventured to look out of the windows saw, in the blue brilliancy of the quick-following jets of lightning, the lake at the foot of the rock, ordinarily so still and so dark, lighted up, not on the surface only, but down to half its depth; so that, as it tossed in the wind, like a tortured sea of writhing flames, or incandescent half-molten serpents of brass, they could not tell whether a strong phosphorescence did not issue from the transparent body of the waters, as if earth and sky lightened together, one consenting source of flaming utterance.

Sad was the condition of the late plastic mass of living form that had flowed into shape at the will and law of the music. Broken into individuals, the common transfusing spirit withdrawn, they stood drenched, cold, and benumbed, with clinging garments; light, order, harmony, purpose departed, and chaos restored; the issuings of life turned back on their sources, chilly and dead. And in every heart reigned that falsest of despairing convictions, that this was the only reality, and that was but a dream. The eldest sister stood with clasped hands and down-bent head, shivering and speechless, as if waiting for something to follow. Nor did she wait long. A terrible flash and thunder-peal made the castle rock; and in the pausing silence that followed, her quick sense heard the rattling of a chain far off, deep down; and soon the sound of heavy footsteps, accompanied with the clanking of iron, reached her ear. She felt that her brother was at hand. Even in the darkness, and amidst the bellowing of another deep-bosomed cloud-monster, she knew that he had entered the room. A moment after, a continuous pulsation of angry blue light began, which, lasting for some moments, revealed him standing amidst them, gaunt, haggard, and motionless; his hair and beard untrimmed, his face ghastly, his eyes large and hollow. The light seemed to gather around him as a centre. Indeed some believed that it throbbed and radiated from his person, and not from the stormy heavens above them. The lightning had rent the wall of his prison, and released the iron staple of his chain, which he had wound about him like a girdle. In his hand he carried an iron fetter-bar, which he had found on the floor of the vault. More terrified at his aspect than at all the violence of the storm, the visitors, with many a shriek and cry, rushed out into the tempestuous night. By degrees, the storm died away. Its last flash revealed the forms of the brothers and sisters lying prostrate, with their faces on the floor, and that fearful shape standing motionless amidst them still.

Morning dawned, and there they lay, and there he stood. But at a word from him, they arose and went about their various duties, though listlessly enough. The eldest sister was the last to rise; and when she did, it was only by a terrible effort that she was able to reach her room, where she fell again on the floor. There she remained lying for days. The brother caused the doors of the great suite of rooms to be closed, leaving them just as they were, with all the childish adornment scattered about, and the rain still falling in through the shattered windows. "Thus let them lie," said he, "till the rain and frost have cleansed them of paint and drapery: no storm can hurt the pillars and arches of these halls."

The hours of this day went heavily. The storm was gone, but the rain was left; the passion had departed, but the tears remained behind. Dull and dark the low misty clouds brooded over the castle and the lake, and shut out all the neighbourhood. Even if they had climbed to the loftiest known turret, they would have found it swathed in a garment of clinging vapour, affording no refreshment to the eye, and no hope to the heart. There was one lofty tower that rose sheer a hundred feet above the rest, and from which the fog could have been seen lying in a grey mass beneath; but that tower they had not yet discovered, nor another close beside it, the top of which was never seen, nor could be, for the highest clouds of heaven clustered continually around it. The rain fell continuously, though not heavily, without; and within, too, there were clouds from which dropped the tears which are the rain of the spirit. All the good of life seemed for the time departed, and their souls lived but as leafless trees that had forgotten the joy of the summer, and whom no wind prophetic of spring had yet visited. They moved about mechanically, and had not strength enough left to wish to die.

The next day the clouds were higher, and a little wind blew through such loopholes in the turrets as the false improvements of the inmates had not yet filled with glass, shutting out, as the storm, so the serene visitings of the heavens. Throughout the day, the brother took various opportunities of addressing a gentle command, now to one and now to another of his family. It was obeyed in silence. The wind blew fresher through the loopholes and the shattered windows of the great rooms, and found its way, by unknown passages, to faces and eyes hot with weeping. It cooled and blessed them.—When the sun arose the next day, it was in a clear sky.

By degrees, everything fell into the regularity of subordination. With the subordination came increase of freedom. The steps of the more youthful of the family were heard on the stairs and in the corridors more light and quick than ever before. Their brother had lost the terrors of aspect produced by his confinement, and his commands were issued more gently, and oftener with a smile, than in all their previous history. By degrees his presence was universally felt through the house. It was no surprise to any one at his studies, to see him by his side when he lifted up his eyes, though he had not before known that he was in the room. And although some dread still remained, it was rapidly vanishing before the advances of a firm friendship. Without immediately ordering their labours, he always influenced them, and often altered their direction and objects. The

209

change soon evident in the household was remarkable. A simpler, nobler expression was visible on all the countenances. The voices of the men were deeper, and yet seemed by their very depth more feminine than before; while the voices of the women were softer and sweeter, and at the same time more full and decided. Now the eyes had often an expression as if their sight was absorbed in the gaze of the inward eyes; and when the eyes of two met, there passed between those eyes the utterance of a conviction that both meant the same thing. But the change was, of course, to be seen more clearly, though not more evidently, in individuals.

One of the brothers, for instance, was very fond of astronomy. He had his observatory on a lofty tower, which stood pretty clear of the others, towards the north and east. But hitherto, his astronomy, as he had called it, had been more of the character of astrology. Often, too, he might have been seen directing a heaven-searching telescope to catch the rapid transit of a fiery shooting-star, belonging altogether to the earthly atmosphere, and not to the serene heavens. He had to learn that the signs of the air are not the signs of the skies. Nay, once, his brother surprised him in the act of examining through his longest tube a patch of burning heath upon a distant hill. But now he was diligent from morning till night in the study of the laws of the truth that has to do with stars; and when the curtain of the sun-light was about to rise from before the heavenly worlds which it had hidden all day long, he might be seen preparing his instruments with that solemn countenance with which it becometh one to look into the mysterious harmonies of Nature. Now he learned what law and order and truth are, what consent and harmony mean; how the individual may find his own end in a higher end, where law and freedom mean the same thing, and the purest certainty exists without the slightest constraint. Thus he stood on the earth, and looked to the heavens.

Another, who had been much given to searching out the hollow places and recesses in the foundations of the castle, and who was often to be found with compass and ruler working away at a chart of the same which he had been in process of constructing, now came to the conclusion, that only by ascending the upper regions of his abode, could he become capable of understanding what lay beneath; and that, in all probability, one clear prospect, from the top of the highest attainable turret, over the castle as it lay below, would reveal more of the idea of its internal construction, than a year spent in wandering through its subterranean vaults. But the fact was, that the desire to ascend wakening within him had made him forget what was beneath; and having laid aside his chart for a time at least, he was now to be met in every quarter of the upper parts, searching and striving upward, now in one direction, now in another; and seeking, as he went, the best outlooks into the clear air of outer realities.

And they began to discover that they were all meditating different aspects of the same thing; and they brought together their various discoveries, and recognized the likeness between them; and the one thing often explained the other, and combining with it helped to a third. They grew in consequence more and more friendly and loving; so that every now and then, one turned to another and said, as in surprise, "Why, you are my brother!"—"Why, you are my sister!" And yet they had always known it.

The change reached to all. One, who lived on the air of sweet sounds, and who was almost always to be found seated by her harp or some other instrument, had, till the late storm, been generally merry and playful, though sometimes sad. But for a long time after that, she was often found weeping, and playing little simple airs which she had heard in childhood—backward longings, followed by fresh tears. Before long, however, a new element manifested itself in her music. It became yet more wild, and sometimes retained all its sadness, but it was mingled with anticipation and hope. The past and the future merged in one; and while memory yet brought the rain-cloud, expectation threw the rainbow across its bosom—and all was uttered in her music, which rose and swelled, now to defiance, now to victory; then died in a torrent of weeping.

As to the eldest sister, it was many days before she recovered from the shock. At length, one day, her brother came to her,

211

took her by the hand, led her to an open window, and told her to seat herself by it, and look out. She did so; but at first saw nothing more than an unsympathizing blaze of sunlight. But as she looked, the horizon widened out, and the dome of the sky ascended, till the grandeur seized upon her soul, and she fell on her knees and wept. Now the heavens seemed to bend lovingly over her, and to stretch out wide cloud-arms to embrace her; the earth lay like the bosom of an infinite love beneath her, and the wind kissed her cheek with an odour of roses. She sprang to her feet, and turned, in an agony of hope, expecting to behold the face of the father, but there stood only her brother, looking calmly though lovingly on her emotion. She turned again to the window. On the hill-tops rested the sky: Heaven and Earth were one; and the prophecy awoke in her soul, that from betwixt them would the steps of the father approach.

Hitherto she had seen but Beauty; now she beheld truth. Often had she looked on such clouds as these, and loved the strange ethereal curves into which the winds moulded them; and had smiled as her little pet sister told her what curious animals she saw in them, and tried to point them out to her. Now they were as troops of angels, jubilant over her new birth, for they sang, in her soul, of beauty, and truth, and love. She looked down, and her little sister knelt beside her.

She was a curious child, with black, glittering eyes, and dark hair; at the mercy of every wandering wind; a frolicsome, daring girl, who laughed more than she smiled. She was generally in attendance on her sister, and was always finding and bringing her strange things. She never pulled a primrose, but she knew the haunts of all the orchis tribe, and brought from them bees and butterflies innumerable, as offerings to her sister. Curious moths and glow-worms were her greatest delight; and she loved the stars, because they were like the glow-worms. But the change had affected her too; for her sister saw that her eyes had lost their glittering look, and had become more liquid and transparent. And from that time she often observed that her gaiety was more gentle, her smile more frequent, her laugh less bell-like; and although she was as wild as ever, there was more elegance in her motions, and more music in her voice. And she clung to her sister with far greater fondness than before.

The land reposed in the embrace of the warm summer days. The clouds of heaven nestled around the towers of the castle; and the hearts of its inmates became conscious of a warm atmosphere—of a presence of love. They began to feel like the children of a household, when the mother is at home. Their faces and forms grew daily more and more beautiful, till they wondered as they gazed on each other. As they walked in the gardens of the castle, or in the country around, they were often visited, especially the eldest sister, by sounds that no one heard but themselves, issuing from woods and waters; and by forms of love that lightened out of flowers, and grass, and great rocks. Now and then the young children would come in with a slow, stately step, and, with great eyes that looked as if they would devour all the creation, say that they had met the father amongst the trees, and that he had kissed them; "And," added one of them once, "I grew so big!" But when others went out to look, they could see no one. And some said it must have been the brother, who grew more and more beautiful, and loving, and reverend, and who had lost all traces of hardness, so that they wondered they could ever have thought him stern and harsh. But the eldest sister held her peace, and looked up, and her eyes filled with tears. "Who can tell," thought she, "but the little children know more about it than we?"

Often, at sunrise, might be heard their hymn of praise to their unseen father, whom they felt to be near, though they saw him not. Some words thereof once reached my ear through the folds of the music in which they floated, as in an upward snow-storm of sweet sounds. And these are some of the words I heard—but there was much I seemed to hear, which I could not understand, and some things which I understood but cannot utter again.

"We thank thee that we have a father, and not a maker; that thou hast begotten us, and not moulded us as images of clay; that we have come forth of thy heart, and have not been fashioned by thy hands. It *must* be so. Only the heart of a father is able to create. We rejoice in it, and bless thee that we know it.

213

We thank thee for thyself. Be what thou art—our root and life, our beginning and end, our all in all. Come home to us. Thou livest; therefore we live. In thy light we see. Thou art—that is all our song."

Thus they worship, and love, and wait. Their hope and expectation grow ever stronger and brighter, that one day, ere long, the Father will show himself amongst them, and thenceforth dwell in his own house for evermore. What was once but an old legend has become the one desire of their hearts.

And the loftiest hope is the surest of being fulfilled.

214

The Story of Tuan Mac Cairill

James Stephens

James Stephens (1882–1950) was arguably one of the most important members of the Celtic revival. A friend of AE's, who influenced his early poetry profoundly, he produced some of the finest literary works based on ancient Irish myth and folk-lore. The Crock of Gold *(1912), his best known work, mixes fantasy, humour and vision in a rich brew. His other books include* The Demi Gods *(1914),* Deirdrie *(1923) and* In the Land of Youth *(1924). His collection of Irish fairy tales from which the following story is taken, reworked the old tellings in a new and original way, bringing them to life and injecting a sense of the sacredness of all life which colours so much of Celtic literature. As well as a fine literary stylist, Stephens was also a broadcaster, critic, journalist, lecturer and dramatist. Like many of the writers involved in the Revival, he was a student of the ancient Celtic literature and language, as well as a Theosophist closely involved with the work of Yeats, Russell and George Moore. The story printed here is one of the oldest and most mysterious of Irish myths in which we read of the semi-divine bard Tuan, who is said to have lived for many hundreds of years, and to have passed through several forms both animal and human. As a result of his long life, he is said to have preserved the visionary history of Ireland which he here relates to the Christian Abbot of Moville.*

From *Irish Fairy Tales*. Macmillan, London 1920.

Arthur Rackham

The Story of Tuan Mac Cairill

I

Finnian, the Abbot of Moville, went southwards and eastwards in great haste. News had come to him in Donegal that there were yet people in his own province who believed in gods that he did not approve of, and the gods that we do not approve of are treated scurvily, even by saintly men.

He was told of a powerful gentleman who observed neither saint's day nor Sunday.

"A powerful person!" said Finnian.

"All that," was the reply.

"We shall try this person's power," said Finnian.

"He is reputed to be a wise and hardy man," said his informant.

"We shall test his wisdom and his hardihood."

"He is," that gossip whispered—"he is a magician."

"I will magician him," cried Finnian angrily. "Where does that man live?"

He was informed, and he proceeded in that direction without delay.

In no great time he came to the stronghold of the gentleman who followed ancient ways, and he demanded admittance in order that he might preach and prove the new God, and exorcise and terrify and banish even the memory of the old one; for to a god grown old Time is as ruthless as to a beggarman grown old.

But the Ulster gentleman refused Finnian admittance.

He barricaded his house, he shuttered his windows, and in a gloom of indignation and protest he continued the practices of ten thousand years, and would not hearken to Finnian calling at the window or to Time knocking at his door.

But of those adversaries it was the first he redoubted.

217

Finnian loomed on him as a portent and a terror; but he had no fear of Time. Indeed he was the foster-brother of Time, and so disdainful of the bitter god that he did not even disdain him; he leaped over the scythe, he dodged under it, and the sole occasions on which Time laughs is when he chances on Tuan, the son of Cairill, the son of Muredac Red-neck.

II

Now Finnian could not abide that any person should resist both the Gospel and himself, and he proceeded to force the stronghold by peaceful but powerful methods. He fasted on the gentleman, and he did so to such purpose that he was admitted to the house; for to an hospitable heart the idea that a stranger may expire on your doorstep from sheer famine cannot be tolerated. The gentleman, however, did not give in without a struggle: he thought that when Finnian had grown sufficiently hungry he would lift the siege and take himself off to some place where he might get food. But he did not know Finnian. The great abbot sat down on a spot just beyond the door, and composed himself to all that might follow from his action. He bent his gaze on the ground between his feet, and entered into a meditation from which he would only be released by admission or death.

The first day passed quietly.

Often the gentleman would send a servitor to spy if that deserter of the gods was still before his door, and each time the servant replied that he was still there.

"He will be gone in the morning," said the hopeful master.

On the morrow the state of siege continued, and through that day the servants were sent many times to observe through spy-holes.

"Go," he would say, "and find out if the worshipper of new gods has taken himself away."

But the servants returned each time with the same information.

"The new druid is still there," they said.

218

All through that day no one could leave the stronghold. And the enforced seclusion wrought on the minds of the servants, while the cessation of all work banded them together in small groups that whispered and discussed and disputed. Then these groups would disperse to peep through the spy-hole at the patient immobile figure seated before the door, wrapped in a meditation that was timeless and unconcerned. They took fright at the spectacle, and once or twice a woman screamed hysterically, and was bundled away with a companion's hand clapped on her mouth, so that the ear of their master should not be affronted.

"He has his own troubles," they said. "It is a combat of the gods that is taking place."

So much for the women; but the men also were uneasy. They prowled up and down, tramping from the spy-hole to the kitchen, and from the kitchen to the turreted roof. And from the roof they would look down on the motionless figure below, and speculate on many things, including the staunchness of man, the qualities of their master, and even the possibility that the new gods might be as powerful as the old. From these peepings and discussions they would return languid and discouraged.

"If," said one irritable guard, "if we buzzed a spear at that persistent stranger, or if one slung at him with a jagged pebble!"

"What!" his master demanded wrathfully, "is a spear to be thrown at an unarmed stranger? And from this house!"

And he soundly cuffed that indelicate servant.

"Be at peace all of you," he said, "for hunger has a whip, and he will drive the stranger away in the night."

The household retired to wretched beds; but for the master of the house there was no sleep. He marched his halls all night, going often to the spy-hole to see if that shadow was still sitting in the shade, and pacing thence, tormented, preoccupied, refusing even the nose of his favourite dog as it pressed lovingly into his closed palm.

On the morrow he gave in.

The great door was swung wide, and two of his servants carried

Finnian into the house, for the saint could no longer walk or stand upright by reason of the hunger and exposure to which he had submitted. But his frame was tough as the unconquerable spirit that dwelt within it, and in no long time he was ready for whatever might come of dispute or anathema.

Being quite re-established he undertook the conversion of the master of the house, and the siege he laid against that notable intelligence was long spoken of among those who are interested in such things.

He had beaten the disease of Mugain; he had beaten his own pupil the great Colm Cillé; he beat Tuan also, and just as the latter's door had opened to the persistent stranger, so his heart opened, and Finnian marched there to do the will of God, and his own will.

III

One day they were talking together about the majesty of God and His love, for although Tuan had now received much instruction on this subject he yet needed more, and he laid as close a siege on Finnian as Finnian had before that laid on him. But man works outwardly and inwardly, after rest he has energy, after energy he needs repose; so, when we have given instruction for a time, we need instruction, and must receive it or the spirit faints and wisdom herself grows bitter.

Therefore Finnian said: "Tell me now about yourself, dear heart."

But Tuan was avid of information about the True God.

"No, no," he said, "the past has nothing more of interest for me, and I do not wish anything to come between my soul and its instruction; continue to teach me, dear friend and saintly father."

"I will do that," Finnian replied, "but I must first meditate deeply on you, and must know you well. Tell me your past, my beloved, for a man is his past, and is to be known by it."

But Tuan pleaded:

220

"Let the past be content with itself, for man needs forgetfulness as well as memory."

"My son," said Finnian, "all that has ever been done has been done for the glory of God, and to confess our good and evil deeds is part of instruction; for the soul must recall its acts and abide by them, or renounce them by confession and penitence. Tell me your genealogy first, and by what descent you occupy these lands and stronghold, and then I will examine your acts and your conscience."

Tuan replied obediently:

"I am known as Tuan, son of Cairill, son of Muredac Red-neck, and these are the hereditary lands of my father."

The saint nodded.

"I am not as well acquainted with Ulster genealogies as I should be, yet I know something of them. I am by blood a Leinsterman," he continued.

"Mine is a long pedigree," Tuan murmured.

Finnian received that information with respect and interest.

"I also," he said, "have an honourable record."

His host continued:

"I am indeed Tuan, the son of Starn, the son of Sera, who was brother to Partholon."

"But," said Finnian in bewilderment, "there is an error here, for you have recited two different genealogies."

"Different genealogies, indeed," replied Tuan thoughtfully, "but they are my genealogies."

"I do not understand this," Finnian declared roundly.

"I am now known as Tuan mac Cairill," the other replied, "but in the days of old I was known as Tuan mac Starn, mac Sera."

"The brother of Partholon," the saint gasped.

"That is my pedigree," Tuan said.

"But," Finnian objected in bewilderment, "Partholon came to Ireland not long after the Flood."

"I came with him," said Tuan mildly.

The saint pushed his chair back hastily, and sat staring at his host, and as he stared the blood grew chill in his veins, and his hair crept along his scalp and stood on end.

IV

But Finnian was not one who remained long in bewilderment. He thought on the might of God and he became that might, and was tranquil.

He was one who loved God and Ireland, and to the person who could instruct him in these great themes he gave all the interest of his mind and the sympathy of his heart.

"It is a wonder you tell me, my beloved," he said. "And now you must tell me more."

"What must I tell?" asked Tuan resignedly.

"Tell me of the beginning of time in Ireland, and of the bearing of Partholon, the son of Noah's son."

"I have almost forgotten him," said Tuan. "A greatly bearded, greatly shouldered man he was. A man of sweet deeds and sweet ways."

"Continue, my love," said Finnian.

"He came to Ireland in a ship. Twenty-four men and twenty-four women came with him. But before that time no man had come to Ireland, and in the western parts of the world no human being lived or moved. As we drew on Ireland from the sea the country seemed like an unending forest. Far as the eye could reach, and in whatever direction, there were trees; and from these there came the unceasing singing of birds. Over all that land the sun shone warm and beautiful, so that to our sea-weary eyes, our wind-tormented ears, it seemed as if we were driving on Paradise.

"We landed and we heard the rumble of water going gloomily through the darkness of the forest. Following the water we came to a glade where the sun shone and where the earth was warmed, and there Partholon rested with his twenty-four couples, and made a city and a livelihood.

"There were fish in the rivers of Eirè, there were animals in her coverts. Wild and shy and monstrous creatures ranged in her plains and forests. Creatures that one could see through and walk through. Long we lived in ease, and we saw new animals grow,—the bear, the wolf, the badger, the deer, and the boar.

"Partholon's people increased until from twenty-four couples there came five thousand people, who lived in amity and contentment although they had no wits."

"They had no wits!" Finnian commented.

"They had no need of wits," Tuan said.

"I have heard that the first-born were mindless," said Finnian. "Continue your story, my beloved."

"Then, sudden as a rising wind, between one night and a morning, there came a sickness that bloated the stomach and purpled the skin, and on the seventh day all of the race of Partholon were dead, save one man only."

"There always escapes one man," said Finnian thoughtfully.

"And I am that man," his companion affirmed.

Tuan shaded his brow with his hand, and he remembered backwards through incredible ages to the beginning of the world and the first days of Eirè. And Finnian, with his blood again running chill and his scalp crawling uneasily, stared backwards with him.

V

"Tell on, my love," Finnian murmured.

"I was alone," said Tuan. "I was so alone that my own shadow frightened me. I was so alone that the sound of a bird in flight, or the creaking of a dew-drenched bough whipped me to cover as a rabbit is scared to his burrow.

"The creatures of the forest scented me and knew I was alone. They stole with silken pad behind my back and snarled when I faced them; the long, grey wolves with hanging tongues and staring eyes chased me to my cleft rock; there was no creature so weak but it might hunt me; there was no creature so timid but it might outface me. And so I lived for two tens of years and two years, until I knew all that a beast surmises and had forgotten all that a man had known.

"I could pad as gently as any; I could run as tirelessly. I could be invisible and patient as a wild cat crouching among leaves; I could smell danger in my sleep and leap at it with wakeful claws; I could bark and growl and clash with my teeth and tear with them."

"Tell on, my beloved," said Finnian; "you shall rest in God, dear heart."

"At the end of that time," said Tuan, "Nemed the son of Agnoman came to Ireland with a fleet of thirty-four barques, and in each barque there were thirty couples of people."

"I have heard it," said Finnian.

"My heart leaped for joy when I saw the great fleet rounding the land, and I followed them along scarped cliffs, leaping from rock to rock like a wild goat, while the ships tacked and swung seeking a harbour. There I stooped to drink at a pool, and I saw myself in the chill water.

"I saw that I was hairy and tufty and bristled as a savage boar; that I was lean as a stripped bush; that I was greyer than a badger; withered and wrinkled like an empty sack; naked as a fish; wretched as a starving crow in winter; and on my fingers and toes there were great curving claws, so that I looked like nothing that was known, like nothing that was animal or divine. And I sat by the pool weeping my loneliness and wildness and my stern old age; and I could do no more than cry and lament between the earth and the sky, while the beasts that tracked me listened from behind the trees, or crouched among bushes to stare at me from their drowsy covert.

"A storm arose, and when I looked again from my tall cliff I saw that great fleet rolling as in a giant's hand. At times they were pitched against the sky and staggered aloft, spinning gustily there like wind-blown leaves. Then they were hurled from these dizzy tops to the flat, moaning gulf, to the glassy, inky horror that swirled and whirled between ten waves. At times a wave leaped howling under a ship, and with a buffet dashed it into air, and chased it upwards with thunder stroke on stroke, and followed again, close as a chasing wolf, trying with hammering on hammering to beat in the wide-wombed bottom and suck out

224

the frightened lives through one black gape. A wave fell on a ship and sank it down with a thrust, stern as though a whole sky had tumbled at it, and the barque did not cease to go down until it crashed and sank in the sand at the bottom of the sea.

"The night came, and with it a thousand darknesses fell from the screeching sky. Not a round-eyed creature of the night might pierce an inch of that multiplied gloom. Not a creature dared creep or stand. For a great wind strode the world lashing its league-long whips in cracks of thunder, and singing to itself, now in a world-wide yell, now in an ear-dizzying hum and buzz; or with a long snarl and whine it hovered over the world searching for life to destroy.

"And at times, from the moaning and yelping blackness of the sea, there came a sound—thin-drawn as from millions of miles away, distinct as though uttered in the ear like a whisper of confidence—and I knew that a drowning man was calling on his God as he thrashed and was battered into silence, and that a blue-lipped woman was calling on her man as her hair whipped round her brows and she whirled about like a top.

"Around me the trees were dragged from earth with dying groans; they leaped into the air and flew like birds. Great waves whizzed from the sea: spinning across the cliffs and hurtling to the earth in monstrous clots of foam; the very rocks came trundling and sidling and grinding among the trees; and in that rage, and in that horror of blackness, I fell asleep, or I was beaten into slumber."

VI

"There I dreamed, and I saw myself changing into a stag in dream, and I felt in dream the beating of a new heart within me, and in dream I arched my neck and braced my powerful limbs.

"I awoke from the dream, and I was that which I had dreamed.

"I stood a while stamping upon a rock, with my bristling head swung high, breathing through wide nostrils all the savour of the world. For I had come marvellously from decrepitude to strength. I had writhed from the bonds of age and was young again. I smelled the turf and knew for the first time how sweet that smelled. And like lightning my moving nose sniffed all things to my heart and separated them into knowledge.

"Long I stood there, ringing my iron hoof on stone, and learning all things through my nose. Each breeze that came from the right hand or the left brought me a tale. A wind carried me the tang of wolf, and against that smell I stared and stamped. And on a wind there came the scent of my own kind, and at that I belled. Oh, loud and clear and sweet was the voice of the great stag. With what ease my lovely note went lilting. With what joy I heard the answering call. With what delight I bounded, bounded, bounded; light as a bird's plume, powerful as a storm, untiring as the sea.

"Here now was ease in ten-yard springings, with a swinging head, with the rise and fall of a swallow, with the curve and flow and urge of an otter of the sea. What a tingle dwelt about my heart! What a thrill spun to the lofty points of my antlers! How the world was new! How the sun was new! How the wind caressed me!

"With unswerving forehead and steady eye I met all that came. The old, lone wolf leaped sideways, snarling, and slunk away. The lumbering bear swung his head of hesitations and thought again; he trotted his small red eye away with him to a near-by brake. The stags of my race fled from my rocky forehead, or were pushed back and back until their legs broke under them and I trampled them to death. I was the beloved, the well known, the leader of the herds of Ireland.

"And at times I came back from my boundings about Eirè, for the strings of my heart were drawn to Ulster; and, standing away, my wide nose took the air, while I knew with joy, with terror, that men were blown on the wind. A proud head hung to the turf then, and the tears of memory rolled from a large, bright eye.

"At times I drew near, delicately, standing among thick leaves or crouched in long grown grasses, and I stared and mourned as I looked on men. For Nemed and four couples had been saved from that fierce storm, and I saw them increase and multiply

226

until four thousand couples lived and laughed and were riotous in the sun, for the people of Nemed had small minds but great activity. They were savage fighters and hunters.

"But one time I came, drawn by that intolerable anguish of memory, and all of these people were gone: the place that knew them was silent: in the land where they had moved there was nothing of them but their bones that glinted in the sun.

"Old age came on me there. Among these bones weariness crept into my limbs. My head grew heavy, my eyes dim, my knees jerked and trembled, and there the wolves dared chase me.

"I went again to the cave that had been my home when I was an old man.

"One day I stole from the cave to snatch a mouthful of grass, for I was closely besieged by wolves. They made their rush, and I barely escaped from them. They sat beyond the cave staring at me.

"I knew their tongue. I knew all that they said to each other, and all that they said to me. But there was yet a thud left in my forehead, a deadly trample in my hoof. They did not dare come into the cave.

" 'Tomorrow,' they said, 'we will tear out your throat, and gnaw on your living haunch.' "

VII

"Then my soul rose to the height of Doom, and I intended all that might happen to me, and agreed to it.

" 'To-morrow,' I said, 'I will go out among ye, and I will die,' and at that the wolves howled joyfully, hungrily, impatiently.

"I slept, and I saw myself changing into a boar in dream, and I felt in dream the beating of a new heart within me, and in dream I stretched my powerful neck and braced my eager limbs. I awoke from my dream, and I was that which I had dreamed.

"The night wore away, the darkness lifted, the day came; and from without the cave the wolves called to me:

" 'Come out, O Skinny Stag. Come out and die.'

"And I, with joyful heart, thrust a black bristle through the hole of the cave, and when they saw that wriggling snout, those curving tusks, that red fierce eye, the wolves fled yelping, tumbling over each other, frantic with terror; and I behind them, a wild-cat for leaping, a giant for strength, a devil for ferocity; a madness and gladness of lusty unsparing life; a killer, a champion, a boar who could not be defied.

"I took the lordship of the boars of Ireland.

"Wherever I looked among my tribes I saw love and obedience: whenever I appeared among the strangers they fled away. Ah, the wolves feared me then, and the great, grim bear went bounding on heavy paws. I charged him at the head of my troop and rolled him over and over; but it is not easy to kill the bear, so deeply is his life packed under that stinking pelt. He picked himself up and ran, and was knocked down, and ran again blindly, butting into trees and stones. Not a claw did the big bear flash, not a tooth did he show, as he ran whimpering like a baby, or as he stood with my nose rammed against his mouth, snarling up into his nostrils.

"I challenged all that moved. All creatures but one. For men had again come to Ireland. Semion, the son of Stariath, with his people, from whom the men of Domnann and the Fir Bolg and the Galiuin are descended. These I did not chase, and when they chased me I fled.

"Often I would go, drawn by my memoried heart, to look at them as they moved among their fields; and I spoke to my mind in bitterness:

"When the people of Partholon were gathered in counsel my voice was heard; it was sweet to all who heard it, and the words I spoke were wise. The eyes of women brightened and softened when they looked at me. They loved to hear him when he sang who now wanders in the forest with a tusky herd."

VIII

"Old age again overtook me. Weariness stole into my limbs, and anguish dozed into my mind. I went to my Ulster cave and dreamed my dream, and I changed into a hawk.

"I left the ground. The sweet air was my kingdom, and my bright eye stared on a hundred miles. I soared, I swooped; I hung, motionless as a living stone, over the abyss; I lived in joy and slept in peace, and had my fill of the sweetness of life.

"During that time Beothach, the son of Iarbonel the Prophet, came to Ireland with his people, and there was a great battle between his men and the children of Semion. Long I hung over that combat, seeing every spear that hurtled, every stone that whizzed from a sling, every sword that flashed up and down, and the endless glittering of the shields. And at the end I saw that the victory was with Iarbonel. And from his people the Tuatha Dè and thc Andè came, although their origin is forgotten, and learned people, because of their excellent wisdom and intelligence, say that they came from heaven.

"These are the people of Faery. All these are the gods.

"For long, long years I was a hawk. I knew every hill and stream; every field and glen of Ireland. I knew the shape of cliffs and coasts, and how all places looked under the sun or moon. And I was still a hawk when thc sons of Mil drove the Tuatha Dè Danann under the ground, and held Ireland against arms or wizardry; and this was the coming of men and the beginning of genealogies.

"Then I grew old, and in my Ulster cave close to the sea I dreamed my dream, and in it I became a salmon. The green tides of Ocean rose over me and my dream, so that I drowned in the sea and did not die, for I awoke in deep waters, and I was that which I dreamed.

"I had been a man, a stag, a boar, a bird, and now I was a fish. In all my changes I had joy and fullness of life. But in the water joy lay deeper, life pulsed deeper. For on land or air there is always something excessive and hindering; as arms that swing at the sides of a man, and which the mind must remember. The stag has legs to be tucked away for sleep, and untucked for movement; and the bird has wings that must be folded and pecked and cared for. But the fish has but one piece from his nose to his tail. He is complete, single and unencumbered. He turns in one turn, and goes up and down and round in one sole movement.

"How I flew through the soft element: how I joyed in the country where there is no harshness: in the element which upholds and gives way; which caresses and lets go, and will not let you fall. For man may stumble in a furrow; the stag tumble from a cliff; the hawk, wing-weary and beaten, with darkness around him and the storm behind, may dash his brains against a tree. But the home of the salmon is his delight, and the sea guards all her creatures."

IX

"I became the king of the salmon, and, with my multitudes, I ranged on the tides of the world. Green and purple distances were under me: green and gold the sunlit regions above. In these latitudes I moved through a world of amber, myself amber and gold; in those others, in a sparkle of lucent blue, I curved, lit like a living jewel: and in these again, through dusks of ebony all mazed with silver, I shot and shone, the wonder of the sea.

"I saw the monsters of the uttermost ocean go heaving by; and the long lithe brutes that are toothed to their tails: and below, where gloom dipped down on gloom, vast, livid tangles that coiled and uncoiled, and lapsed down steeps and hells of the sea where even the salmon could not go.

"I knew the sea. I knew the secret caves where ocean roars to ocean; the floods that are icy cold, from which the nose of a salmon leaps back as at a sting; and the warm streams in which we rocked and dozed and were carried forward without motion. I swam on the outermost rim of the great world, where nothing was but the sea and the sky and the salmon; where even the wind was silent, and the water was clear as clean grey rock.

230

"And then, far away in the sea, I remembered Ulster, and there came on me an instant, uncontrollable anguish to be there. I turned, and through days and nights I swam tirelessly, jubilantly; with terror wakening in me, too, and a whisper through my being that I must reach Ireland or die.

"I fought my way to Ulster from the sea.

"Ah, how that end of the journey was hard! A sickness was racking in every one of my bones, a languor and weariness creeping through my every fibre and muscle. The waves held me back and held me back; the soft waters seemed to have grown hard; and it was as though I were urging through a rock as I strained towards Ulster from the sea.

"So tired I was! I could have loosened my frame and been swept away; I could have slept and been drifted and wafted away; swinging on grey-green billows that had turned from the land and were heaving and mounting and surging to the far blue water.

"Only the unconquerable heart of the salmon could brave that end of toil. The sound of the rivers of Ireland racing down to the sea came to me in the last numb effort: the love of Ireland bore me up: the gods of the rivers trod to me in the white-curled breakers, so that I left the sea at long, long last; and I lay in sweet water in the curve of a crannied rock, exhausted, three parts dead, triumphant."

X

"Delight and strength came to me again, and now I explored all the inland ways, the great lakes of Ireland, and her swift brown rivers.

"What a joy to lie under an inch of water basking in the sun, or beneath a shady ledge to watch the small creatures that speed like lightning on the rippling top. I saw the dragon-flies flash and dart and turn, with a poise, with a speed that no other winged thing knows: I saw the hawk hover and stare and swoop: he fell like a falling stone, but he could not catch the king of the salmon: I saw the cold-eyed cat stretching along a bough level with the water, eager to hook and lift the creatures of the river. And I saw men.

"They saw me also. They came to know me and look for me. They lay in wait at the waterfalls up which I leaped like a silver flash. They held out nets for me; they hid traps under leaves; they made cords of the colour of water, of the colour of weeds—but this salmon had a nose that knew how a weed felt and how a string—they drifted meat on a sightless string, but I knew of the hook; they thrust spears at me, and threw lances which they drew back again with a cord.

"Many a wound I got from men, many a sorrowful scar.

"Every beast pursued me in the waters and along the banks; the barking, black-skinned otter came after me in lust and gust and swirl; the wild-cat fished for me; the hawk and the steep-winged, spear-beaked birds dived down on me, and men crept on me with nets the width of a river, so that I got no rest. My life became a ceaseless scurry and wound and escape, a burden and anguish of watchfulness—and then I was caught."

XI

"The fisherman of Cairill, the King of Ulster, took me in his net. Ah, that was a happy man when he saw me! He shouted for joy when he saw the great salmon in his net.

"I was still in the water as he hauled delicately. I was still in the water as he pulled me to the bank. My nose touched air and spun from it as from fire, and I dived with all my might against the bottom of the net, holding yet to the water, loving it, mad with terror that I must quit that loveliness. But the net held and I came up.

" 'Be quiet, King of the River,' said the fisherman, 'give in to Doom,' said he.

"I was in air, and it was as though I were in fire. The air pressed on me like a fiery mountain. It beat on my scales and scorched them. It rushed down my throat and scalded me. It weighed on me and squeezed me, so that my eyes felt as though they must burst from my head, my head as though it would leap from my body, and my body as though it would swell and expand and fly in a thousand pieces.

"The light blinded me, the heat tormented me, the dry air made me shrivel and gasp; and, as he lay on the grass the great salmon whirled his desperate nose once more to the river, and leaped, leaped, leaped, even under the mountain of air. He could leap upwards, but not forwards, and yet he leaped, for in each rise he could see the twinkling waves, the rippling and curling waters.

" 'Be at ease, O King,' said the fisherman. 'Be at rest, my beloved. Let go the stream. Let the oozy marge be forgotten, and the sandy bed where the shades dance all in green and gloom, and the brown flood sings along.'

"And as he carried me to the palace he sang a song of the river, and a song of Doom, and a song in praise of the King of the Waters.

"When the king's wife saw me she desired me. I was put over a fire and roasted, and she ate me. And when time passed she gave birth to me, and I was her son and the son of Cairill the king. I remember warmth and darkness and movement and unseen sounds. All that happened I remember, from the time I was on the gridiron until the time I was born. I forget nothing of these things."

"And now," said Finnian, "you will be born again, for I shall baptize you into the family of the Living God."

So far the story of Tuan the son of Cairill.

No man knows if he died in those distant ages when Finnian was Abbot of Moville, or if he still keeps his fort in Ulster, watching all things, and remembering them for the glory of God and the honour of Ireland.

The Weird of Fionavar

Ella Young

Ella Young (1867–1956) was born in the village of Feenagh, County Antrim, Ireland. A gifted story-teller who remembered the tales "told by the peat fires" in her childhood, she became active in the Celtic revival after meeting George Russell, Standish O'Grady and W.B.Yeats in 1903, at which time she also joined the Theosophical Society in which Russell was also active. Later, she moved to America, where she met Kenneth Morris and encouraged him to pursue his writing career. Her works are imbued with a graceful and sensitive use of the natural rhythms of speech, and with a visionary beauty which enriches the original tales while never diverging far from their roots. The brief sequence of poems published here appeared originally in 1922. It re-tells the tragic story of Fionavar (originally Findbhair, or "Fair Eyebrows"), the daughter of King Aillil and Queen Maeve, ancient rulers of Connaught. Ella Young draws a delicate love story from the threads of Irish mythology, weaving themes and characters now long forgotten even in their own land. It is, so far as I am aware, the only volume of poems she published.

From *The Weird of Fionavar*, a pamphlet published by the Talbot Press, Dublin and T Fisher Unwin, London 1922.

The Weird of Fionavar

The tragic story of Fionavar, the Princess, daughter of Aillil and Medb, is set in the heroic legends like a strange jewel from a far country set in the boss of a war-shield—a jewel that wrought more havoc than the sword, and left a memory that disputes precedence with the hero-vaunt of Cu Chulainn.

Druid-woman, sombre eyed,
Turn the spindle at your side,
Spin a doom for Fionavar.

I spin gold and silver flame,
The world's joy when she came,
I spin for Fionavar.

Love I spin that wearieth:
White beauty quenched in death
I spin for Fionavar.

Clash of swords and reddened spears,
And slow-dropping bitter tears
I spin for Fionavar.

A king's son out of the South
To die for one kiss of her mouth
I spin for Fionavar.

Sun and moon and flowering grass,
Songs that live and songs that pass
I spin for Fionavar.

On my spindle gold and red,
Silver, green, and purple thread
And black—for Fionavar.

Aibric's song for Fionavar

She is the slender blossomed thorn,
She is the heart-beat of the Spring,
The faint sweet music before morn,
She, the light swallow on the wing.

She is the maid-moon young and white,
The queen that has the heavens for home—
I am the lonely wind of night,
I am the spent sea's bitter foam.

A song that Aibric made for Fionavar

Gold leaves and leaves of silver
On every tree,
White lilies in the lake-water—
And love is gone from me !

She was the sweet wind blowing
In April from the South,
Redder than quicken berries
The redness of her mouth.

She was the wild swan flying
Far-off when winds are chill:
She was the cloud at sunrise
On the dark crest of the hill.

A song that Trostan made

If I were a king's son
I would give you a white hound
In a leash of silver,
I would give you a white stallion
From over the sea.
I would give you a cloak of purple
Wrought with findruiny,
And shoes of white bronze,
If I were a king's son.

You would talk with me
In the bright-coloured palace:
You would be glad at my coming,
If I were a king's son.

Trostan made this

The hawk in the cliff of Ben Edair
Knows that I am stricken.

The otter knows
In the pool by the hurdles.

Love has a short blossoming—
But the dead remember it.

Fardia speaks

Like the young crescent moon,
Like a star in still water,
Like a sword, is Fionavar:
Redder than dawn she is,
Stranger than death.

A song that Aibric made

Long-legged heron
If you had a wish
You would ask the gods
For one small fish:
And the gods might give you one.
I would ask the sun
Out of the sky,
The gods would laugh
And pass by.

Ardan made this

With chains of silver two and two
Bound together I gave you
Fifty snow-white hounds.

You gave me the sun and moon.
Angus has not in his dùn
Or Mananann beneath the sea
Half the treasure you gave me.

But ah, my grief ! would I had known
What your gift was, and kept my own !

Aibric's Song

Folk of the Sidhe-Mound under the hill,
I hear their music when the wind is still.

Fionavar, Fionavar,
You need not fear the drifting snow
Fionavar, the road you go.

I hear their high sweet voices singing
When the wind goes past:
I hear their secret laughter bringing
You home at last.

Fionavar, Fionavar,
You need not fear the burning sun
Fionavar, when day is done.

Fionavar's Lover

On every yett of his horse's mane
He had nine bells of gold;
The purple sea-stain in his cloak
Wrought with white findruiny.

"Now who is this," the proud Queen said,
"Some rover from the South!"
But Fionavar stepped lightly down
And kissed him on the mouth.

Maeve shook out on her shoulder
Her twisted locks of hair,
"O many a king has knelt to me
For Fionavar the Fair.

"But will you swim the wan water
Where the druid hazels are
And break a branch of the crimson fruit
For love of Fionavar ?"

He set himself to the wan water
No living man had crossed;
She watched him grasp the crimson fruit—
She knew who plucked was lost!

The Piast of the wan water
Rose up through the dark tide:
"A kiss ! a kiss to me, King's Son,
Before you mount and ride !"

Her loathly body round his feet
Was strong as iron bands:
He took the druid branch in his teeth
And fought her with his hands.

Fionavar lifted his sword—
O but her face was wan !
She cried to him with a great cry:
Cried and ran.

Her mother caught her as she passed
By the long locks of her hair:
"The tide runs deep in the Kelpies' Pool,
You'll tryst no lover there !"

The white wave lipped him cheek and chin,
The black wave lipped his head:
The third wave held him at her feet
When he was drowned and dead.

Fionavar

O Flame blown out of Tir-nan-Og,
White Flame borne on enchanted air,
O heart's delight and heart's despair,
    O Fionavar ! O Fionavar!

Draw the white shroud above her face
And cover up her close-shut eyes,
She will not hear a voice that cries
    O Fionavar ! O Fionavar!

O Love that none of us might win,
By strange lone ways to us you came,
And lone you go, White Heart of Flame,
    O Fionavar! O Fionavar!

Pale face that held our hearts in thrall,
Pale face, made paler by our love,
We could but draw the shroud above,
    O Fionavar! O Fionavar!

Frail hands no mortal lover kissed,
Fair-folded now as Death beseems,
You hide away the Dream of Dreams,
    O Fionavar! O Fionavar !

"O sorrow on you for this ill deed,
Black sorrow on your pride !
You put death-bands on your own daughter
By the wan water side !"

"Red fruit that's red with my Love's blood,
Stain red, stain red my mouth!
And let the hearts that longed for me
Be emptied of love's drouth.

My tryst and troth I'll keep with him
That was my only love,
Though the river sand is under his head
And the wan water above."

Aibric is reconciled

Day by day the sun
Climbs the wide sky,
The little stream has its song,
The wind goes by.

The earth that is wise and old
    Dreams and stirs in her sleep—
How could we mortals hold
    A treasure she wished to keep?

All loveliness to dust at last,
    All loveliness goes down they say
Like roses when the Summer's past
    And Love and Wisdom die away.

And yet I think the Earth is glad
    For joy that old-time lovers had,
And Autumn burns a fiercer red
    For sake of lovers that are dead.

The White Hound of the Mountain

Thomas J Kiernan

Thomas Joseph Kiernan (1897–1967) wrote only one volume of stories, from which the one included here, the title story, comes. For most of his life he was a senior diplomat, holding the office of Irish Ambassador to the Vatican State in 1941, and subsequently in Austria, West Germany, Canada and Washington DC. Other than the volume from which this story comes, he wrote only books on national finance and administration, a literary portrait of Pope Pius XII and one historical novel. But like many of the writers in this collection, although his life took him far from his homeland he never quite lost touch with the deepest strata of all—the mythological. The stories which make up The White Hound of the Mountain, *Kiernan's last book, are more than simple retellings of old folk tales—they breathe out the mists and wonders of Ireland. The collection is almost unique in having a commentary by the author, in which he reveals the breadth of his reading and study in the area of myth and legend, and the subtlety with which he saw the patterns underlying the story he chose to re-tell. In fact the interpretation is a very modern one, being based largely on Jungian ideas. This is interesting as it is somewhat at variance with the mystical quality of the stories. Kiernan seems to have seen them as doubly significant because of this, conscious of the fact that the stories resonated in more than one area of human awareness.*

Kiernan returned to Ireland at the end of his life and died in Dublin in 1967. His wife was well known as a ballad singer under her maiden name of Delia Murphy.

From *The White Hound of the Mountain*. Devin-Adair Co, New York 1962, by permission of the publisher.

Elizabeth Rivers

The White Hound Of The Mountain

There was a King in Ireland long ago, and long ago it was—if I had been alive then, I wouldn't be here now. I was never without a story, new or old, and maybe it's better like that than being without any story—and he had three daughters. There was a well in his garden and a seat on the cover of the well. Nobody who ever sat in the seat and made a request of God and Mary and the saint of the well was denied it, and the King was not giving the key of the door of the garden to anybody but keeping it in his own pocket always for fear that any one of his three daughters should make a request that would not please him.

He left home one day and he mislaid the key on the kitchen table and he did not remember to put it in his pocket when he was going out. The eldest daughter found the key on the table, took it up and called the other two sisters and went out. She took the lock off the door of the garden and the youngest of the three daughters said that she would have something to tell her father when he came home. They went into the garden, the three of them. The eldest daughter sat in the seat and she asked God and Mary and the saint of the well that the King of the Eastern World should come seeking her in marriage before a year had passed.

"I'll have something to tell my father when he comes home," said the youngest woman.

The second-eldest sat in the seat and she made a request of God and Mary and the saint of the well that the King of the Western World should come seeking her in marriage before six months had passed. Then they asked the youngest to sit in the chair and she said that she wouldn't, but that she would have something to tell her father when he came home.

They told her again to sit in the seat and again she said that she would not. The two sisters then got hold of her and said that they would throw her on her head down into the well and that she would be drowned unless she sat in the chair as they had sat and made her request. Rather than be drowned, she sat in the

247

seat, very much annoyed. She made a request of God and Mary that the White Hound of the Mountain should come seeking her in marriage before a month had passed. He was a white hound that used to be going on the mountains in the daytime to be seen by everybody and nobody knew what kind of hound he was or in what place he stayed at night-time.

When the King came home each daughter told her own story, and the youngest told how the two others had forced her to sit in the chair against her will and that in her annoyance the request she had made was that the White Hound of the Mountain should come asking for her. "It's a bad thing you've done, daughter," said her father; "it would have been better for you to have made any other request than the request you have made."

"I don't know at all what kind of thing the White Hound of the Mountain is," said the daughter. "I was so annoyed that I didn't care what I did with myself or what request I made."

Before the month was out, during the dark of the night, the White Hound of the Mountain came to the door.

"King and Prince," said the White Hound of the Mountain, "send out my woman to me, or if you don't, I will knock down your court and your city on you."

The daughter of the *Cailleach na gCearc*—the hen woman— was dressed up and was sent out to him. He seized her and brought her to a court with a fine castle, and thinking that he had taken the right woman, he put her sitting on a seat in the kitchen. He himself stood up as a fine man, and he put the back of his legs against the fire and asked her what jewel of a king or great prince throughout the courts and cities that night she would rather have.

"There is no jewel of a king or prince I would prefer," she said, "than to be in that yard outside at the back of the court and a couple of hundred hens belonging to me, and to be giving them food from morning till night."

"If that's true," he said, "it isn't the right woman was sent to me.". He took hold of her shoulder and he dragged her through fences and through briars and through bushes until he left her at the door of the King. She was bruised and cut, and in very bad shape.

248

On the following night the White Hound of the Mountain came to the door of the King's house. "King and Prince," he said, "send my woman out to me, or I will knock down your house."

The daughter of the cleaning woman was dressed up. She was dressed like a lady and she was put outside for him, and he took her to his court and his mansion. He put her sitting on a chair in the kitchen. He himself stood up with his back to the fire, a fine man. He asked her what jewel of a king or fine prince throughout the courts and cities of the world she would rather have.

"There is no jewel of a king or a prince I would prefer," she said, "to yonder big tub to be full of clothes and I to be washing them from morning till night."

"If that's right," he said, "'tisn't the right woman I have at home with me tonight." Then he caught hold of her by the shoulder and he dragged her out through briars and fences and bushes and every way that was worse than the other till he took her to the door of the King's house and left her in the place where he found her.

On the next night the White Hound of the Mountain came to the door of the King's house. "King and Prince," he said, "send my woman out to me."

"I have already sent her to you," said the King.

"You haven't," said he. "Send her out to me quickly, or if you don't, I will knock your castle to the earth." When they would not send her out to him, he put his shoulder to the castle and he shook the whole building.

"'Tis better for us," said the King, "to send her out than to have the house fall on top of us." So the daughter of the king was sent out to him then, and he took her home to his court and his mansion. Then he put her sitting on a seat in the kitchen and he stood up before her and he asked her what jewel of a king or prince throughout the courts of the world she would rather have with her.

She answered that there was no jewel of a king or mighty prince in the world that she would rather have than himself.

"That's true," he said; "I have the right woman at last. Which would you rather," he said, "that I am a hound at night-time and a man in the day, or a man at night-time and a hound in the day?"

"The night is lonely," she said, "and I'd rather you were a man at night-time and a hound in the day."

"I will be like that," he said, "a man during the night and a hound during the day."

They lived together like that, he and she, and it was the life of a king's daughter for her till she was about to have a baby. She said to him then one day that she would very much like it if he brought her to the house of her father. "If you take my advice," he replied, "you will stay where you are."

"I would like to go home," she said, "in case I die. I am far from people here, and far away from my family; I have nobody here except you."

"I will leave you home," he said, "since you ask it; but the baby that you will bear in your father's house will be taken from you between its birth and baptism, and if it is, there is no harm done and don't be troubled at all about it; and don't pretend that it happened, and don't ever tell who took it from you. They will be asking you what sort of place you have here and what kind of life you lead and what sort is the White Hound of the Mountain. Don't tell them a word in answer to their questions. If you do you won't lay sight on me ever again."

Then he went and brought her to her home and her people did not notice her coming till she was amongst them in the house. There was a great welcome for her, and after a couple of nights she had a young son. On the night after its birth, when everybody in the house was asleep, a fine woman came and started to take the baby with her. When the mother saw the child being taken off a tear dropped from her eye, and the moment it dropped one eye fell out of the baby's head. She picked up the eye and put it in a strongbox and then put the box in her pocket as the other woman departed with the baby.

When the people of the house awoke the child was gone and was not to be found. They asked her where was the child. She said she didn't know. They said to her that she must tell. She said she wouldn't. They asked her what kind of man she had and what sort was the White Hound of the Mountain and what kind of life had she been leading and where was she, in what kind of dwelling place. "There is no good in your asking me questions," she replied. "You won't get any information of that sort from me."

When she was recovered and back on her feet, the White Hound of the Mountain came and took her home, and she was with him until she was about to have a second baby. Once more she said to him that she would like to be brought to the house of her father. "I want to go to my people," she said.

"If you will take my advice," he replied, "you will stay where you are. The child you are carrying will be taken from you as the other one was, and even if it is, there is no harm done; and don't pretend that it has been taken, and above all things don't drop a tear from your eye when you see it going. And if you tell of your circumstances here, or about me, you won't lay sight on me ever again."

On the following day he left her at her home. There was a great welcome for her, everybody in the family asking her what kind of home she lived in and what sort of person the White Hound of the Mountain was. She told them that she wouldn't give them information about anything of that kind and that there was no good in their asking her.

A week later a young son was born. When he was a couple of nights old and everybody in the house was asleep except herself, a fine woman came and took up the child and brought it away with her. When the mother saw him going a tear dropped from her eye and an eye fell from the baby. She took the eye and put it in her strongbox and put that in her pocket. When the other people in the house awoke the child wasn't to be found. Everybody was asking her where was the child, where had it gone to, or who had taken it away.

She said she did not know and if she did she would not tell them. A week later when she was up again the White Hound of the Mountain came and took her home. "You are a good woman," he said, "not to have told them anything."

When she was about to have the third baby she told him to

bring her home. "If you take my advice," he said, "you will stay where you are, but since you say so, I will leave you at your father's home, but of all you ever saw don't tell what kind I am or your life here, or if you do you won't see me ever again."

He left her at home then and told her that the child would be taken from her as the other two were. "And even if it is, it is no harm and don't tell who took it from you; if you do you won't ever see me again." All her people were asking her what kind of life she had and what kind of dwelling place and what sort of thing was the White Hound of the Mountain.

"Don't keep on asking me," she said; "I won't tell you anything." A couple of days later, a girl child was born, and in the night when everybody in the house was asleep a fine lady came and took the child with her, and when the mother saw the child being taken away, a tear dropped from her eye and an eye fell from the child. She took the child's eye and put it in the strongbox and again she put the little box in her pocket.

When the people of the house awoke the child was gone and not to be found. Her people told her that it was easy for them to see that her man wasn't a good man since she would not tell them anything about him and her children disappearing as they were, without anybody knowing where they were gone or what was happening to them. "If you don't tell now," said her father, "what kind of life you have led, and what kind of being the White Hound of the Mountain is, and what has happened to your children, a fire will be lighted and you will be burnt in it." Again she said that she would not tell.

On the following morning, a fire was lighted, and when the fire was red, they caught her, swung her up and down, right and left, to throw her into the fire. Rather than be burnt she told them, from beginning to end, what kind of life she had been leading and about the court and about the fine mansion and the food and drink she had, and that the White Hound of the Mountain was the grandest man in the world and that he was a fine man at night-time and a hound in the daytime as they themselves saw him.

They released her then and they were satisfied to know the kind of life she had. The White Hound of the Mountain came to the place then as a fine man, dressed like the son of a king the finest in the world, and he took her with him to his court and mansion, and he told her that he would never spend another night with her, except that one night, since she had not kept secret that the *geasa*[*] were lifted from him at night; that these the *geasa* had been put on him by the Queen of the Black Cloak, who was in the lower world, and he would have to go to her now.

They spent that night together, sorrowful and troubled. He rose in the morning and shook hands with her and bade her goodbye, and told her that she was finished with him now for ever.

He turned himself into a black crow, went out the door and went flying into the sky. She walked out after him and always watched him as she covered mountains and hills, and she went by every way that the black crow went, keeping after him. She didn't see a house or a place throughout the day, a person or people, but kept her eye on the black crow always till evening came. Then she saw a fine court a distance away from her on the side of a hill, and as night fell she saw the black crow going into the court. She followed him and went in, and she asked lodgings from the woman of the house till morning. The woman of the house granted her this, for she was tired and worn out after having been running from early morning.

There was a fine young lad on the kitchen floor with a hurling stick of gold in his hand and a silver ball, and he was playing with them. "That is a fine little boy, God bless him," she said. "He is," said the woman of the house, "but it's little his mother has done for his upbringing." The boy was one-eyed. She didn't get a glimpse of the black crow from the time she had gone into the house.

When he (that is, the black crow) was eating his supper he cut a full plate of every kind of the best that was on the table. He handed the plate to the serving maid and told her to bring it to

[*] *Geas* (plural, *geasa*): "a solemn injunction, esp. of a magical kind, the infringement of which led to misfortune or even death, a tabu, spell or prohibition" (*Dincen's Irish-English Dictionary*, pub. for the Irish Texts Society, Dublin, Educational Company of Ireland, 1927).

the person whom he was seeing but who was not seeing him. The girl brought the plate to her and she ate her fill, and it was little of it she left.

When he was eating his breakfast next morning he cut a plateful of everything that was best on the table and he ordered the girl to bring the plate to the person on whom he was looking and who was not looking at him. The girl did so, and that person satisfied her appetite and little she left.

When she had eaten, she saw the black crow going down the room and out through the door. She got up. "Don't go out yet," said the woman of the house. "Here is a scissors for you, and perhaps you will find work for it later." She took the scissors and put it in her pocket, and walked out after him.

The black crow was rising, flying into the sky, and she, going along on the ground, followed after him over bogs and mountains, through glens and through hills, keeping her eyes fixed all the time on the black crow before her.

She didn't see a house or a place, a person or people to whom she could speak a word throughout the entire day, till dark evening overtook her. Then she saw a fine court at a distance down in the valley and she saw the black crow going in by the door. She walked in after him and asked lodgings for the night from the woman of the house, and she got that and welcome.

There was a fine little boy on the floor there, with a hurling stick of gold in his hand and a ball of silver, and he was playing with them. "That is a fine little boy," she said, "God bless him."

"He is," said the woman of the house, "but it's very little his own mother has ever done for him." The child was one-eyed.

When the black crow was eating his supper, before he ate anything, he cut a full plate of the best of the food on the table, and he ordered the plate to be given to the person on whom he was looking and who did not see him. The plate came and she ate her fill, and it was little she left after the long amount of walking she had been doing during the day. When he was eating his breakfast on the following morning, he cut another full plate of the best of the food, and ordered that it be given to the person on whom he was looking and who did not see him.

254

When he had eaten his breakfast, he came down the room as a black crow and he went out by the kitchen door. She got up. "Don't go yet," said the woman of the house. "Here is a comb for you, and maybe you will find use for it later on." She took the comb and put it in her pocket, and walked out after the crow. He was going before her, flying into the sky, and she walked behind him on the ground, through hills and mountains and through the wildest and remotest places till evening came dark on her; and she saw a fine court at a short distance, and she saw the black crow making for the court, she never taking her eyes off him till she saw that he was going in.

She herself went in the same way and she asked lodging of the woman of the house till morning. "You will have that and welcome," said the woman of the house. "It is late to send anybody out till morning."

She didn't see sight of the black crow from the time she came in.

There was a little girl walking on the floor. "That's a fine child, God bless her," she said.

"She is," said the woman of the house, "but little trouble her mother has taken about her." The child had only one eye.

When the black crow went to eat his supper, he cut up a full plate of the best food on the table. "Give that," he said to the girl, "to the person I am looking at and who is not seeing me." The girl took it and brought it to her and she ate all she wanted and left little. She was tired and worn out, overcome and downcast, and her heart was broken after all the walking.

When he was eating his breakfast fairly early next morning, he cut a plateful of the food and sauces and said to the girl: "Give that to the person on whom I am looking but who is not looking at me." The girl did that and she ate a little of it, very little. When she was finished, the black crow came down the room and struck her a blow of his wings on the cheek, and he went out the door and she walked out after him.

"Don't go yet," said the woman of the house, handing her a small wooden peg for winding thread. "Here, put this in your pocket," she said, "and perhaps you will need it later on." She took the winding peg and put it in her pocket.

He went before her into the sky, flying, and she kept following him and watching him, and at last when a good part of the day was done, he went out of her sight and she couldn't trace him any more.

Then she began wailing and shouting, crying and beating her fists and tearing the hair of her head in her grief and distress and misery. She went on then in the direction where she had last seen him, but she failed completely to get a sight of him anywhere. In the early evening she saw him in the distance, and he was lying on the top of a little hill. She came up to him, and as soon as she reached him, he became as fine a man as he had ever been.

She sat down beside him then, he sat beside her, and he put his head in her lap and they began talking and chatting and sharing each other's complaints. He told her to return home, that there was no use in her following him any longer, that the journey she had made so far was nothing compared with the way that lay before her.

He said: "I have now to swim across that narrow sea, and when I reach land on the other side, do you see the hill across yonder?"

"I see it," she said.

"I've got to go up to the top of that hill, and there is a hole on the top of that hill; I must go down in that hole. There are stairs going down there, and I must go down that way till I come to the underworld, the place where the Queen of the Black Cloak is, and I must stay with her. That is a way that you would not be able to travel. There is a stair for every day in the year, and a serpent will be there before you on every one of those stairs if you try the way and will swallow you up."

She shed a wave of blood on the breast of his shirt. He rose up, bade her farewell, and went away from her, and she kept watching after him till he swam across the sea. She kept him in sight as he walked on the ground beyond the sea and as he went up the hill until he passed out of her vision.

Then she cried and beat her hands and tore her hair till she was like a wild person. She said to herself that it was all the same to her whether she was alive or dead, that she must get across that sea.

She went and gathered a bundle of rushes. She tied the rushes together, put them down on the sea, and placed her two feet on them, and the sheaf of rushes took her to the land on the far side.

She didn't find a house or a place there, and night came on and she had to spend the night sleeping in the open.

She awoke early in the morning and started walking, and she kept going till she came to a big town. She went into one of the houses; and the kind of house it was a baker's shop.

The baker asked her what brought her that way. She said that she was looking for domestic work. "I would need a servant girl," said the baker, "if you aren't too dear."

"I'll not be dear," she said, "but what kind of business do you carry on?"

"I'm a baker," he said, "and I would want you to keep the women of the house company and do all kinds of work in connection with the kitchen. How much will you be asking for a year?"

"I'll be asking you," said she, "nothing more than my keep and a threepenny loaf of bread for every day till the end of the year."

"You will get that," said the baker.

She put in the year in the baker's house. The baker then gave her her pay, that is, a loaf of bread for every day of the year, and she took with her that amount of bread to the top of the hill. When she came to the first stair, the serpent was lying there and its mouth opened to swallow her. She threw a loaf into his mouth, and the serpent swallowed it and she went past. She kept on throwing loaves into the mouths of the serpents, one after the other, and going past each one till she had thrown the last of the loaves in and was beyond all the serpents then and was in the underworld.

She was walking in the underworld, then, till she came to the brink of a river, and there were two girls washing clothes in the river. They had a shirt on which there was blood on the breast, and they were finding it impossible to take the blood out of the front of the shirt. She was standing watching them, and she asked them why they were unable to get the blood out. "Give it

257

to me," she said to one of the women, "and perhaps I may get it out." The woman handed her the shirt. She took it and dipped it into the water, and she gave it only two dips in the water when the blood went out of it. She asked them why there was blood on that shirt of all the shirts they were washing.

One of the girls said that about a year ago a strange young man had come to that big house up there and that that was the shirt he was wearing when he arrived, and that not even the best of the cleaning women had been able to remove the blood from the shirt until she had done so.

"Is that man living in the house?" she asked.

"Yes," said the girl. "He is married to an old Queen there, and she is the owner of this whole estate."

"Don't tell her that you've met the likes of me. She will ask you," she said, "how you have succeeded in getting the blood from the front of the shirt. You will say to her that a crow flew over your head carrying a white bone in his mouth, and that the bone fell out of its mouth in the place where you were washing; that when you had failed to get the blood out of the breast of the shirt, one of you took the bone without thinking what you were doing and rubbed it on the shirt, and the moment you rubbed, the front of the shirt was as clean as the rest of it, and the sharpest eye would not notice that there had ever been any colour of blood on it."

The girls went home to the old Queen, glad enough, as they had the shirt cleaned. She asked them had they taken the blood out of the front of the shirt.

"Yes," said one of the girls.

"How did you get it out?"

"When we had failed, a crow flew over our heads with a white bone in his mouth, and the bone fell from him. One of us took the bone kind of heedlessly and rubbed it on the front of the shirt, and the moment it was rubbed it cleaned the blood from the front of the shirt."

"That's true," said the old Queen, "that's one of the bones of the woman who put the blood in the shirt. It wouldn't be possible to get the blood out of the shirt ever till she had a hand in the

258

rubbing of it," said she, "or one of her bones. That is one of her bones that the crow had, and she is a long time dead." The old Queen was delighted then. She no longer feared her.

She went then and came to the house of the hen woman, as it was near the big house, and she asked a place from her for a week. The hen woman gave her that and welcome.

"It's a great wonder," said the hen woman, "that a fine woman like you would be asking a place in such a mean house as this."

"Oh, it is quite good enough," said she.

She stayed there till the following morning, and the scullery maid from the big house came into the hen woman's house, and the clothes she had on her were torn and raggedy and dragging behind her, some of them sweeping the ground. "Come here to me," said she to the scullery maid, "till I cut some of those rags off you."

The woman came to her and she put her hand in her pocket and took out her scissors, and she cut off plenty of the rags that were dragging on the ground. Silken clothing then grew over the scullery maid, finer than any lady's in the world, with golden lace and of the most elegant fashion. She ran up to the big house in great joy and pride on account of the fine clothing. When she came in twelve didn't recognize her for the one that did, she was so dressed up. They all asked her where she got the clothing. She said that it was a fine woman who was in the hen woman's house when she herself had come in, who had taken a scissors out of her pocket and begun cutting the rags off her, and that this clothing had grown on her just then. "Go down there," said the old Queen, "and tell her to send that scissors up to me at once." The scullery maid went down.

"My mistress said to you," said she, "to send that scissors to her at once."

"Tell her I will," she said, "if she lets me sleep tonight with her man." The scullery maid went back and she told that conversation to the old Queen.

"Go back down," says she, "and tell her that I will grant her request rather than be without the scissors."

She went down and told that talk to the other woman, and

she gave the scissors to her on that condition. The maid returned and handed the scissors over to the old woman, the Queen. When night came, the other went up to the house. "You old harlot," said the old Queen, "go up and sleep. My man is in bed before you." He was there, with a drug-drink given to him by the old Queen.

The creature went up, and she took off her clothes and she went in beside him in the bed, and she began telling him that it was she who was there, and the way she had come and everything they had gone through, and her mouth didn't shut till morning talking to him, and he gave neither echo nor answer to her. The deadly sleep was on him, and he didn't know that she was there at all.

When daybreak came the old Queen came to the bed. "You dirty whore," said she, "get out of there! You have no shame, sleeping with my man since the night began!" The poor woman got up and she put on her clothes, and she walked down to the hen woman, and her good article lost and not a thing for it.

During that day, a young girl who was bald from scab came into the house of the hen woman. Her head was broken out in scabs. "Come over to me till I comb your head!"

She went over to the other woman, who put her hand in her pocket and brought up the comb, and she drew it a couple of times on the skull of the scabby-headed woman. The most beautiful head of hair that was on any woman in the world grew, the colour of gold, and it grew on her down to her knees.

The scabby woman ran up to the big house in great pride and joy on account of the fine head of hair she had. Twelve did not recognize her then for the one that did. You'd never get tired looking at her beautiful hair. The Queen of the Black Cloak asked her who had put that fine head of hair on her. She told her that it was a fine woman who was in the house of the hen woman, who had been staying there for a couple of nights, who had rubbed a comb she had on her diseased head and that that fine head of hair had grown on her.

"Go down at once," said she, "and tell her to send that comb up here to me!"

The scabby woman went down and told the other woman. She said that she would send her the comb provided she had tonight in one bed with her husband. The scabby woman went back and told the Queen of the Black Cloak. She said: "Rather than be without the comb, she will have that." So the scabby woman went and told the woman in the hen woman's house that her wish was granted. She gave her the comb and the scabby woman gave the comb to the Queen of the Black Cloak.

At the coming of night, the Queen of the Black Cloak said to her husband to go to bed, and he went to bed. When he was in bed, she gave him a sleeping draught, and he fell asleep, and he was unconscious till the following morning. He was like a man who was dead. She came in at nightfall. "Go up and sleep with my man, you old harlot!" said the Queen of the Black Cloak.

She went, she took off her clothes and she lay down beside him till morning. She began telling him everything she had gone through from beginning to end, and explaining to him the way she had come, and telling him how she had earned him up to then. But she didn't get a sign or answer or word from him by morning. And at the first sign of daylight, the Queen of the Black Cloak came to her. "You dirty whore," said she, "it's time for you to get up and get out this moment! Little shame you have, sleeping with my husband all night."

The creature got up, heavy and weary and her two good articles lost and nothing for her as a result. The poor woman went then to her lodging where she had been before, and she took out her winding peg and began reeling golden threads of silk till she had six or seven bundles of these golden silk threads made, the finest that the human eye had ever seen. The boy in charge of the pigs arrived then, and he was watching her for a while winding the thread off the reel. He went out and didn't stop till he told the Queen of the Black Cloak about it.

"Go back," said she, "and tell that hussy to send that reel here to me!" The boy went to her and told her that the Queen said she was to give him the reel so that he could bring it to her. "Tell her I will give it," said she, "if she lets me sleep with her man till morning!"

261

The boy went back and he told the conversation to the Queen of the Black Cloak. "Sooner than be without the reel," she said, "say I agree!" The boy went back and told her this, and she gave him the reel on that condition.

When night came, the Queen of the Black Cloak put her husband to bed, and she stuck a sleeping pin in his head and he fell into a deep sleep till morning. The other woman came, and she ordered her to go up and sleep. She went and took off her clothes and stretched beside him in the bed. She began telling him from beginning to end everything he had gone through and that she had gone through, and that this was the third night that she was with him in bed, telling him about the lost scissors and about the lost comb and that the reel was now lost for the sake of this night, and that she had no other means of having any other night with him. She warbled her torment, and as you can imagine he didn't hear a single word she said the three nights, as he was in a deep sleep.

With the first coming of day, the Queen of the Black Cloak came to them. She told her, "Old harlot, get up out of there," that she was a shameless woman to have been sleeping with her husband for these three nights. The poor creature got up, heavy and weary and sick at heart, and there was nothing she could do but beat her face with her hands, her three good articles lost and nothing as a result. She went to her lodging as before.

When the old Queen found her gone, she took the sleeping pin from his head and he wakened and he hadn't the slightest recollection that the other woman had been with him. But the butler had been listening to every word that had been said during the three nights. His bed was in the room nearest them.

During the day, the butler asked his master a question: "I will put a problem to you and solve it!" said the butler. "Had you ever a woman other than the Queen of the Black Cloak?" He said he had. Said the butler: "She has been in bed with you for the past three nights."

"She was not," he said, "for she is a long time dead."

"Be certain," said the boy, telling him every detail of her talk during the three nights.

"That's true then," said he. "Nobody could know of that kind of conversation, nobody that ever drew breath, but herself and myself. Wasn't it a great sleep was on me when I didn't feel her!"

"Why wouldn't you sleep since the Queen of the Black Cloak gave you drugged drinks on the two first nights, and put a sleeping pin in your head last night, which she took out today when she found herself gone from you?"

"Like a good man," said he to the butler, "she is in the dairy now, eating meat there. Go in and stick a bone down in her throat, and call me then!" In went the butler. The Queen was there before him. He got a big bone and put it into her mouth, and he forced it down into her throat. He shouted for his master that she was close to being choked. The master came. Neither he nor the butler left the place till they had choked the Queen of the Black Cloak.

They put a report throughout the court that she had been choked from eating the meat. Said one of her waiting-women: "May God not relieve her. There was never a day that she wasn't evil!" They waked her for two nights and two days, and buried her.

No sooner was the Queen choked than he walked to the house of the hen woman, and he took her in his arms—that is, the first wife. He smothered her with kisses, he drowned her with tears, and he dried her with his cloak of fine silk and satin. He took her with him straight up to the court then, and they spent those two nights cheerfully at the wake of the Queen of the Black Cloak.

When they had her buried, they sold up the court and all that was in it and outside it, and they took their journey home to Ireland. They brought the butler with them; they wouldn't leave him behind. They didn't stop or stay till they came to the last house they had left—that is, the house of the woman who had given her the reel.

When they went in there, the little girl was on the floor, and she with one eye. Herself put her hand in her pocket and took up the box and opened it, and the eye jumped into the head of the child and was as good as the other eye.

They spent that night in three portions: a third in romances, a third in storytelling, and a third in placid slumber and long sleep—till the next morning. That was the house of a sister of his that they had spent that night in. They made their farewells and departed, and brought the little girl with them; she was their own daughter.

They were at night in the house where they had spent the second night when they were adventuring, and there was a boy on the floor with one eye. She put her hand in her pocket, took the box out, and opened it, and the eye jumped into the head of the boy and was as good as the other eye. They spent the night in that house, and got ready fairly early, themselves and the butler, the little girl and the boy, and they said goodbye.

They were that night in the first house where the black crow and herself had stayed when they were on their travels. As they came in, there was a fine boy on the floor with a hurling stick of gold in his hand and a silver ball, and he was playing; and he had one eye. She looked at him, put her hand in her pocket, took out the strongbox, and opened it, and the eye jumped into the head of the boy and was as good as the other eye.

They spent that night in three thirds: a third with romancing, a third with news-telling, and a third with pleasant long sleep—till day came on the following morning. They got ready, prepared for the journey, and said goodbye.

Those were three sisters of the White Hound of the Mountain, one in each of the houses where they spent the three nights.

"Each of them," he explained, "took one of the children from you between the time of its birth and its baptism, and they brought them up well till then in order to lift the *geasa* from their brother."

They and the three children and the butler, went on and did not stop or tarry till they were that night in their own court and city. That was the house where the White Hound of the Mountain had brought the King's daughter at the beginning.

They kept the butler with them in the same company as themselves, eating food at the same table, with the freedom of the house and the court and permission to do anything he liked there, just like themselves; there was no distinction made between him and them, and he was in their company till death parted them. They spent a long life with great prosperity together, cheerful and gay. They had satisfaction of everything as long as they lived, and that is the end of the story of the White Hound of the Mountain.

COMMENTARY ON THE WHITE HOUND OF THE MOUNTAIN

The theme of this story is the same as that of the Amor and Psyche tale told by Apuleius in The Golden Ass. *In his editorial note to the transcription of the story in* Béaloideas, *Professor Duilearga lists nine Irish variants, and he later published in* Béaloideas *one of these, from County Kerry, called "Bull Bhalbhae." They belong to a family of folk tales going back the to matriarchal Mediterranean cultures, and their theme is the feminine psychic development.*

The main course of the stories is consistent, and in this main course what is most striking is that the woman is the active agent who decides, acts, suffers, pursues. The male partner tells her that she will see him no more. She keeps after him. He tells her to go home, "that there was no use in her following him any longer, that the journey she had made so far was nothing compared with the way that lay before her." In the "Bull Bhalbhae" version, there is still more stress on this male resistance: "He went off and she followed him. After some time he waited till she came up to him and he told her to return home, that it was useless for her to keep following him, that she would see him no more. She said that she would not return, and he went off, and she kept following him till night came. He waited for her then, and told her that she had better go home."[*] It is only when her initiative has deprived her of all she has, when her patient and intelligent toils and sufferings have left her with no resource except her love, that she is redeemed.

The story tells of woman's way toward completion, of her heroic and stubborn struggle for redemption of her love, and therefore of her self.

[*]*Béaloideas,* VI: 1, p. 76.

Her way and her weapons are altogether different from man's: there is no pride in adventurous and gallant fight, her only guide is love, and her instruments are the secret, deep-buried and then awakened forces which are part of her being of the female principle. And it is only through activating these forces that she is capable of the double redemption.

The story starts with a king who has three daughters. There is no mention of a mother, but he is the ruler over the sacred well in his garden over which is a seat, and if you sit in this seat your life wish becomes true. As stated by Neumann: "The symbolic character of sitting is still evident in such terms as sitzen, 'to sit'; besitzen, 'to possess'; Besitz ergreifen, 'to seize possession'; and besessen sein, 'to be possessed'. Similarly the Sitz, 'seat,' and Wohnsitz, 'home' or 'seat', of a tribe refer to the region whence it came or where it became ansässig, 'settled'. In ritual and custom, to sit on something has the significance of 'to take possession' of it."[*]

There is no need then for a Great Mother beside the Great Father, because the sacred well of life stands for the Great Mother principle, the source of Full Life. This king, therefore, is the ruler of life, the divine father. He knows that his daughters are not mature enough to take possession of the life wishing well, so he hides the key. But he leaves the key on the kitchen table one day. That means that his children find the key to the source of life in their ordinary life surroundings (and it could not be made clearer by the simple Irish storyteller, because all daily life centred in the kitchen, just as later in the story the White Hound of the Mountain brings his brides into his kitchen). With this key, the daughters can now open the forbidden door to the garden with the holy well.

When Psyche was ready for the opening of her drama, Eros came to her. Just so, the White Hound comes for "his woman." It was the wish of the woman, spoken at the magic well, the life source, that brought the male principle into activity.

Twice the White Hound rejected the substitutes sent out to him from the paternal stronghold. He wanted "his woman," not a wife to look after his chickens or one to clean the house.

[*] Erich Neumann, *The Great Mother*, Bollingen Series XLVII, New York, Pantheon, 1955, p. 98.

Three times, each time when she was in need of security, she returned to her "home." She ignored the request of her man that she stay with him. The contrast between this attitude and her later behaviour when she insisted on following him and he could not shake her off is meaningful when it is understood that the loss of her lover meant the beginning of her love, while for the White Hound of the Mountain it meant the loss of the woman he had taken externally, even arrogantly—"Send her out to me quickly, or if you don't, I will knock your castle to the earth."

In the three years "they lived together like that," both were in darkness, each to the other. As the "Bull Bhalbhae" story puts it, "she did not know anything concerning him except that he was a bull in the day and a man in the night." In that way the man wished to continue, his days in the freedom of the White Hound of the Mountain, by nights in the seclusion of the dark, "to have and to hold till death do us part." But there was nothing much to part since there was no union deeper than that which is told as being three procreations of the woman, who is shown to be as innocent and childlike as when she made her childlike wish; so it was that each time she had to return to her father's house for security.

The climax of this part of the psychic unfolding of the woman is the expulsion. Eve was not expelled from the Garden of Eden more roughly than the daughter from the carefree indifference of her father's stronghold. While there, she had not needed even to think much about the fate of her missing babies. The threat of destruction, posed by the fire prepared for her, was a real one unless she performed the act necessary to put an end to her mere animal-subordination life. That end was mandatory to create the crisis for the beginning of her knowledge of love as separation, struggle, and suffering, to achieve by her initiative, positive and single-purposed, the redemption not only of her new self, conscious of love, but of her half-man.

The process is explained by Neumann in Amor and Psyche:

Psyche's act leads, then, to all the pain of individuation, in which a personality experiences itself in relation to a partner as something other, that is, as not only connected with the partner. Psyche wounds herself and wounds Eros, and through *their related wounds their original, unconscious bond is dissolved. But it is this two-fold wounding that first gives rise to love, whose striving it is to reunite what has been separated; it is this wounding that creates the possibility of an encounter, which is prerequisite for love between two individuals. In Plato's* Symposium *the division of the One and the yearning to reunite what has been sundered are represented as the mythical origin of love; here this same insight is repeated in terms of the individual.*[*]

There is to be noted this essential difference of purpose in achievement between the male development stories, Conn-Ide and Niall, and the present story of female development. In the former, the purpose achieved is not an end in itself but is the finding of a life source to which to return for sustenance, and is not a total victory but only an essential part of total achievement. In the woman's story, everything is contained in her struggle to learn, for herself and her lover, to separate from the solely animal and routine association and, having forced the separation, to reunite on a fully conscious plane, so that in place of the part-human, part-animal, there is substituted the part-human, part-divine. This is an end in itself. It is peculiarly the function of the feminine principle, whether in the female or the male.

"They spent that night together, sorrowful and troubled." That is the turning point of the tale.

In "Bull Bhalbhae," we have the tantalizing account of the three-day pursuit by the woman, when he would run and then wait for her to overtake him, only to tell her to go away home. "He waited for her always, and when she came up to him he would tell her always to go home,"[†] thinking she was the woman who had always been returning to her father's court before. But she was now a woman conscious of and driven by love. Do what he could, the bull could not get rid of her; and when all fruit failed, he became a crow.

The scissors and comb and reel (in "Bull Bhalbhae," a skein of

---

[*] Erich Neumann, *Amor and Psyche*, Bollingen Series LIV, New York, Pantheon, 1956, pp. 85–86.

[†] *Béaloideas*, VI: 1, p. 77.

thread) represent processes in the separation toward putting in order: scabby hair replaced by golden tresses, rags by rich clothes, or as the ordering in the Psyche story of the pile of seeds, "Sort out the different kinds, stack them in separate little heaps."[*]

The blood which she shed on the breast of his shirt has a parallel in "Fáinne Oir" in the Curtin collection of Irish folk tales. Failing to awaken the sleeping woman, her lover, the king's son, "stooped down to kiss her. With the first kiss blood came from his nostril and fell on her robe in a round spot. At the second kiss he bled in the same way, and the blood went through her clothes to her body. At the third kiss the blood fell on her breast and remained there." When at the end of the story a crisis arose as prelude to the union, it was solved by this blood: "The son of Red Breast, King of Three Seas, kissed her and that moment every trace of blood disappeared from her."[†]

The parallel is useful in interpreting the meaning of the blood shed by the woman on the breast of the man's shirt. When she had succeeded in following her man to the underworld, it was the blood that formed the first link in the circle that ended in the completion. During her year of separation from him, his year with the Queen of the Black Cloak, the blood was a torment to the old Queen because it represented the living love that sought actively to liberate the man who, from the immaturity of his animal existence, had fallen into the dark unconscious and could not return. To redeem him and make possible the return, he had as help the strength and persistence of the woman, spiritualizing her animus, to use Jung's concept, at this stage of the story, and at a later stage the wakefulness and shrewdness of his "shadow" figure, his "servant."

The heroine of the story, bereft at the river's edge, finds her self at last. We are now at the beginning of the preparation of the woman for the final union. She has followed the male up to now, given birth to children whom in her immaturity she unwittingly maims, lamented her losses, and still followed the man, till the final break and her pouring out of her heart's blood. Now at last she has strength enough, having nothing left, "all the same to her whether she was alive or dead," to act on her own initiative, from conscious volition, to make

[*] Apuleius, The Golden Ass, tr. Robert Graves, New York, Penguin, 1954, p. 148.

[†] Jeremiah Curtin, Irish Folk Tales, Dublin, Talbot, 1956, pp. 116, 123.

with her hands and skill from reeds the means of crossing the river that separated her from knowledge of her male part or partner.

The year of preparation was a year of service. In that time she mastered the means of satisfying the serpents barring the way down to the "other world," the unconscious realities of being. There was no celestial compulsion here such as Venus put on Psyche, but the inner compulsion of the feminine developing to its full capacity of transforming character; and in that process, she had to know and acknowledge "evil," to work in service to gain the means (the loaves of bread) to take the evil out of evil. There was no hesitancy about her actions when she was ready. "When she came to the first stair, the serpent was lying there and its mouth opened to swallow her. She threw a loaf into his mouth, and the serpent swallowed it and she went past. She kept on throwing loaves into the mouths of the serpents, one after the other, and going past each one till she had thrown the last of the loaves in and was beyond all the serpents then and was in the underworld."

At the brink of the river, the end of the pursuit, the metamorphoses of hound and bird also end. The pressing insistence of the feminine principle at work, the male anima, acting from the depths of the unconscious, has brought the man to the mature stage where he can reach down to the unconscious, where it is a new kind of world "out of this world." It cannot be called unreal since it is there that everything happens to solve the dramatic life agonies. During this period of solution, it is indeed the only worthwhile reality.

Down there we are introduced to the other woman. Here is the loathsome old hag of the male stories, who repelled the young man. Her influence on the man is so negative, as seen in the feminine story of the White Hound, that it is necessary to destroy her. In the male stories, it is not so much a matter of destroying her as of transforming her.

The heroine is completely and cleverly successful up to the time of her encounter with the dark-cloaked Queen, the woman-image of the man which had restrained and restricted him from before he had heard the call from the wishing well. Three times, and therefore finally as far as her own efforts could go, the heroine fails. Her precious stratagems, the magic comb and scissors and reel, are lost, and there is

270

nothing left for her except to stay passive after all her torment of activity. Yet it was because of these labours, remaking herself, that it was possible for the "friend" of the man, the "shadow" figure, to emerge from his hidden place close to the man in his sleep, awake for him in his sleep.

The struggle between the dark Queen of the underworld and the heroine is not as one-sided as might at first appear. Indeed, the battle is won from the moment the heroine washes the blood from the shirt. From then on, she is in charge of the situation, being herself completed for the unique personal relationship toward which all her travail of development has been oriented. If it were only a matter of her own preparedness, the dark woman would fade away at this stage, for she is the lower or more primitive of the two characters of the feminine, the untransformed female animus; and though she is still very much alive in the life of the man, the heroine has proved herself the transformative character, which is her later stage of maturity.

She goes through the actions of trying to awaken the man—the reverse of the sleeping beauty theme of folk tales. She succeeds because she awakens the "servant," who tells his "master." Just as the dark woman of the unconscious is the woman of the story, nebulous and unknown at first but gradually brought nearer and nearer to consciousness as the journey of the tale progresses till the two women, who are one, meet for the showdown, so are servant and master one—horse, hound, servant in the Niall story; hound, crow, and servant in this. The "servant" proves indispensable for the solution on the male side.

This explains why the heroine is "in the wings" of the drama when it comes to its climax. There she can wait confidently for the destruction of the dark feminine figure, the collective, unpersonalized female impact on the male. In the dark of the unconscious, it is the "servant" who must find the dark Queen and disable her, so that the "master" (of himself) can safely see the end of his being "possessed" by the unconscious.

Better than the more widely known Apuleius story of Psyche and Amor, we have here the intertwined story of the development, in their different ways, of the male and the female from the collective unconscious, a primitive stage, to the later stage where a unique

271

personal relationship is possible. The lines of the story are not cluttered up by the introduction of the male as a god. The story keeps on the proper human level, without whimsy, and is all the more telling for that.

There is none of the pretty ending as in Lewis's spiritual parody **Till We Have Faces,** *where "two figures, reflections, their feet to Psyche's feet and mine, stood head downward in the water. But whose were they? Two Psyches, the one clothed, the other naked? Yes, both Psyches, both beautiful (if that mattered now) beyond all imagining, yet not exactly the same."* [*]

The "Bull Bhalbhae" version of the Irish story makes the psychological mistake of leaving the united couple in the lower world where "they lived in comfort and pleasure for the rest of their lives." [†]

While the dark and negative character of the feminine is conquered and destroyed, the White Hound story is insistent in its reminders that the "servant" remained. On the "return" from the underworld of the unconscious, "they brought the butler with them; they wouldn't leave him behind." As modern psychologists pursue their researches, they find this character and use the name "friend" as description. How close he remained in the after experience of the wholeness climaxed in the story is clearly stated in the final paragraph. He was part of the unity, "in the same company as themselves, eating food at the same table, with the freedom of the house and the court and permission to do anything he liked there, just like themselves."

The dark woman has been cheerfully waked and buried. The children are made whole, since all is now for wholeness—which is the meaning of holy; and "they took their journey home to Ireland."

---

[*] C. S. Lewis, *Till We Have Faces*, London, Bles, 1956, p. 319.

[†] *Béaloideas*, VI: 1, p. 87.

Princes of the Twilight

Henry Treece

*Henry Treece (1911–1966) is the youngest of the writers included
here, but he belongs firmly in their ranks and his work is very much a
part of the Celtic literary revival, keeping it alive into the present
century. Though Treece is best known as an historical novelist and
writer of children's books, he was also a fine poet, and in his youth
was a founding member of the New Apocalypse movement, a group of
young poets—whose numbers included Dylan Thomas—dedicated to
bringing to their work a deeper understanding of myth and its
relationship to everyday life. This is born out in all of Treece's work,
though he soon left the movement behind. His best works are his Celtic
and Dark Age novels, including* Red Queen, White Queen
(1958), The Great Captains *(1956), and* The Green Man
*(1966). His poetry is contained in four volumes, of which the present
dark and evocative piece comes from* The Haunted Garden *(1947).
His poem "The Warrior Bards" (1942) quoted at the opening of this
book, evokes as vividly as any one ever has, the world of Celtic myth.*

From *The Haunted Garden.* Faber & Faber, London 1947, by permission of the
publisher.

Elizabeth Rivers

Princes of the Twilight

I

First the frost, kissing the anguished root
And striking terror in the seed's soft heart
With winter breath, turning all water iron.

Then the thaw and Spring's soft courtier
Dancing in green across the merry fields,
Gold torque and harp all glittering in the sun.

And last the summer weather in the vine,
Covering the bones from sight with scented moss,
With bugloss and poppy and the rich red corn.

It was well in the old days, before the knife had lost its edge and the dog turned on his master.

Then the sky was always blue and crimson pennants waved in the mild air.

And the lords and the ladies galloped on white horses over the rolling heather towards the sea, laughing and singing, their gay cloaks streaming out behind them.

And in the halls, minstrels sang and jugglers tossed bright swords into the air; and sometimes, at midnight, the grandson of the ancient Oak-men would appear before the window, and with his dark art would set the flowers to ring like convent bells, or fetch a cloud of white doves out of the fire-smoke, or call in strange tongues from behind the flapping tapestry.

And in the hovel the goose-girl dreamed of silken sheets and gay laughter, of golden bowls and red wine, as she laid out the thin cold body in its threadbare shift.

It was well in the old days, for then men looked to a time of freedom, when the wolves would go back to the hills and the raiding long-boats would leave the coasts and founder, farther away than even the wild geese knew.

II

First desire, and sweet seduction's play,
The mad blood racing through the veins
To tear the rind and lay the soft fruit bare.

Then pride, striding like famine through the land
With golden staff to slash the heads from flowers,
Or choosing ripe plum here, rejecting there.

And last, mere usage, long habit turning grey
Love's multi-coloured tapestry, and birds
Suddenly sweeping songless through the air.

The Queen, Gwynhyvar, sat smoothing her golden hair with a comb of jet. At her small feet lay a hunting hound.

From time to time her sea-blue eyes strayed to the waxen image of the tall king, dressed in the cloak of the Red Dragon, and then her long white fingers snatched up the silver bodkin and thrust it again and again through the body and the eyes and the legs of the still image.

Looking into her mirror, the Queen saw the thick curtains part, and her red lips drew back to show her teeth, sharp and white as a cat's.

In the doorway stood the tall king, dressed in the cloak of the Red Dragon.

And Gwynhyvar turned to him and held out her long hands in yearning.

"My love," she sang, "Why have you stayed away from me, to whom every moment of your absence is a needle through my eyes?"

III

First the mood, a wind shaking the trees
Or stirring in some distant sullen plain,
With a swirl of dust and quiver of dead leaves.

And then the act, quick as a viper's tongue,
Catching the devil on the knife's sharp edge
Before he could escape, letting red rain fall.

And last repentance in her rough grey shift,
Hiding her tears with soiled and broken hands,
Listening for larks where no birds ever sang.

Under the feathered tree, seven Princes sat, listening to the harper and drinking from golden horns.

And their words flew in and out of the branches like coloured birds, climbing and soaring, swooping and striking, skimming from head to head and hardly ever perching in the heart.

And at last, when the sun had gone and the last minstrel had been dismissed, that Prince with the jet-black hair and the full red lips of a girl spoke to his peers in this manner:

"Dogs mate not with wolves the wise ones say,
Nor is man born who has seen moon by day
But from a pit or from the wormy grave.
Who here will call himself the black bear's slave?"

As the last word fell from the cherry lips, each Prince drew his bright knife and thrust it to the hilt in the daisy-damasked lawn. Then the young one, with the hair of jet and the girl's treacherous lips, lifted his head as the dusk fell and howled like a wolf between his jewelled hands.

The six Princes saluted him, then turning they flung back their velvet cloaks and shot seven arrows into the round moon's white face.

IV

First, the three gaunt birds waiting for Spring
On blackened bough, staring across the waste,
Watching for sun to break the purple mist.

Then the summer wood, full of a million sighs,
And the wings of a thousand coloured birds, where
In moon-time the pale man whispers with the moths.

Last, the robin, frost on his scarlet breast,
Making his quaint runes across the snow,
And mistletoe swinging in the Atlantic wind.

The three dark women stood by the table, watching the King as he lolled, his great golden head sunk in his tired hands.

"Do not despair," they chanted, "For every winter has its Spring, and not a sword but comes to rust at last."

And Arthur, his heart lighter, rose and walked by night in the woods, and learned a lesson from the flickering moths.

And at last he came to where the rocky cliffs fall down to the great sea, and he looked towards the land where his kinsmen still lived. Then he shouted into the blustering wind, hoping that his words would carry across the wide water to where his folk waited:

"Men of Armorica, Comrades, Cymry!
Come now if you will ever come,
And we will tread the serpents in the fire,
And we will drive the wolves back to the sea!"

He listened, expecting a titanic reply. But his ears caught only the mad violence of the wind, and his kingly words fell from the air, torn and shrivelled, down the rock-face and into the sea-shore spume.

And a bird, his small breast bleeding from the barb, hobbled behind him through the snow, and the marks that his feet made spelled the history of despair.

V

The fifth sad season is a pæan of pain,
Nothing so simple as mere toothless death,
But pitched right at the point of stark corruption

Where every cell shrieks for another dawn
And breath of parsley underneath the moon,
While womb's walls writhe that their dear day is done.

The last decaying hair, the crumbling jaw,
Ask no broad freedom, crave no fragrant grove,
Beg only the soft motion sea-sand knows.

The old man took the little Prince by the hand and led him down the worn stone steps into the vault below the chapel.

A bat flew out of the shadows and brushed across the boy's face. A grey rat scuttled over his feet and was lost in the darkness. Above, in the world of men, the Atlantic roared and broke its hyaena-teeth against the gaunt cliffs.

"This is your kinsman," said the priest, lifting the stone lid of a great coffin. "This is Uther Pendragon, whose banner you will one day carry through the land."

The boy looked at the writhing mass and shuddered.

"Look long on this great one, boy," said the old man, "and say a prayer."

The boy bent his head and thought of men chained in a burning cage.

When the two had climbed the stone steps, back into the light, three old women, dressed in black, came out of the shadows and peered about. They lifted the heavy coffin-lid and plunged their yellow hands inside. Standing on the rocks above the churning sea, they threw their horrid load to the hungry breakers.

A black seal raised his head above the waves, and recognizing the falling failing gift, dived deep to carry word to the green eminence.

279

And a dying raven, wandering towards oblivion in the upper air, swooped and carried off in his dry beak the ring-finger of the ancient King.

VI

Love-in-dream, the golden pinnacles
Piercing the cotton-wool to a cobalt sky,
And the goose-girl climbing the palace's jade steps.

Love-in-life, the winter afternoons
When log-fires throw their shadows on the wall
And wind howls in the chimney like a wolf.

Love-in-death, the white child in the wood,
Walking among the drooping aconite
And listening for voices that will never come.

And so he lay, the last of the Romans, and listened to the battle rolling away from him across the rocky field.

And Arthur leaned on his withered arm and wept to hear the bright blood streaming from his side.

And as he stayed, bound to earth, the vetch and the convolvulus crept through his open, gasping wounds into his head; and he remembered Olwen, the goose-girl, who had come bare-foot to Camelot to conceive his child.

And he remembered the long, warm, dusky afternoons they had spent together, between battles, in a shepherd's hut above Vricon.

And last of all, he remembered his son, who might have saved the land, but who was lost, no-one knew where, and now would never know the light ecstasy of victory, or the weight of a crown.

And Arthur reached out for his sword, to put an end to his suffering in the old Roman way.

But his fingers were already dead, and his eyes filled with blood.

"Bedwyr," he called, as faint as conscience in a drunken dream, "Bedwyr, my friend, come to me now."

There was a rustle in the sedges by the lake, then silence.

VII

Between fate and falcon's falling, screaming, tearing,
Cleaving the still cloud to deliver death,
Swirls in the upper air a sword-like will.

Somewhere between the rolling weed-grown wave
And craters pocking the green ocean bed,
Sways mercy in a labyrinthine shell.

The will to kill no less than will to die
Swings in the dusk of mindless ecstasy,
Mocking the three crosses on the hill.

Then the tall Queen, the darkest of the three, who sat like a dream of monoliths in the stern of the boat, quietly drew a long knife from her breast, and slowly cut the pale, bruised head from the defeated body. Holding it by the tattered golden hair, she let it drop silently into the black lake.

Only a single ripple hurt the stillness, and then a cloud moved westward across the moon.

VIII

Who is the pale hunter dressed in green,
The white stranger with the death-pale hands;
And why does he carry that bright golden spear?

Who is the dark soldier dressed in red,
The black watcher with the bloody hands;
And why does he wear that gleaming silver star?

The hunter is desire, who waits the winter moon;
The soldier, love, who moves towards the sun.
Why stare they at each other's hands in fear?

In a small clearing of the frozen forest, a little lad tumbled on all fours, among the volcanic stones.

He wailed as he played, and said, "If I am indeed the son of a King, as they say, why then is my body clothed with hair, and my hands armed with curling claws?"

The dying raven watched him, with glazed eyes, from the broken bough of a tree. For a moment it remembered its own heritage, and saw itself seated on velvet at a golden board, with the sad harps wailing the song of the midsummer sacrifice by the great fire. A wolf howled from the depths of the wood.

The little lad stopped in his play of gnawing a snail-shell and shambled towards the sound.

"I am coming, Mother," he sobbed. "Have patience with the weak. Pity the sons of Kings, for they must play."

Further Reading

The following represents a small selection only of what is a truly vast subject. The first section lists some of the books more readily available which give the background to Celtic literature, its origins and development. The second half lists works by the writers represented in this selection and by others who are not included. Most of them wrote many more works than are listed here: those selected are considered to contain their finest writing.

The Celtic Tradition

Alaya, F. *William Sharp–Fiona Macleod: 1855–1905.* Cambridge, Mass, 1970.

Arnold, M. *The Study of Celtic Literature.* London, 1905.

Fisher, M. *Henry Treece.* London, 1969.

Hyde, D. *A Literary History of Ireland.* London & New York, 1937.

Krissdotir, M. *John Cowper Powys and the Magical Quest.* London & Sydney, 1980.

McFate, P. *The Writings of James Stephens.* London, 1979.

Macleod, F. *The Winged Destiny: Studies in the Spiritual History of the Gael.* New York, 1974. (Reprint)

Matthews, C. *The Celtic Book of the Dead.* London & New York, 1992,

——, *Elements of the Celtic Tradition.* Shaftesbury, 1990.

Matthews, J. *Taliesin: Shamanism and the Bardic Mysteries in Britain & Ireland.* London, 1992.

——(Ed), *A Celtic Reader.* London, 1991.

O'Driscoll, R. (Ed), *The Celtic Consciousness.* Edinburgh and Portlaoise, 1982.

Sharp, E. (Ed), *Lyra Celtica.* Edinburgh, 1896.

Summerfield, H. *That Myriad Minded Man: A Biography of G.W. Russell.* Gerrards Cross, Bucks, 1975.

Tarrant, D. *James Branch Cabell: The Dream & the Reality.* Norman, Oklahoma, 1967.

The Celtic Renaissance

Collins, W.J. Townsend. *Tales from the New Mabinogion.* London, 1923.

Colum, Padraic, *The King of Ireland's Son*. London, 1930; Edinburgh, 1986.

——, *Orpheus, Myths of the World*. New York, 1930; Edinburgh, 1991.

De Blacam, Aodh, *The Druid's Cave*. Dublin, 1920.

Dunsany, Lord, *The Charwoman's Shadow*. London, 1926,

——, *A Dreamer's Tales*. New York, 1912,

——, *The Gods of Pegana*. Boston, 1919,

——, *The Last Book of Wonder*. Boston, 1910,

——, *The Sword of Welleran*. Boston, 1907,

——, *Time and the Gods*. Boston, 1905,

——, *To Awaken Pegasus*. Oxford, 1949.

Ferguson, Sir Samuel, *Congal*. London, 1872,

——, *A Hibernian Night's Entertainment*. Dublin, 1887,

——, *Lays of the Red Branch*. New York, 1893.,

——, *Aideen's Grave*. Dublin, 1925.

Jones, Thomas Samuel Jr. *Leonardo & Other Sonnets*. New York, 1930,

——, *The Rose Jar*. New York,

——, *Sonnets of the Cross*. New York, 1922,

——, *The Unicorn & Other Sonnets*. New York, 1931,

——, *The Voice in the Silence*. New York, 1911.

Joyce, Robert Dwyer, *Blanid*. Boston, 1879,

——, *Deirdrie*. Boston, 1879.

Macdonald, George, *At the Back of the North Wind*. London, 1871,

——, *The Gifts of the Christ Child* (2 Vols) London & Oxford, 1973,

——, *Lilith*. London, 1895,

——, *Phantastes*. London, 1858,

——, *The Princess and Curdie*. London, 1883, 1949.

——, *The Princess and the Goblin*. London, 1872, 1949.

Machen, Arthur, *The Great Return*. London, 1920,

——, *The Hill of Dreams*. London, 1907,

——, *Holy Terrors*. London, 1946,

——, *The Secret Glory*. New York, 1922,

——, *The Shining Pyramid*. London, 1925.

Macleod, Fiona, *The Divine Adventure*. London, 1900,

——, *The Dominion of Dreams*. London, 1899,

——, *From the Hills of Dream*. Edinburgh, 1896,

——, *Green Fire*. New York, 1896,

——, *Iona*. London, 1900; Edinburgh, 1982, reprinted 1991.

——, *Laughter of Peterkin*. London, 1895,

——, *Pharais.* Derbyshire, 1894,

——, *The Sin-Eater and Other Tales,* Edinburgh, 1895,

——, *Ulad of Dreams.* Portland, 1907,

——, *Vistas.* Chicago, 1894,

——, *The Washer at the Ford.* Edinburgh, 1895,

——, *Where the Forest Murmurs.* London, 1910.

Macpherson, James, *Fragments of Ancient Poetry Collected in the Highlands.* London, 1760,

——, *Fingal.* London, 1762,

——, *Temora.* London, 1763.

Milligan, Alice, *The Last Feast of the Fianha.* London, 1900.

Morris, Kenneth, *Book of the Three Dragons.* New York & Toronto, 1930,

——, *The Chalchuhuite Dragon.* New York, 1942, (reprinted 1991),

——, *The Fates of the Princes of Dyfed.* Port Loma, California, 1904, (reprinted 1974).

O'Connor, N. J. *Battles & Enchantments.* Dublin, 1924.

O'Grady, Standish James, *Ulrick the Ready.* London, 1896,

——, *The Departure of Dermot.* Dublin, 1917.

Parsons, E.B. *Tales of Tara.* Dublin, 1933,

——, *Dusk of the Druid.* London, 1935.

Powys, John Cowper, *Atlantis.* 1954,

——, *Brazen Head.* London, 1956,

——, *A Glastonbury Romance.* New York, 1932,

——, *Homer and the Aether.* London, 1959,

——, *Maiden Castle.* New York, 1936,

——, *Morwyn.* London, 1937,

——, *Porius.* London, 1951,

——, *Weymouth Sands.* New York, 1934,

——, *Wolf Solent.* London, 1929.

Rinder, Edith Wingate, *The Shadow of Arvor.* Edinburgh, n.d.

Russell, George ['AE'], *The Avatars.* London, 1933,

——, *The Candle of Vision.* London, 1918,

——, *Collected Poems.* London 1926,

——, *Song and its Fountains.* London, 1932.

Ryan, W.P. *The Celt and the Cosmos.* London, 1914,

——, *From Atlantis to the Thames.* London, 1926,

——, *Plays for the People.* Dublin, 1904,

——, *King Arthur in Avalon.* London, 1934.

Stephens, James, *The Crock of Gold.* London & New York, 1913,

——, *Deirdrie.* London, 1923,

——, *The Hill of Vision.* Dublin & New York, 1912,

——, *In the Land of Youth.* London, 1924.

Treece, Henry, *Collected Poems.* New York, 1946,

——, *The Dark Island.* London & New York, 1952,

——, *Electra.* London & New York, 1963,

——, *Golden Strangers.* London & New York, 1956,

——, *The Great Captains.* London & New York, 1956,

——, *The Green Man.* London & New York, 1966,

——, *Jason.* London & New York, 1961,

——, *Oedipus.* London & New York, 1964,

——, *Red Queen, White Queen.* London & New York, 1958.

Yeats, W.B. *The Celtic Twilight.* London, 1893,

——, *The Secret Rose.* London, 1897,

——, *Stories of Red Hanrahan.* London, 1897.

Young, Ella, *The Coming of Lugh.* Dublin, 1909,

——, *Celtic Wonder Tales.* Dublin, 1910; Edinburgh, 1985,

——, *The Wonder Smith and His Son.* Dublin, 1927; Edinburgh, 1992,

——, *The Tangle-Coated Horse.* Dublin, 1929; Edinburgh, 1991.

——, *The Unicorn With Silver Shoes.* Dublin, 1920.

286